MIND MAGIC

MIND MAGIC

The Neuroscience of Manifestation

and How It Changes Everything

DR JAMES R DOTY

yellow
kite

Published by arrangement with Avery, an imprint of Penguin Publishing Group, a division of Penguin Random House LLC. First published in the United States in 2024

First published in Great Britain in 2024 by Yellow Kite
An imprint of Hodder & Stoughton Limited
An Hachette UK company

2

Copyright © James Doty 2024

The right of James Doty to be identified as the Author of the Work has been asserted by him in accordance with the Copyright, Designs and Patents Act 1988.

All rights reserved. No part of this publication may be reproduced, stored in a retrieval system, or transmitted, in any form or by any means without the prior written permission of the publisher, nor be otherwise circulated in any form of binding or cover other than that in which it is published and without a similar condition being imposed on the subsequent purchaser.

A CIP catalogue record for this title is available from the British Library

Paperback ISBN 978 1 399 73786 9
ebook ISBN 978 1 399 71097 8
Audiobook ISBN 978 1 399 71098 5

Typeset in Arno Pro by Shannon Nicole Plunkett

Printed and bound in India by Manipal Technologies Limited

Hodder & Stoughton Limited
Carmelite House
50 Victoria Embankment
London EC4Y 0DZ

www.yellowkitebooks.co.uk

To all of those throughout my life who have helped me along my journey and so often have shown me the path.

To my wife, Masha, and my children, Jennifer, Sebastian, and Alexander, who every day are an inspiration.

CONTENTS

INTRODUCTION: THE REAL SECRET — ix

Chapter 1
**OUT OF THE WRECKAGE:
WHAT AM I ALREADY MANIFESTING? — 1**
Practice: What Am I Already Manifesting? — 16

Chapter 2
**NETWORKS AND VIBRATIONS:
THE PHYSIOLOGY OF MANIFESTING — 21**
Practice: Relaxing the Body — 44

Chapter 3
STEP ONE: RECLAIM YOUR POWER TO FOCUS YOUR MIND — 55
Practice: Building Inner Power — 74

Chapter 4
STEP TWO: CLARIFY WHAT YOU TRULY WANT — 77
Practice: What Does Success Look Like for You? — 81
Practice: Eliciting a Positive Emotion — 91

Chapter 5
STEP THREE: REMOVE THE OBSTACLES IN YOUR MIND — 101
Practice: Beliefs and Their Opposites — 116
Practice: Self-Compassion — 124

Chapter 6
**STEP FOUR:
EMBED THE INTENTION IN YOUR SUBCONSCIOUS — 132**
Practice: Visualizing Your Intention — 153

Chapter 7
STEP FIVE: PURSUE YOUR GOAL PASSIONATELY — 158
Practice: How Does My Intention Benefit Life? — 167
Practice: Scanning for Synchronicity — 174

Chapter 8
STEP SIX: RELEASE EXPECTATIONS AND OPEN TO MAGIC — 179
Practice: Let Go of Attachment and Open to Magic — 196

CONCLUSION: THE JOURNEY HOME — 202

MIND MAGIC: A SIX-WEEK PROGRAM TO MASTER MANIFESTATION — 207

ACKNOWLEDGMENTS — 262

NOTES — 264

INDEX — 273

Introduction

THE REAL SECRET

THE UNIVERSE DOESN'T GIVE A FUCK ABOUT YOU.

It may not sound like it, but this is good news. The universe doesn't give a fuck about you, not because you are not worthy or are out of alignment with the cosmos or have been put under a curse for ten generations. No, the universe doesn't give a fuck about you because it has no fucks to give.

Many of us are taught to spend our lives hoping for something outside of ourselves to fix our problems and make us whole: a winning lottery ticket, a wise guide who knows all the answers, a guru, a guardian angel, or some magical being, force, energy, or genie sitting out there in the universe who will make everything work out for us. For years, I longed to believe this, too. I thought there was a stern cosmic parent tracking all our actions and deciding if we were worthy to receive our dream house or to meet our soulmate or to be cured of cancer. As a neuroscientist and physician, I know today that we have no proof of such a force or being but we have a great deal of scientific evidence of the power of our own minds to produce changes in our lives that may at first appear impossible. This is the practice of manifestation.

There is much confusion about manifestation in popular culture, so before I go any further, here is what I mean by the term: *manifesting* is defining an intention such that it gets embedded into our subconscious, which functions below the level of consciousness. By doing so, we activate brain networks associated with goal orientation that make an intention important, salient, or noteworthy. In practice, this means that regardless of whether or not that intention is present on a conscious level, brain mechanisms that remain focused on the goal are activated around the clock. Our inner intention now guides our life. By using our inner power to tap the vast resources of our own brain, we gradually decrease the impact of our external environment and begin living from our deepest intentions.

In fact, the first step in successfully manifesting is to separate yourself from the belief that there is an external source for solving your problems, and that this external source is what is manifesting in your life. If you want to lead a rich, meaningful, and prosperous life, you do not have to appease any power beyond yourself. You simply must believe that the source of your well-being and success is nothing other than the power of your own mind. The reality is that the same mind that creates the obstacles to the life you want is also the source of the intention that will make the life that you want real. This is the real secret.

The fuck you give must be your own. This is the real magic.

I say this to you as a neurosurgeon who has studied and operated on the brain and as a neuroscientist who has spent decades investigating the human mind and brain, as a practitioner of spiritual techniques who has collaborated with the Dalai Lama and other spiritual leaders to teach compassion to thousands of people, and as a human being who has learned it all the hard way.

Manifestation is about cultivating a fierce belief in possibility. As a child I was acutely aware of the power of negative circumstances to limit a human life. I grew up in poverty, with an alcoholic father and a chronically depressed and suicidal mother. I had the feeling that life was a punishment or a curse or, possibly worst of all, a random and chaotic mess without rhyme or reason. Maybe you, too, struggle to find meaning in the events of what feels like a haphazard existence, or you wonder why you and your loved ones have to suffer when there is no good reason to and you feel powerless to help. These struggles begin to limit your vision of what is possible and make it more and more narrow.

For years I allowed my environment to dictate the terms of my life, and I didn't believe I could effect any meaningful change. This is so often the case when we experience trauma: the pain and shock of the traumatic experience take on an exaggerated authority in our minds that is difficult to challenge and frightening to confront. This pain is powerful enough to alter not only our own genes but, as researchers in the field of epigenetics have discovered, the genes of subsequent generations. Our minds and bodies organize around preparations to prevent a similar trauma from happening in the future, and in the process, our consciousness becomes caught in reacting to a frightening and unreliable external world rather than envisioning the changes we can make. In the process, we give away the energy, attention, and focus we possess to make a real difference in our own lives; we are distracted away from our own power. Without knowing it, we trade our innate self-agency for magical thinking. It's a raw deal.

The world can indeed be starkly unfair, and this unfairness can shatter a person's dreams. And as unfair as I once perceived the world to be, I know today that countless other human beings in this world are treated with greater injustice, on both the individual and systemic levels. The societies they live in have created structural roadblocks that limit their ability to manifest, whether due to their race, social class, religion, sexual orientation, gender expression, or other arbitrary criteria. Still other people are afflicted by serious illnesses of the body and the mind and can find little relief from their suffering, which also affects their belief in their ability to manifest. Manifesting is not a cure or a fix for all suffering. Like all human activity, it can be limited by countless factors beyond our control and reality has the final say, regardless of our intention. That being said, if there is a possibility of change, using the techniques of manifesting will more likely than not help bring it about.

I was moved by a story I heard once about a POW during the Vietnam War who practiced an attitude of "long-term nonspecific optimism." He did not know if or when he would be liberated and he recognized that his situation was outside of his control: to fight his captors was to possibly be killed or to lose the will to live from despair. Instead, his conscious practice of optimism allowed him to remain hopeful that his circumstances could change. He used the power of his mind to keep his belief in the possibility of freedom alive. It gave him resilience. And when he was released, his attitude of optimism helped him not to focus on the past but to look forward to future possibilities.

Thus I see manifesting as, at its heart, a practice of well-being, engagement with the world, and living a good life. By practicing it, we cultivate *dispositional optimism*, defined as a generalized tendency to expect good outcomes across important life domains. Research has shown a staggering number of health benefits associated with dispositional optimism, from improvements in cardiovascular health to how quickly wounds heal to slower disease progression. Where some may believe that the only measure of a successful manifestation is the material results it delivers, I consider this view to be misguided. The true gift of visualizing our intentions again and again is to go through life with a buoyant sense that things will work out for us, which liberates us to be both responsive and resilient no matter what our external circumstances bring.

The practice of manifestation dates back thousands of years. Much of what we associate today with manifesting derives from the Vedic scriptures of the Hindu tradition. The Mundaka Upanishad, for example, states, "Whatever world a man of pure understanding envisages in his mind and whatever desires he cherishes, that world he conquers and those desires he obtains" (3.2.10). The Buddha similarly commented on the powerful ability of thoughts to shape our experience of the world when he said, "Whatever a monk keeps pursuing with his thinking and pondering, that becomes the inclination of his awareness."

In the nineteenth century, the spiritual movement known as New Thought drew from a wide variety of religious and philosophical sources, including alchemy, New England transcendentalism, the Christian gospels, and Hinduism to formulate the notion of the "Law of Attraction." At its core, the Law of Attraction is the belief that our thoughts determine the nature of the experiences that come into our lives: positive thoughts bring positive experiences and negative thoughts bring negative ones. New Thought served as the foundation for much of the popular literature on manifesting in Western culture, from Napoleon Hill's *Think and Grow Rich* (1937) to Norman Vincent Peale's *The Power of Positive Thinking* (1952) to perhaps the most well-known and notorious, Rhonda Byrne's *The Secret* (2006).

The notion of the Law of Attraction has led to many unfortunate misunderstandings on the nature of manifestation. First, it has become associated with a self-serving prosperity gospel promoted by our materialist culture that makes you believe that by becoming rich, living in a mansion, and driving an expensive car, you will create happiness and find the behavioral changes that are required to realize our desires. And perhaps most damaging, it has spread the idea that the painful and unjust circumstances we experience are entirely the result of our own thinking. I hope that what I share with you in this book will reframe your conception of manifestation as a path to a life of meaning and purpose and, at the end of the day, help you to realize what is truly important.

Manifesting has long been confined to the same New Age territory as astrology, tarot cards, and belief in the power of crystals, full of pseudoscience and platitudes. Until recently, it was not possible to scientifically study the concrete processes by which the brain turns intention into reality. But significant developments in imaging have revolutionized our ability to watch the brain transform on a cellular, genetic, and even molecular level. We can now speak about manifestation in terms of cognitive neuroscience and the function of large-scale brain networks. This has allowed us to demonstrate that manifesting is neither a get-rich-quick scheme nor a misguided wish-fulfillment system but is part of the brain's extraordinary ability to change, heal, and remake itself, known as *neuroplasticity*.

Neuroplasticity is the umbrella term for the brain's ability to modify, change, and adapt both structure and function throughout life and in response to experience, as well as through repetition and intention, enabling the brain to form new circuits and to prune away old ones that no longer serve us. By redirecting our attention, we can literally change our brains, creating more gray matter in the very areas that help us learn, help us perform, and allow us to manifest. As the brain adapts, it makes alterations that can produce dramatic and positive effects on everything from Parkinson's disease to chronic pain to attention deficit hyperactivity disorder (ADHD). And the same neuroplasticity is how we change our brains using intention and practice to manifest the reality we envision.

Manifesting is essentially the process of intentionally embedding the thoughts and images of the life we desire into our subconscious. We are all manifesting intentions in an untrained and uninformed way already, and the results are often haphazard, vague, and unfocused. To manifest consciously, we must learn how to reclaim and direct the power of our attention and understand the physiological mechanisms that allow us to direct that attention, as well as the obstacles and false beliefs that limit our power to do so. When we consciously direct our attention toward our desired goals, those goals become important to the brain. The way our goals get embedded is through a process called *value tagging*, the brain's way of deciding what is significant enough to be imprinted at the deepest levels of the subconscious. When we practice visualization, we conjure powerful positive emotions, and these cue the *selective attention system* to tag the goals we desire as highly valuable and associate them with our reward system. Visualization works because, amazingly, the brain does not distinguish between an actual physical experience and one that is intensely imagined.

Once the goal is embedded in our subconscious, our brain works like a bloodhound seeking opportunities to bring it about in reality, putting the full force of our conscious and subconscious minds behind the search. As opportunities arise, we notice them and respond, taking the necessary action to further our goal. We repeat this process of embedding our intention many, many times. Once we have done everything we can to manifest our goal, we must accept that is all we can do and no longer have attachment to the outcome. Manifestation has its own timeline that may or may not correspond with ours. Also, the reality is that not all of our goals will manifest, and often there are many reasons why that is the case, which are not apparent at the time.

In my first book, *Into the Magic Shop*, I told the story of the fateful meeting I had as a child that would change my life forever. Growing up in poverty and stuck in a painful family situation in the High Desert of California, I believed I was under a kind of curse that would keep my life small and at the mercy of my circumstances. Then one summer day while my parents were arguing, I got on my bike and rode as fast and as far as I could from my house and, with dust in my mouth, wandered into a magic shop. I met a kind woman named Ruth, who wore a blue muumuu and looked up from the paperback she was reading. Her glasses were perched on her nose and held by a chain around her neck. Ruth gave me an incredibly radiant smile. The very nature of her smile made me feel OK: she made me feel safe. She told me it was her son's shop, and she didn't know anything about magic. After we spoke for about twenty minutes, Ruth indicated that she would be in town for six weeks that summer and offered to teach me about another type of magic if I came to the shop every day. Over those six weeks, Ruth fed me a bottomless supply of Chips Ahoy! cookies and taught me what she called "real magic": techniques I could use to relax my body, tame my mind, open my heart, and clarify and visualize my intention. Those happy hours I spent in the back room of the magic shop sitting across from Ruth in a metal chair on the brown shag carpet were my first experiences of neuroplasticity. Her kindness and attention rewired my brain.

Despite my initial hesitation, confusion, and fear, Ruth taught me to detach from my thinking enough to see it for what it was: just thoughts, one after the other, passing through my mind and disappearing. At first I would react with fear or aggression to the frightening voice and images of disaster coursing through my mind, but I learned I could replace the negative thoughts with positive, self-affirming ones; I could let go of the voice that told me "People like you never amount to anything" and replace it with the voice of the person I wanted to be living the life I wanted to live. I discovered I had a brain that could be reshaped to form new pathways through repetition and intention toward my own healing. With her help, I realized my own inner power.

What I didn't understand at the time was that what Ruth was teaching me was effectively what today we would call manifestation. Though there was indeed something magical about Ruth and what she had to share, her advice was very practical—in a way, she was helping me study the power of the human brain and heart long before I became a physician and neurosurgeon. Buoyed by Ruth's kindness and care, I devoted myself to my vision of the future I wanted, and this was the first step in truly manifesting into reality the life I desired. I went from taking all my cues from the world outside of myself to making choices based on an intimate inner dialogue with myself that I practiced daily.

It was hard work, and I often wanted to give up. When I became impatient, I remember Ruth telling me, "Jim, be patient, be patient. You just have to be patient. Changing your brain takes time."

It was hard to be patient. Especially because I didn't know exactly what was happening or was going to happen. But I learned patience and I learned how to be present and listen. Or, at the time, I thought I had listened.

Ruth's kindness, presence, and patience changed the trajectory of my life, and her lessons became the basis for practically everything I went on to achieve in life. Ultimately, I used Ruth's practices to get myself out of my hometown in the High Desert and into college, then on to medical school and later training as a neurosurgeon, and subsequently to an endeavor as a successful medical entrepreneur. But somewhere along the way I lost touch with my own heart, and this cost me gravely—not only financially, but in my most intimate human relationships.

Ruth's emphasis was unfailingly on the importance of opening the heart. Whatever goal I sought, whatever lofty object I desired to achieve, she always brought my mind back to a heartfelt connection with myself and others. And so I've often found it disheartening that this magic that is within every human being has been so frequently misunderstood, commodified, or presented as something only certain people can access. While manifesting is commonly understood in our culture as a way of gaining great wealth and possessions, available only to the lucky few, I see it as a daily practice of well-being that promotes thriving, wholeness, and an openhearted engagement with our world. And where the so-called prosperity gospel would have us believe that our desire is the primary engine of manifesting, I am here to tell you that it is in fact our ability to direct our attention.

When I first wrote *Into the Magic Shop*, I had no idea of the impact it would have. I had no expectation that the most popular K-pop band today, BTS, would use my book as inspiration for their third album, *Love Yourself: Tear*, or record the song

"Magic Shop" inspired by the book, or that I would find myself discussing a movie adaptation of my story with the actor Jon Hamm, or that a sixteen-year-old girl would be inspired to make a phone app based on my alphabet of the heart concept. I honestly thought that, whether my book sold any copies or not, if it affected one person's life for the better, that would be enough. Since the book's publication, I've received thousands of messages from readers. Even now, two hundred to three hundred new messages arrive via email every month. Others come handwritten on sheets torn from yellow legal pads or in calligraphy on beautiful handmade paper. They come from Japan and Romania, sub-Saharan Africa, and next door to me in Northern California. These heartfelt responses to my story have taught me to believe with confidence that we are not alone, even in our deepest moments of hopelessness, despair, and fear. Everyone has wounds, and when we share them honestly, they become the means for deep connection between all of us.

As I listen to readers' responses to my work, I notice that a significant percentage of the messages I receive are from people who are suffering in their lives and looking for their power to heal their own wounds and change their situations for the better. Their circumstances are vastly different, but their longings are strikingly similar. In particular, they want to know how visualization works to manifest their dreams. *Into the Magic Shop* was the story of my own personal journey of manifesting myself out of poverty, into wealth, out of it again, and, finally, back to the heart of compassion at the center of what Ruth taught me. It was one person's story, with all its uniqueness: its highs and lows, advantages and setbacks.

But *Mind Magic* is about *your* journey. In this book, I am going to show you how to harness your brain's power to make your intention reality and explain exactly how it works from the perspective of neuroscience. I will guide you through the six steps I and many others follow to manifest our intentions. These are informed by a lifelong practice of studying the mind as a neuroscientist and as a meditation practitioner myself. These six steps cover every aspect of the manifesting process: reclaiming our power to focus our mind; clarifying what we truly want; removing the obstacles in our mind; embedding the intention in our subconscious; pursuing our goal passionately; and letting go of our attachment to the outcome. Additionally, I have also included different kinds of stories of manifestation in the hope of inspiring you to start living and writing yours.

Even a few years ago, it was not possible to fully present a framework for how manifesting works that was grounded in the latest insights of neuroscience. Now it is possible to cut through the pseudoscience and mysticism and reveal the concrete brain mechanics that underlie the relaxation, detachment, compassion, and visualization that Ruth taught me. My hope is that a clear presentation of the science behind manifesting will empower readers not only to trust the practices, but to use them to heal themselves, change their lives, and understand their power to change their world.

Contrary to what it might seem in *The Secret*, manifesting is not limited to a few or controlled by a secret society of one-percenters. Manifesting is a radically equitable practice available to all, which has the potential to go beyond one's immediate physical, mental, and emotional circumstances. Accordingly, this book will also be filled with the stories of a great variety of people and how they use principles consistent with what we now know about neuroscience to manifest their intentions, from aspiring medical students, to neurodivergent teenagers, to master Polynesian navigators, to Hollywood megastars.

Lastly, I hope that by being open about my mistakes, I will help spare my readers from making the same ones, especially when it comes to deciding what is truly worth wanting and what will bring true happiness.

A final word before getting started. Throughout the book I have included practices to help you clarify where you are now and move forward to where you want to go. I have placed them where they made sense in the course of my explanations. In the last section, however, I have combined and arranged them into a six-week program for readers who would like to make a more formal commitment.

Chapter 1

OUT OF THE WRECKAGE

What Am I Already Manifesting?

It is in the knowledge of the genuine conditions of our life that we must draw our strength to live and our reason for acting.
—Simone de Beauvoir

YOU MAY NOT REALIZE IT OR BELIEVE IT, BUT YOU ARE ALREADY manifesting your life. The question is, is it the life you want?

It was 2000, and the dot-com bubble had just burst. One morning, I woke up worth $78 million, with a villa in Florence and a 7,500-square-foot Cape Cod–style mansion on a bluff overlooking Newport Bay, and with a Ferrari, Porsche, Mercedes, BMW, and Range Rover in my multicar garage. I had just made a down payment on a 6,500-acre island in New Zealand. Yes, my own personal island, with four homes and beaches lapped by deep turquoise water and complete privacy. I thought I had left the poverty of my childhood far behind.

It seemed that everything I had wanted and worked for had materialized, but like so many others who had believed in the limitless possibilities that Silicon Valley offered, I found the harsh reality as my entire net worth vanished in six weeks. It was like a nightmare but I was wide awake, and every day brought more bad news.

I had borrowed $15 million from a Silicon Valley bank for which I had used my stock in a medical technology company as collateral. I hadn't talked to my banker for several months, but when my cell phone rang one morning for the millionth time, I knew there was no avoiding the inevitable.

"Hello?"

"Jim," he said in a voice feigning banker cheerfulness. "How are you?"

He knew the answer. He had followed the dot-com crisis and was well aware that my collateral was worth next to nothing. He informed me of what I already knew.

"Jim, unless you have other assets of which I'm not aware, you're broke and in debt." And after a pause, "What are we going to do?"

"Sell everything," I answered abruptly.

"Sounds like you don't have a choice," he said. "Let's talk in a few weeks and we'll have a better idea where things are going."

Shortly afterward, I was forced to sell the villa in Florence, cancel the purchase of "my" island in New Zealand, sell all my cars except for one, and put my mansion overlooking Newport Bay on the market. No one was living in the house then. I was separated from my wife at the time, my daughter was away at college, and I was living in Silicon Valley as the CEO of a medical technology company a friend had founded. Reluctantly, I returned to the empty house to prepare it for sale and was met by all the harsh evidence that almost all of my dreams had failed. As I drove up, I saw the garden my wife had planted with such enthusiasm and care. What had once grown was now wilted and dead. Yellow-leaved azaleas and drooping camellias betrayed the lack of attention the garden had been getting from the gardener who had promised to check in. The house looked abandoned.

What hurt most was who was absent from the house. Throughout the rooms were nails or picture hooks screwed into the walls, but without pictures. When my wife left, she took all the family photographs, and with them, any reminder that a family had lived in this house. In the central living room, above the mantel, there was a rectangular sun-shadow and a hook where a framed picture had hung. This had been our prized botanical print of iris bulbs by the Bavarian master Basilius Besler, which we had discovered in a tucked-away antiquarian print shop in Florence on one of our print-hunting adventures.

Those were happier times. At the same store, we found a number of old maps from the sixteenth and seventeenth centuries that we loved and that I bought. I remembered feeling happy at the time, and that I was making her happy. I remembered how we had flown first class and stayed in a five-star hotel. How my wife had turned to me and said, "Thank you."

How different those distant memories were to the silence that had formed between us, fraught with resentment, as we grew further and further apart. I winced at the recollection of the painful lack of intimacy between us at the end, how I took on extra surgeries and used the long hours as an excuse not to try to repair the lost connection between us, and how she had told me, "I don't know you anymore."

I passed my daughter's room still filled with furniture. I went over and sat on the bed and thought of her and how many memories we had from the house. But I also remembered her telling me "I won't miss this place" when she left. I didn't understand at first, but I later realized her feelings were a result of the reality of my relationship with her mother. I had somehow begun living at a distance from my own life. Even in the midst of my family life, my mind was elsewhere: tugged back to painful or idealized memories of the past or leaning into the future toward my next surgery, my next financial milestone, the shining moment to come when I could finally have enough to be OK. In the process, I forgot to enjoy what I had and to connect with the people I wanted to build that life with.

As I walked through the formal living room and then the informal living room, my mind ran through a slideshow of a life that was now over. I passed my study with its grand navy-blue wing chair with brass studs, where I had drunk port and smoked cigars from my humidor with friends, the humidor that I had purchased at an auction for Big Brothers Big Sisters of America, of which I was the event chair. My name was engraved on a plaque on the top. When I'd sat in that chair and looked at the plaque as I got a cigar, I'd felt important. I sat in that chair again and rubbed my fingers across the plaque. I felt neither important nor powerful. I felt small.

Now that I was the only one there, the house felt ridiculous and ostentatious. The rooms seemed oversized and inflated, full of hot air, full of nothing. I was like a miniature person roaming through a vast dollhouse of unneeded accessories. The furniture itself seemed strangely insubstantial. From deep inside me, a sense memory floated up of my childhood. Poverty is a paradox: on the one hand, the air is full of a heaviness so great, it can feel like an inescapable weight; but on the other, everything is touched with a strange lightness, as if it were all about to blow away.

I had worked so hard to build a solid foundation for my family because my own had been uprooted so often. Nothing was more degrading or humiliating for me than being evicted from our home. The deputy sheriff coming to our door with the eviction order. Our belongings on the sidewalk. Neighbors watching with curiosity or pity and me thinking, *I hope my mom can find us a place to stay.* I remember sitting on our couch by the curb with all our belongings and my mom next to me. By this time, my sister had moved out and my brother wasn't home. He always left in these moments, perhaps to protect himself or not be embarrassed or ashamed by sitting in front of the neighborhood spectators.

My mom put her arm around me and said, "It's OK, son. It will all be alright. We'll find a place."

When I was a kid, I used to sneak into my older brother's room when he wasn't home and flip through old copies of *Architectural Digest* that I found in the pile of books and magazines he gathered for artistic inspiration. My brother was an amazing artist, and he was always finding treasures to spark his creativity. When I saw a home whose details struck me as particularly cozy or dramatic—with a widow's walk overlooking the sea, or a prominent hearth to warm family gatherings—I'd secretly tear out the page to add to my collection, which I kept in a green cardboard folder in my sock drawer. Of course, these magazines were from the 1960s and early '70s, when the image of the perfect American family reigned without mercy over my childhood imagination. But still, over the years I compiled quite the archive of architectural details, so when Ruth asked me to envision the home I wanted, I had a vast store of images to draw from.

The image that formed in my mind was of myself standing on the balcony of a Cape Cod–style mansion overlooking the dark blue waves of a body of water. Night after night, I had pictured myself there, feeling the bite of the sea breeze against my cheeks, tasting the snap of salt on my tongue, gazing into the depths of the swirling tides. In fact, I'd experienced the scene so vividly, with all my senses so fully engaged, that when I found myself standing on the widow's walk of my Cape Cod–style mansion on a bluff overlooking Newport Bay in reality, I almost wasn't surprised. Or more accurately, my brain settled in and received the experience with a comforting sense of familiarity and recognition.

Through all those early mornings and sleepless nights of doing my meditation and visualization practice, I'd rewired my brain to get comfortable with my dream. This is one of the paradoxes of manifesting: long before I bought it, the image of my mansion, the widow's walk, and the sea breeze had gone from an unthinkable fantasy to a tangible reality. By the time I walked out onto the balcony in real life, my brain *expected* me to be there. Its expectation, and the accompanying twenty-four-hours-a-day focus on my vision by my subconscious, had made my mansion a self-fulfilling prophecy.

Weighed down by my tour, I sat at the top of the stairs, in the heart of the house, with my head in my hands, wondering what to do next. My shoulders rose with resentment at my wife for the emptiness she left behind and all the painful, difficult tasks she had left me with. My throat contracted with longing for my daughter, who was now at college. And my jaw tightened with rage at myself for somehow engineering this entire mess.

My mind raced, jumping from tasks to bitterness to worry about the future. But ultimately, one question rang inside my mind: *What had I missed?* It was as if a patient had died under my care even though I had administered their treatment to the letter. I had done everything right and gotten everything I wanted, but instead of succeeding, I had somehow failed. The success I achieved should have been the peak experience of my life, but it felt just like rock bottom.

The answer came while I was trying to complete my to-do list. After slogging my way through my many tasks, I found myself in a closet with a few boxes of old belongings. I shifted a box of books, and my eye fell on something of much greater value. It was the cigar box I'd used to hold my prized objects when I was that twelve-year-old boy. I hadn't opened it since college. I sat on the floor of the closet, propped the box on my lap, and removed the lid. The faint musk of the past wafted up. Inside the box I found my Lancaster High School class ring with its cut-glass ruby; the wrinkled fake plastic thumb tip I used in sleight of hand tricks to make a scarf or cigarette disappear; and, most precious of all, the tattered black-and-white composition notebook that contained all my notes from my time with Ruth.

I flipped through the pages of the notebook and found my list of wishes.

Go to college.
Be a doctor.
A million dollars.
Rolex.
Porsche.
Mansion.
Island.
Success.

I saw other phrases in my childhood handwriting that I recognized as scraps of Ruth's wisdom:

Compass of the heart. What you want isn't always what you need.
Those who hurt people are often those who hurt the most.

I looked down at the cigar box holding my cherished objects. My heart clenched at the realization that despite all the things I had managed to accumulate, in a sense, this thin twelve-inch box contained everything I had ever truly possessed. A person can't possess more than they can love, and I had not opened my heart any wider than when I first wrote my list. My mansion, my island, my cars, even my family could not fit in the narrow space inside me, and now they were moving on, possibly to be found by those who could truly hold them.

At first, my mind rushed to find someone or something to blame. As it began piecing through my memories, it struggled to find any culprit it could solidly grasp. For much of my life, I was waiting for a father figure who would tell me what to do in any situation, look out for me, love me, and teach me how to become the person I wanted to be. My own father was not able to fill this role: a barely functioning binge drinker, he (and therefore my family) lived paycheck to paycheck when he did work. He'd be in a job for a few months, and we would start to feel almost safe, and then he would go on a binge, spend every penny, and come home drunk or just disappear for days. Invariably, the binge was almost always related to him losing his job for some reason unknown to any of us and him feeling afraid and ashamed to come home and face us, so he would start drinking. We moved often, from one nondescript apartment in a place where I didn't want to live to another, always hoping he would find a stable job. But that never happened.

Even worse, my mother had suffered a debilitating stroke and spent most of her time hiding from the world in bed, and when her depression bottomed out, which it frequently did, she would attempt suicide, usually overdosing on her sleeping pills. I often felt like a leaf being blown by an ill wind, or a child actor in a '50s sitcom in which everything goes disastrously wrong. I felt at odds with the universe, as if I had done something to offend it; that somehow the whole situation was all my fault, yet I couldn't identify my crime or how to set it right. Without a grown-up to look out for me, I developed an overblown sense of responsibility and a serious chip on my shoulder. Without my knowing it, my negative thinking hummed in my mind like the cruel DJ of an underground radio station. These thoughts affected most of my interactions and produced experiences that gave rise to an unceasing series of painful and unhappy events. And these negative thoughts, circulating back to my brain and throughout my body, kept my negative view of the world feeling solid and real.

I had achieved all of the external trappings I associated with success; I wanted to believe Ruth's magic had healed me. I wanted to believe that I had given up my childish hope for a better or different past, taken all my power back, and moved on. If that hadn't worked, something else must be the problem. So I next tried to blame my brain. But it wasn't my brain's fault: after all, my brain and subconscious had dutifully carried out the directives I gave them and produced material results beyond my wildest dreams. The gold Rolex was wrapped heavily around my wrist, the Ferrari and BMW and Porsche were parked in my garage. The mansion itself could have jumped from the pages of the *Architectural Digest* I had so lovingly studied in the tiny apartment in the High Desert whose only view was either of the drab beige back side of another apartment complex lined with garbage cans or the endless desert filled with tumbleweeds. Faithful servant, my brain had only done what I asked, without questioning my intention or motivation.

My brain was just doing its job. It requires tremendous discipline and diligent repetition to create new neural pathways in the brain, and if they are not tended, they will become overgrown like any forest trail. Although it was Ruth's techniques that had brought me so much prosperity and success, by the time I reached bankruptcy it had been years since I'd practiced them. As I achieved item after item on my list, I felt more and more confidence in my ability to manifest my desires and less urgency to stay connected with Ruth's message: as a result, I practiced Ruth's techniques less and less often. You, too, may have been introduced to a practice years ago or had a spiritual experience that changed who you thought you were, but today you find yourself drifting away from it or struggling to keep it a part of your life. It's like an addiction: the longer you are sober, the more confident you feel that you don't need to go to AA. In retrospect, I'd forgotten how important Ruth's lessons had been.

Without the clarity and comfort of the practices to keep me tied to my transformative experience with Ruth, I faced alone the dissolution of my family, the loss of my fortune, and the liquidation of my assets. Most significantly, I had to face that I had lost touch with the powerful habit of opening my heart that had temporarily enabled me to quiet the cruel negative monologue about myself running through my mind. Without a steady drip of the medicine of compassion, my deep-seated habit of self-criticism and self-doubt had returned with a vengeance: *You're not good enough. People like you never amount to anything. You'll never make it.* For a while, the trumpet of my material success drowned out the rumbling of my inner critic. But then I began to hear it, like a menacing inquisitor murmuring in the back of my mind, as I attended a fancy gala or drove one of my sports cars along the coast. And finally, it pushed to the forefront and berated me, just like it had when I was a boy.

This voice, arising out of what Ruth called the "wounds of the heart," frightened me and drove me to prove it wrong. If I could only get the world to believe I was good enough, to believe I had made it, I could silence the voice once and for all, or so I believed. More than anything else, my pursuit of material success came down to my desperate desire to escape my own inner tormentor, the voice of my inner shame. Ironically, as I rushed toward each new acquisition, I forgot to be present for my own pain, which was driving the desire for each new shiny thing. I remembered the one time I lied to Ruth, when I promised her that I had opened my heart before setting my intention. What I did not realize was I had been persisting in that lie ever since.

Today, as a physician, I can look back and see myself as a patient undergoing the journey of a serious illness. The illness was shame and the primary symptom was lack of self-worth. As a twelve-year-old, I was not qualified to make an accurate diagnosis, and so I assumed my illness was poverty itself. Based on this, I then assumed the proper course of treatment was the accumulation of all the markers of success by the standards of society. I prescribed to myself a single-minded, unrelenting path of material achievement, driven by the prodding of my inner critic. However, because I had diagnosed only the surface problem and not the root, the problem persisted and, over years of going untreated, grew worse until it came to a head as I wandered through the wreckage of my life.

If you had significant narrowing of an artery in your heart, the common treatment would be angioplasty. This involves the insertion of a tiny balloon into the artery to expand it, followed by the placement of a wire-mesh stent. An angioplasty and stent placement will only take away the chest pain and provide temporary relief, but unless the habitual behaviors and emotional distress that caused the plaque in the first place are addressed, the stent will often need to be replaced within a year. Eventually, you are faced with a choice: address the underlying problem or die.

The material successes I pursued were essentially no more than stents offering temporary relief from my sense of shame. All the while, the illness of shame continued to impede my innate sense of self-worth. I had somehow bypassed my true affliction. The fact is that I was not alone. Millions of us live in a fog of denial and false hopes, not quite knowing what ails us (or not wanting to know), stumbling through our days and wishing for the best, then unraveling when we find ourselves reliving the same story over and over in bewilderment. For many of us, we are manifesting our own unhappiness.

Sitting on the floor of the closet, I finally *saw* my life and what had become of it. I saw my graduation from college and then from medical school, my wedding, my hopes for the future, the birth of my daughter, my career as a neurosurgeon, my success as an entrepreneur, my divorce, my estrangement from my daughter, and now my loneliness and failure. I had devoted so much time to vividly picturing my future successes that I had never vividly witnessed my life in the present. In that moment, sitting at the top of the stairs, twelve-year-old Jim and forty-four-year-old Jim met each other in their shared bewilderment: *What had I missed?*

As I began to cry, I saw what I had missed. I had wanted a big enough house to put all my family's suffering to right, and in this sense, I had gotten what I wanted. In my mind, I created a mansion, not a *home*. But deeper down, it was this experience of *home* I most deeply longed for: safety, belonging, connection, and warmth. An experience of being present for the ones I loved, caring for them and being cared for by them, and sharing their struggles. I had manifested the outer trappings of my dream but had forgotten to fill that dream with the people and loving relationships that gave it meaning. I had forgotten to satisfy my heart's longing.

I went up to the widow's walk to look out on the bay one last time. When I had first imagined the home where I would eventually live, the image that stood out was of standing on a balcony looking out over Newport Bay. And I had manifested that vision into reality. There was Lido Isle, and there was Balboa Peninsula ringed with the stately sailboats that announced their owners' lives of luxury and leisure.

There was a lone chair on the balcony and I sat down for a few moments. I closed my eyes to think, and suddenly I heard a noise behind me. I looked over and there was a nest of possums burrowed in a crevice under an overhang and behind a fire extinguisher.

The empty house must have been an inviting refuge for the mother possum. A baby possum's cry sounds like a human's sneeze, and sitting there in that chair, I felt as if I were overhearing a child's birthday party where everyone has a cold. As I faced the task of dismantling my home, I marveled at the possum's diligence in assembling hers. How she had painstakingly carried bits of leaves, grass, twigs, moss, and bark in her tail; how, with no degree in architecture or interior design, she had created a structure perfectly suited to shelter her young until they were ready to venture out on their own.

I knew I was in free fall, and my mind latched on to the first tender thing it could find: What was I going to do about the possum's nest? It could take forever to get animal control to come and look, and even then, would their methods be humane? I couldn't just cast the defenseless young out into the elements to be starved, frozen, or devoured. The house was the last remaining thing holding me to my old life, and keeping me from my new one, whatever that might look like. As long as the nest was there, I wasn't leaving the house. And I did not have the heart to move it.

"Goddamn it, you bastards!" I screamed at the possums, not caring if my neighbors heard me or thought I was crazy.

Just let me go, please, I thought to myself. But I knew I couldn't just walk away.

It was time to face my reality and take responsibility for my life just as it was. I had gotten the things I thought I wanted, and they had brought with them a whole host of unanticipated problems. I had manifested them and now it was my task to deal with them. In fact, I could not start my new life, whatever form it might take, without dealing with the problems of my old one. My life might have fallen apart externally, but internally, despite all emotional evidence to the contrary, I was still OK. It was possible to separate my consciousness from the negative emotional reactions the situation was causing in my mind and body. The only way for my nervous system to believe this was if I calmed down. I needed to relax, breathe deeply, and exhale, letting go of the tension before I could think clearly.

After a bit of research, I set up a live trap for the mother possum: a bed of torn-up newspapers with a few apple slices inside. Possums are nocturnal, so I had to stay up and make sure she got inside. Then, wearing gardening gloves, I made sure none of her babies had been left in the nest or on the balcony behind the fire extinguisher. When I was confident everyone was accounted for, I loaded the trap into my car and drove it to a wooded area down the coast. I set the cage on the ground and opened the trap. Cautiously, the mother crawled out, sniffing along the ground, her bald tail curled above her, her babies tucked inside her pouch. In a few short weeks, the babies, who start life the size of a honeybee and can neither hear nor see, would be independent, venturing out on their own. Their instincts were powerful and reliable, and they did not question them. Whereas we humans, with our abnormally large brains and years of responding and adapting to our environment, need to fight for our natural wisdom, for our ability to hear and listen to our inner compass.

I wished the possums the best for their new life and returned to my empty house to start mine.

Humans are imperfect creatures, and our desires are often imperfect, too. When we picture owning a Ferrari, we envision ourselves cruising down the highway at top speed, relishing the devil-may-care freedom that we believe wealth gives us. We do not imagine the pain of having no one to share our adventure with. And when we picture a mansion to live in, we see a warm and vibrant scene of family life. We do not imagine our family fractured by a lack of intimacy, and ourselves alone facing the sale of our home. We imagine the things we want, but not the complexities they bring. We imagine the widow's walk, but not the possums.

Before I could think about what I wanted to manifest in the next stage of my life, I had to understand what I had *already* manifested, and assess its value with a clear head and an open heart. What had worked and what hadn't? What was my role in manifesting the empty mansion, the broken family, the dead end? How had my thinking, my unexamined beliefs, and my unfinished business with my heart contributed to this quagmire?

PRACTICE:
What Am I Already Manifesting?

In this practice, I invite you to assess your current situation with clarity and compassion. The intention here is to be as objective as possible about your circumstances without any judgment. As you uncover the aspects of your life you are already manifesting, you will discover the places from which you may be withholding your inner power. Don't worry about changing anything right now. All you need to do is offer a kind and clear awareness.

1. GET YOURSELF READY

   A. Find a time and a place to do this practice so that you will not be interrupted.

   B. Do not start this practice if you are stressed, have other matters that are distracting you, have drunk alcohol or used recreational drugs in the last twenty-four hours, or are tired.

   C. Have a pad of paper and a pen near you.

2. START TO RELAX

   A. Sit in a relaxed position with your eyes closed for a few minutes, allowing your thoughts to settle.

B. Now sit up straight with your eyes still closed and take three breaths slowly in through your nostrils and slowly out through your mouth. Repeat until this type of breathing feels comfortable for you and is not distracting.

C. Beginning with your toes, start to relax the muscles of your body all the way to the top of your head, feeling more and more at ease as you focus on relaxing your body. You will find that as you do so, there is a sense of calmness that envelops you, and you feel safe. You are no longer worrying about people judging you or criticizing your dreams and aspirations as you slowly continue to breathe in and out.

D. You are comfortable and relaxed as you continue to slowly breathe in and out.

3. VISUALIZE YOUR LIFE

A. Gently call to mind your life in its broad strokes. What are your primary relationships? What is your work? What are the locations where your life takes place? Notice the emotions that arise as you consider these questions. Don't specifically fixate on one image or thought but let your thoughts loosely touch on the major elements that make up your life today for a few minutes.

B. Allow any emotions that come up to run their course naturally. You may notice a range of feelings: joy, contentment, sadness, frustration, boredom, anger. Just be with them and the details of your life for a few more moments.

4. VISUALIZE A BIT MORE FULLY

A. Continue to move through the images of your life. You might reflect on these questions: Who are the people who are important to you, who matter? Do you feel truly connected with them? What is your work? Does it provide you with what you need to live? If you have others who depend on you, does your work provide for them? Does how you spend your day feel meaningful and fulfilling to you? What about the locations in which your life takes place? How does it feel for you to be in those places?

B. Visualize yourself within your life and note whatever these images evoke. Watch your life in your mind's eye. Try to imagine every detail as you slowly breathe in and breathe out. Slowly breathe in and breathe out.

C. Now that you can see every detail, slowly open your eyes and continue to slowly breathe in and out, in and out. You are relaxed and you are calm.

5. RECORD YOUR OBSERVATIONS

A. Take the pen and paper and write for at least five minutes in your own words about what you saw and felt when you visualized your life. Write as many details as possible. Whether it is a few sentences or a paragraph, it only matters that you are writing your life as it is for you and how you feel about it.

B. Now simply sit with your eyes closed, slowly breathing for three to five breaths in through the nose and out through the mouth, and then open your eyes.

6. REVIEW YOUR WRITING

A. First, silently read what you wrote.

B. Then read what you wrote aloud to yourself.

C. Sit with those images of your life for a few moments with your eyes closed.

7. REFLECT ON YOUR LIFE

A. Take a few moments to reflect on how your own choices have brought about the life you are living. Where have you made conscious decisions? Where have you allowed others to choose for you, or just taken the path of least resistance?

B. If your life is not how you once expected and imagined it would be, what was your role in how it actually turned out? There is no need to be afraid or condemn yourself for any part of your life today. This is simply a fact-finding practice. It may not feel like it, but you are taking the first step to reclaim your own inner power to shape your life.

8. APPRECIATE YOUR PRACTICE

A. Feel the empowerment and agency that come with examining your life truthfully. Your life is already starting to transform.

What did you notice? Are there areas of your life that elicited a strong emotion when you reflected on them? If an area is painful to contemplate, you may want to make it the focus of your manifesting. If an area was warm and joyful to reflect on, I invite you to consciously bring these images to mind from time to time and feel gratitude, as these feelings can become a powerful support for you.

Keep the notes that you wrote from this practice with you as you proceed through this program. For better or worse, your life today will become the fundamental ground of the new life you aspire to manifest. You may want to read what you wrote to a trusted friend or mentor and share how your discoveries made you feel. This will give you a sense of accountability and enlist the external support you may need when you are facing resistance, fear, and doubt. By the end of the program, you will likely be surprised by how much has already changed, and your work with this practice will be a good benchmark for your progress.

You may also discover how much you are already manifesting and then take an opportunity to express appreciation for your efforts up to this point and gratitude to life for what it has brought you.

Now that we know our starting point and have clearly seen the life we are already manifesting, we can begin the process of creating the life we want to work toward. But before we embark on our manifestation journey, we need to understand the hardware we are working with, how it was designed, and how it works together.

Chapter 2

NETWORKS AND VIBRATIONS

The Physiology of Manifesting

Any man could, if he were so inclined, be the sculptor of his own brain.
—Santiago Ramón y Cajal

WHEN I WAS IN HIGH SCHOOL, I KNEW A GUY NAMED GEORGE Calloway. Your school may have had someone like him, too. George was a Renaissance man: straight-A student, student council president, and three-sport letterman. He could make a buzzer-beating three-pointer from the corner baseline, hit a grand slam that made everyone in the stands rise to their feet and scream, and then turn around and orate an inarguable rebuttal on why the US Electoral College system should be abolished. Everywhere you looked, George was switching effortlessly between activities. Of course, I envied him and occasionally wished that just once I could watch him flop on his face like an ordinary and fallible human being, but mostly I admired the way he served the greater purpose of whatever team, student committee, or fundraiser needed him at the time.

The brain is full of George Calloways. Our neurons are multisport athletes, constantly forming and changing teams depending on what cognitive activity they need to produce: data interpretation from our five senses, moral reasoning, pattern recognition, memory, intuition. Groups of neurons combine together in identifiable regions, and these regions scale into what are known as *large-scale brain networks*. These networks operate like self-organizing coalitions of Calloways, working in tandem and collaborating to execute high-level tasks and create blindingly complex elements of our consciousness.

From a neuroscience perspective, large-scale or intrinsic networks are collections of widespread brain regions that have been found using scanning techniques such as functional magnetic resonance imaging (fMRI), the electroencephalogram (EEG), positron emission tomography (PET), and magnetoencephalography (MEG). Each network is identified by the role it plays in the overall production of cognition. The regions within a large-scale network display functional connectivity, which means they have been statistically correlated to light up together when the brain is performing certain high-level cognitive activities like processing an image or recalling a memory. Neurons may recombine in service of various mind functions depending on the situation, a bit like the best players in the NBA combining to form an all-star or Olympic team. The large-scale brain networks are the building blocks of a functioning brain, and disruptions in their activity have been implicated in a variety of neuropsychiatric disorders such as depression, Alzheimer's disease, autism spectrum disorder, schizophrenia, ADHD, and bipolar disorder.

Manifesting primarily makes use of four of these large circuits: the default mode network (DMN), the central executive network (CEN), the salience network (SN), and the attention network (AN). It is the interaction of these four primary brain areas, along with the two branches of the vagus nerve, that allows us to give our focused attention to our intentions and make our intentions important enough to the brain to embed them in our subconscious and use its power to manifest them.

Much is known about how these large-scale networks interact, but there remains much that is still unknown. I will give an overview of these different brain networks and how getting them to work together is an integral part of our inner power to maximize our potential to manifest our intentions. To understand how the networks and the nervous system work together, let's consider their role in an actual example of manifesting.

ANULA'S STORY

Anula grew up in Sri Lanka during a time of political and economic upheaval, the result of an ongoing civil war. As the years passed and the bombings intensified, her father worried about the direction the country was heading and began to think more and more about emigrating to the United States. Anula's parents also felt that she and her brother would have better educational opportunities outside of Sri Lanka. The devastating tsunami in 2004 accelerated this process, and finally she and her family emigrated to the United States when Anula was fifteen.

Although her parents' decision to relocate the family was intended to give their children a safer, more resource-accessible environment to thrive in, the family's quality of life was drastically affected by the move in the short term. Her father, who had been a microbiologist working with infectious diseases in Sri Lanka, applied for countless jobs in his profession in America but could only work in a gas station and drive an Uber. Her mother, who had never been employed outside the home before, was also compelled to find work as a daycare provider to help support the family. As a result, they became financially unstable. Adding to the troubles, her mother was diagnosed with breast cancer. Without access to quality healthcare, the family was unable to receive treatment from good doctors and every medical bill was a new reason for dread.

"I remember my mom taking me aside at one point," she recalls, "and telling me, 'You have to make something of yourself because this move is a huge sacrifice for the entire family.'"

The financial insecurity and pressure to succeed weighed heavily on Anula. She had no way to calm herself down. Her amygdala, the almond-shaped mass inside each of the brain's cerebral hemispheres that acts as our threat-detection system, was chronically overactive, filling her mind with anxiety and her body with stress hormones like cortisol. Although she was raised in a country where Buddhism was widely practiced and exposed to meditation—she was even taught it in school—once she arrived in America, her spiritual practice got lost in the worries and problems of daily living. The transition from high school to college was especially difficult for Anula: not only was she away from her family for the first time, but she was also diagnosed with multiple chronic illnesses and began suffering from debilitating anxiety and depression.

"It was like a whirlpool, just being sucked down a hole," she says.

She knew from the start of college that she wanted to go into medicine. However, due to her physical and mental ailments, and the stress of her family's instability, she was not able to perform academically in a competitive way. Whenever she was about to take a test, her anxiety raged, filling her mind with frightening thoughts of failure and vivid images of embarrassment. Because her amygdala was experiencing a constant state of threat, she could not direct her attention toward her intention. Year after year, her pre-med advisers told her, "Your GPA is not good enough for med school." She just had to go on living with the pain of knowing her dream but being unable to pursue it.

After college, she took a job as an associate data manager at a pharmaceutical company with the intention to continue pursuing her goal of becoming a doctor. She tried to take the Medical College Admission Test (MCAT) but was overwhelmed by fear. Her extreme anxiety produced physical symptoms: "I actually wanted to throw up, I would pace, and I couldn't focus. And when the pressure would build up, I couldn't function. It hurt my self-esteem and self-confidence as well. It shook me."

Once, she went through with scheduling the test, but then canceled it at the last minute due to nerves. "At one point," she remembers, "I was like, 'Oh no, I'm not going to get into medical school, and everything is going to come crashing down. I'm going to disappoint my parents. I'm going to disappoint my community. Everything for me is wasted when everyone in the family has suffered so much.'" The physical expressions of Anula's predicament kept her mind locked in the story that she did not feel she had the power to change.

Grasping for something to get her out of her situation, she began exploring spirituality, everything from astrology to life after death to ghosts, and this led her to manifestation. While on a break at her job, without thinking of what she was typing, she Googled "Using magic to get into med school." This led her to my first book, *Into the Magic Shop*, in which I was also repeatedly told by pre-med advisers that I was not good enough to be accepted. In fact, she emailed me and described her desire to attend medical school and her struggles with anxiety. Her story struck me and I responded, which led us to have several telephone conversations about manifestation.

Up to that point, she had thought of manifestation as concerned only with lofty and distant spiritual goals or fantastic displays of wealth. The theme of using manifestation to meet one's immediate needs and achieve one's goals—such as paying rent or getting into medical school—struck a chord with her. When she saw how she could apply the techniques to help her take small steps and make practical improvements in her life, something changed in her belief in herself.

"I mean, it was day and night for me," she told me.

Because of her spiritual background in Buddhism, the meditation practices outlined in my book particularly resonated with her. She quickly took to practicing meditation and relaxation techniques to work with her overwhelming feelings of anxiety and depression. Relaxing her body, part by part, allowed her to calm down, her mind to settle, and her attention to become focused on her breath. It was the first time she had been able to think clearly in a long time.

SYMPATHETIC VS. PARASYMPATHETIC NERVOUS SYSTEM

Human beings were not designed to be stressed out all the time. The state of chronic stress many of us suffer through daily is an unfortunate symptom of the way our nervous system functioning interacts with modern life at the most basic level.

Humans possess a bundle of nerves that originate in the brain stem, the vagus nerve, part of what is called the *autonomic nervous system* (ANS), meaning that it typically works automatically, beneath the level of consciousness. This part of the nervous system developed early in our evolution as a species and has two divisions. The first to evolve was the *sympathetic nervous system* (SNS), whose job it is to ensure our physical survival and the survival of our genes, and whose primary activity is to engage the *fight, flight, or freeze* response. This is where the amygdala reigns. The fight, flight, or freeze response of the SNS has existed in countless species for millions of years. Because it evolved to act in life-or-death situations, it moves along very short neurons and therefore has the power to completely commandeer our physical and emotional resources in a split second, filling our body with stress hormones like cortisol and tensing our muscles for action.

Later, the human nervous system evolved further with the addition of the *parasympathetic nervous system* (PNS), also known as the *rest-and-digest* response, whose job is to return the body to a peaceful resting state, a process known as *homeostasis*. The switch to rest-and-digest is accompanied by a wide variety of physiological changes to promote balance and harmony: our muscles relax, our heart rate and blood pressure decrease, and we produce more saliva for digestion. When we are in rest-and-digest, we feel calm and composed, we are open to connection with others and with our environment, and we have access to the higher-level functions of the neocortex, including abstract planning, creativity, and logical reasoning.

The distinction between the two responses will become crucial for our manifesting process: only when we have shifted into the rest-and-digest response of the nervous system will our brains allow us to reclaim our attention, access the power of our imagination, and unlock our subconscious. There is a quote attributed to Viktor Frankl (although it's only documented in the writings of self-help authors Stephen R. Covey and Wayne Dyer) that says, "Between stimulus and response there is a space. In that space is our power to choose our response. In our response lies our growth and our freedom." It is our ability to choose that allows us to focus our attention and influence our unlocked subconscious to manifest our intention.

As Anula's story of chronic anxiety illustrates, the fight, flight, or freeze response was never meant to be chronically activated. It was designed to produce a short-term physiological response to a stressful situation, say, encountering a rival tribe or outrunning a tiger, and then quickly return to its baseline of homeostasis. On the African savanna where our ancestors evolved, some energy was spent foraging for food, but much of life was spent in downtime. Threats, when they arose, were often lightning fast; they were not chronic and ceaseless as in our modern world. Thus, the body was designed to quickly return to its resting state where it could recover from the drama and release positive neurochemicals such as oxytocin and serotonin, which promote kindness and a sense of healthy connection. To be calm, contented, and caring is the baseline of our species.

The problem is that while evolution takes millions of years to adapt to environmental change, humans have profoundly changed our environment in only a few thousand years. In fact, we lived as hunter-gatherers in groups of fifty to a hundred until only six to eight thousand years ago. Unfortunately, today's fast-paced and anxiety-provoking world is riddled with the sorts of uncertainties and frustrations that trigger the fight, flight, or freeze response and keep it chronically activated by unreal, imagined, or insignificant threats. Essentially, we are responding to a passive-aggressive comment in a colleague's email through the same system that was designed to process a saber-toothed tiger attack. As we will see, the chronic activation of the fight, flight, or freeze response and its release of inflammatory proteins has damaging effects on the body, including an increase in heart disease and a weakened immune system. We pay a huge price in terms of health and longevity because of chronic stress.

At this point in our history, we could say the fight, flight, or freeze response, although associated with our survival as a species, is really a holdover of evolutionary baggage no longer suited to responding to our present world. Although the rest-and-digest response is much more appropriate to flourishing in today's world, it is engaged in a constant struggle for control over the body and mind.

FIGHT, FLIGHT, OR FREEZE VS. REST-AND-DIGEST: PHYSIOLOGY

Division of Autonomic Nervous System (ANS)	Sympathetic Nervous System (SNS)	Parasympathetic Nervous System (PNS)
PRIMARY ACTIVITY	Mobilize the body's fight, flight, or freeze response	Regulate the body's homeostasis and rest-and-digest response
FUNCTION	Control the body's response to perceived threat	Control the body's response while at rest
NEURON PATHWAYS	Shorter neuron pathways = faster response time	Longer neuron pathways = slower response time
BODY RESPONSE	Body speeds and tenses up, becomes more alert; functions not critical to survival shut down	Counterbalance: body restored to a state of calm

Division of Autonomic Nervous System (ANS)	Sympathetic Nervous System (SNS)	Parasympathetic Nervous System (PNS)
CARDIOVASCULAR SYSTEM (HEART RATE)	Increases contraction and raises heart rate	Decreases heart rate
PULMONARY SYSTEM (LUNGS)	Bronchial tubes dilate	Bronchial tubes constrict
MUSCULOSKELETAL SYSTEM	Muscles contract	Muscles relax
PUPILS	Pupils dilate	Pupils contract
SALIVA AND DIGESTION	Saliva secretion ceases	Saliva secretion increases; digestion increases
ADRENAL GLAND	Releases adrenaline	No involvement
NEUROTRANSMITTERS	Epinephrine and norepinephrine (accelerates heart rate)	Acetylcholine (slows down heart rate)
PROTEINS	Proinflammatory	Anti-inflammatory

To more clearly understand how our nervous system works, we must understand how impulses are propagated along the nerves themselves: neurotransmitters. The term *neurotransmitter* is often used interchangeably with *hormones*, but the difference is that neurotransmitters are released from nerve endings in the junction between nerves, called the *synaptic cleft*, while hormones are released into the blood directly. There are over one hundred neurotransmitters in the brain that have evolved to regulate a variety of functions, most of which operate at an unconscious level, including heart rate and blood pressure, digestion and the sense of hunger and thirst, and our response to stress.

Four of these neurotransmitters are primarily responsible for our sense of happiness, well-being, and positive feelings and are, in fact, critical to our survival. These are dopamine, serotonin, oxytocin, and endorphins, which are colloquially called the "happy hormones." Dopamine is often called the "reward chemical," as it is associated with pleasure, satisfaction, and motivation, as well as learning and memory. It is also associated with the *flow state*, which is the experience of being so absorbed by an engaging, enjoyable task that your attention is completely held by it. Serotonin is often called the "mood stabilizer" and is associated with feelings of happiness, sleep regulation, sexual behavior, and appetite. It is also associated with improving one's ability to learn and to improve one's memory. A low level of serotonin is often associated with depression, anxiety, mania, and other mental disorders. Oxytocin is called the "love hormone" because it is associated with romantic attachment, bonding behavior, the sense of intimacy, recognition, connection, trust, and sexual arousal. Endorphins are the body's natural painkillers and are released in response to pain or stress, creating a general feeling of well-being. Most people know endorphins from the so-called runner's high of vigorous exercise, but they are also released by sex, meditation, chocolate, and laughter. As we will see in later chapters, these chemicals play an essential role in the experiences of positive emotion required to teach our brains to classify our intentions as important and worth pursuing.

ANULA'S NEWFOUND POWER

As Anula began to experience some ease and peace in her mind, she found she could reflect more deeply on what she wanted and how to get it. She started writing letters to herself, congratulating herself on the accomplishments she desired, which enabled her to mentally rehearse having already achieved her goals. She started small. First, because she was still experiencing financial insecurity, she experimented with her desire to be promoted at her job. "Congratulations on your promotion, Anula!" she wrote. She folded the letter and carried it in her purse. Whenever she was waiting in line or riding the bus, she took it out and reread it. Each time, she took a deep breath, and visualized the sensations and positive emotions of getting the promotion in reality.

Reading the letter over and over improved her confidence at work. She felt herself tapping into the feeling of *I know this will happen. In fact, it has already happened because I've decided it has.* She began to observe how her tendency to be insecure and second-guess her decisions in her job was becoming drastically reduced. She was more decisive, which in turn improved her confidence and how she carried herself. This newfound confidence inspired respect in her colleagues and supervisors. While participating in team meetings, she had less fear, spoke up more, and ensured her voice was heard. She was starting to embody the leadership aspects that are typically required for the sort of promotion she desired. Normally, such a promotion would take a year or two, but within a few months, she was promoted to full data manager, with an increase in salary of about $20,000.

Even though she was making progress, fears continued to haunt her and hijack her attention. She would take a step toward her goal, then be overcome by self-doubt and images of catastrophe again. "I knew what I wanted," she says, "but I was just not aligned spiritually, physically, or mentally. Instead of living in a manifestation mindset, my life was fear-based."

The change came when she was able to align her personal goal with her ability to contribute to the larger whole of life. "When I was trying to go through the med school process, it was all very me-centered, and coming from a place of fear. I had to break out of that mode, open my heart, and reflect on how much of a difference I could make to my future patients. This allowed me to transform my fear into compassion."

Having a clear mind and a relaxed body enabled her to reconnect with the compassion practice of metta, or lovingkindness, which she was taught at school in Sri Lanka when she was six. She began by offering compassion to herself and gradually expanded the compassion she felt to her loved ones and, ultimately, to the patients she could help in the future if she became a doctor. Whereas to her child self, the practice felt abstract and dry, now it came alive as she envisioned the living and specific human beings she could help deliver from illness to health. She visualized in detail her openhearted compassion for these patients and the care she could offer them. Her chest filled with warmth as she pictured making a correct diagnosis, performing a successful surgery, comforting a frightened family member. Her nervous system released, which allowed her to transcend her self-centered approach and align herself with a larger purpose.

Anula diligently continued practicing her relaxation techniques: she calmed her nervous system by using breath meditation: four-count breaths in, eight-count breaths out. She learned how to tense her entire body intentionally and then release the tension part by part. As her mind and body calmed down, she became able to soothe the voices of fear and shame and reduce their volume. Her ability to focus increased, as did her energy levels, allowing her to take practice MCAT exams. As her practice scores improved, the huge fears she had built up in her head slowly disappeared. The MCAT was no longer a monster; it was simply a step she needed to complete along the way to get to her desired destination.

As she prepared to take the test again, she wrote herself letters congratulating herself on her high score and, later, on being accepted into medical school. Now, though, whenever she took out one of the letters to read, she combined the visualization and relaxation techniques with her openhearted compassion for the suffering people she would be able to treat, and experienced again the deep feelings of connection, service, and joy.

As she directed her attention toward her studies with newfound confidence, she discovered connections she had not perceived before in the material. She was able to gain a more holistic understanding of the systems within the body and how they related to one another. She was also more sensitive to opportunities for support in her environment from teachers, peers, and family members.

"I was no longer drowning in the ocean," she says. "I had learned to surf on the waves that always keep coming. But now, I was supported by a cascade of positive energy that kept coming."

The next time she took the MCAT, she scored well. She completed her application to medical school and miraculously was invited for an interview at her top choice school. It went well, and after months of waiting and continuing to practice her techniques, she finally received the letter she had imagined so many times. She held her acceptance letter in her hand with a strange sensation: it had once seemed like such a long shot, something only on the other side of despair, but now her mind responded as if it had simply expected it all along. The letter was *familiar*.

Anula has now graduated from medical school and continues to practice calming her mind and opening her heart in service of her vocation and the care she will offer to her patients.

THE DEFAULT MODE NETWORK (DMN)

The default mode network is the most thoroughly researched network in the brain. Anatomically, the DMN is also called **the** *medial frontoparietal network* (M-FPN) and is composed of **the** medial prefrontal cortex, the adjacent anterior cingulate cortex, the posterior cingulate cortex/precuneus, and the angular gyrus.

Essentially, the DMN is responsible for brain activity when a person is focused inward, including during wakeful rest, daydreaming, mind-wandering, and reminiscing. It allows us to carry out *self-referential processing*, or the ability to reflect on ourselves. In a sense, it is what lets us narrate the "story of oneself," retrieving and integrating our autobiography stored in our long-term memory and enabling us to take the first-person perspective on that information. It is involved in mental time travel, from recalling past events to envisioning possible events in the future. And it plays a role in how we think about others: considering their thoughts, understanding and empathizing with their emotions, judging whether a behavior is right or wrong, and even perceiving a sense of isolation when we lack social interaction. In our ordinary lives, we experience the workings of the DMN mostly as the incessant chitter-chatter of the mind when it is not occupied with a specific task.

Early researchers noticed that the DMN was deactivated when a person was focused on certain goal-oriented tasks, giving rise to the nickname "task-negative network." This label has since been discarded as misleading because the network is in fact active when we are pursuing *internally* goal-oriented tasks as well as cognitive tasks involving mental concepts. An example would be an introspective meditation session when we focus our attention inward, exploring our thoughts, emotions, and sensations without external distractions. When we are engaged in an external task, DMN can become the commentator that provides detailed thoughts on our performance.

One of the most treacherous mental phenomena is the habitual negative self-talk we call the "inner critic." From a neuroscientific perspective, the inner critic can be seen as an unfortunate collaboration between the default mode network and the SNS. When the DMN gets hooked by the stress response of the SNS, we experience the sort of incapacitating self-consciousness that kept Anula paralyzed. Crucially for our purposes, the DMN is negatively correlated with the attention network (AN), meaning that the more it is activated, the less access we have to the power of our attention. The practices in this book are designed in part to diminish the overpowering sense of self-consciousness that the DMN contributes to our "inner critic."

The DMN has two powerful lessons for us in manifesting: first, experiences such as mind-wandering illustrate that cognition is not always tethered to events in the here and now. As we practice, we will learn to intentionally detach our awareness from whatever is happening in our five senses and direct it toward an imagined experience of the future we envision. Second, when our mind wanders, it inevitably starts to elaborate on internal representations, and this is the foundation of our internal sense of self. While this sense of self is invaluable for all kinds of interactions and daily activities in life, it can gravely interfere with the flow state required to inhabit our vision fully, and so we must learn to turn down its volume.

THE SALIENCE NETWORK (SN)

The salience network is the cognitive system the brain uses to determine what is important. As we will explore in much greater detail later, the brain is bombarded with somewhere between six and ten million bits of information per second, while being able to consciously process only fifty bits per second. This means that about 99.9995 percent of the stimuli reaching our brain are processed below the level of consciousness. Among the overwhelming barrage of internal and external stimuli we are encountering at any given moment, the SN identifies what is most relevant, or *subjectively salient*, and guides behavior accordingly. The SN is involved in detecting, filtering, and determining the relative priority of everything that comes at us from outside and inside, including perceived conflict and discrepancies in information. Our subconscious contains a classification of what we value and what we attend to automatically, and this influences how our SN scans for what is important in our experience. There is some evidence that dysfunction in the SN, such as when our attention is forcibly wrenched away from our conscious direction by compulsive thoughts, may be a core feature of anxiety, depression, pain, and substance disorders.

Salience is usually related to context and is produced by novelty or the unexpected, but it can also be brought about by shifting one's attention consciously toward whatever feature we choose to value. A salient feature can be thought of as the figure that stands out against the background of other non-salient features. Humans have a limited ability to process information; they cannot attend to every aspect of a situation. As we will see in greater detail later, the salience of a thought, idea, or intention determines which bits of information will most likely grab one's attention and have the greatest influence on one's perception of the world. When Anula was reading the letters she wrote congratulating herself, or visualizing herself helping her future patients and rehearsing the associated positive emotions, she was enlisting her SN to teach her brain that these experiences were important. Once that importance was established, her subconscious was primed to bring such experiences about in reality in order to get another hit of the same good feelings. Through repetition, we can make the intention we are attending to salient to the exclusion of other inputs. By doing so, we create what is known as *salience bias* or *cognitive ease*, causing our intention to be one our subconscious cannot ignore.

Structurally, the SN includes the anterior (i.e., front) insula and adjacent inferior frontal gyrus (IFG), the dorsal (i.e., top) anterior cingulate gyrus (ACC), and the amygdala. The anterior insula scans from the bottom up for discrepancies in what we are perceiving, and then coordinates various brain regions together to marshal the resources necessary to respond when a discrepancy is detected. The dorsal ACC is involved in the appraisal of emotional states and conflicts, as well as the use of top-down processing to respond to perceived emotional discrepancies. Part of the ventrolateral posterior frontal cortex (PFC), the left IFG examines new information coming in and helps assimilate it into existing internal models by reappraising its meaning in relation to our preexisting network of associations. The amygdala is part of the SNS and is associated with identifying threats. When the amygdala is activated in a threat response, it negatively impacts the CEN and DMN. When everything is functioning properly, these structures work together to identify something as salient. However, when it is under the influence of the stress response, in the present moment or while recollecting a traumatic event, the SN may erroneously judge the importance of a particular internal or external event, triggering inappropriate autonomic or cognitive-behavioral responses.

Because our brain and nervous system receive such an overwhelming amount of data from both inside and outside the body, we cannot possibly give our attention to every detail. Instead, there is a kind of playbook in our subconscious that manages the precious territory of conscious attention and reroutes everything else into systems of automatic processing. As a result, we miss a shocking amount of information, even when it is blatantly before our eyes.

One of the best-known experiments in psychology is called the Invisible Gorilla experiment or the selective attention test. In this experiment, subjects watch a video in which two groups of students, half wearing black and half wearing white T-shirts, are passing a basketball. The viewers are given two possible directives: count the number of passes made by the people wearing white shirts or keep track of the number of bounce passes versus passes in the air. Then a person dressed in a full-body gorilla suit walks through the scene. At the end, the researchers are asked if they noticed anything unusual taking place in the video. Incredibly, 50 percent of subjects did not report seeing the gorilla.

This experiment emphasizes the nature of directed attention and the phenomenon known as *inattentional blindness*. Subjects who were busy counting the ball passes (the directed salient component on which we focused our attention) missed other aspects of the event going on around them, no matter how bizarre and extraordinary. It also demonstrated how, when we are overwhelmed by too much sensory input, we do not even know how much we are missing.

THE ATTENTION NETWORK (AN)

Within the salience network there is a critical portion whose role is to focus our attention. This is called the *attention network* (AN) and it includes a ventral and a dorsal component. Essentially, the job of these networks is to determine how we pay attention and whether or not to allow our attention to be distracted away from our task.

The dorsal attention network (DAN) is involved in the voluntary, top-down deployment of attention. Within the DAN, the intraparietal sulcus and frontal eye fields influence the visual areas of the brain. These influencing factors allow for the orientation of attention. The ventral attention network (VAN) is the network that primarily includes the temporoparietal junction and the ventral frontal cortex of the right hemisphere. These areas respond when behaviorally relevant stimuli occur unexpectedly. The VAN is inhibited during focused attention in which top-down processing is being used, such as when visually searching for something. This response may prevent goal-driven attention from being distracted by nonrelevant stimuli. It becomes active again when the target or relevant information about the target is found.

Once Anula had calmed her SNS down through relaxation, she was able to carry out the focused attention required to embed her desired intention into her subconscious. And with the intention installed more and more securely, her mind was able to focus more effectively on the tasks required to achieve it. This led in turn to a deeper understanding of the content of her studies with a subtler sense of the connections within it.

THE CENTRAL EXECUTIVE NETWORK (CEN)

The central executive network (CEN) maintains and manipulates information in working memory and is also responsible for decision-making and problem-solving in pursuit of goal-directed behavior. You can think of it as the CEO who gives orders and makes the calls regarding where the rest of the organization is heading. Whereas the DMN shows activation during resting awake states, the CEN shows activation during cognitively and emotionally challenging activities. Its major components include the dorsolateral PFC and the lateral posterior parietal cortex. The dorsolateral PFC manipulates material in working memory and weighs possible behavioral responses. The lateral posterior parietal cortex integrates information from the five senses as well as our internal perception to facilitate sustained attention. CEN hypoactivity is associated with depression and a variety of cognitive disorders.

We need the CEN to help us make wise and appropriate practical decisions, but we also need it for the top-down processing that is necessary to regulate our emotions. When Anula was overwhelmed by stress and doubt, she lost her ability to keep her feelings in perspective, reframe them, redirect her attention to her goals, and talk herself down from the state of chronic SNS activation. When it is operating correctly, the CEN resembles the grounded and stable adult who can soothe the childlike nervous system and defuse its tantrum. This psychological and emotional stability will be essential when we seek to embed our intention in our subconscious, which requires a mental state of calm, ease, and steadiness.

HOW THEY WORK TOGETHER

To manifest with maximum power, the four networks must collaborate effectively in an elegant interplay.

When the process is running smoothly, the SN works in tandem with the AN to determine that a stimulus—in this case, our desired intention—requires higher cognitive processing. This interaction then activates the CEN and deactivates the ceaselessly monologuing default mode network, dynamically allowing us to focus and direct our thinking at will without distraction or self-consciousness. The teamwork of the networks opens a pathway for us to embed our intention in our subconscious, which in turn causes significant resources in the brain to be devoted to bringing it about in reality.

The problem is the SNS, the gatekeeper of our subconscious. There is evidence that when under stress, the overengaged SNS can hijack the default mode network such that our faculty for self-reflection, normally engaged in during safe situations and mediated by the DMN, becomes reactive. When this happens, our sense of being a separate and vulnerable self under threat produces too much rumination and blocks our ability to activate the CEN. This in turn likely undermines the capacity for effective cognitive functioning and embedding of intention while decreasing our ability for emotion regulation. Thus, the embedding of one's intention to manifest must be done in a safe and nonthreatening environment, resulting in maximization of one's cognitive control. The more relaxed our bodies are, and the safer we feel both internally and externally, the less interruption we get from the SNS and the less it prompts an overwhelming torrent of self-reflection from the DMN.

THE GREEN ZONE

Unlike fish and reptiles, whose many young are born immediately self-sustaining and able to seek their own protection, most warm-blooded mammals require significant post-birth parental caring and investment: they need someone to protect them, find food for them, nurture them, and create a safe environment for them as they grow. Therefore, it was necessary for mammals to evolve physiological traits that facilitated approach, contact, and connection. One of the major adaptations was the evolution of the dorsolateral vagal nerve in the myelinated parasympathetic nervous system, which links the organs with the central control systems. The reason this was so significant was that it formed the basis for the affiliative and care response, which, in turn, supplied the physiological pathways for our ability to feel and express compassion. This part of the myelinated vagus nerve is the basis for the *Green Zone* of wellbeing, in which we are calm, focused, in the flow, and able to care responsively for others. The Green Zone is also the state in which our consciousness can be mustered most effectively to visualize and pursue goals.

When the PNS is activated, the tone of the vagus nerve increases. We then enter the Green Zone. This state of well-being facilitates general health; releases beneficial hormones such as oxytocin that are key to the immune and defense systems; helps with learning, critical thinking, and creativity by enabling the flow state; and basically optimizes the human experience. It is also the state that makes manifesting possible by putting our cortex in the driver's seat.

The PNS brings with it the ability to process our emotions, memories, and plans, which then allow us to be much more thoughtful and discerning in our reactions to our experience. This spacious processing ability is the key to claiming your agency to change how you are going to react to the world itself. When we have choices about how we are going to react, those choices affect our physiology, which then affects how we respond to our environment.

So, how do we make the crucial switch from a fight, flight,

or freeze response to a rest-and-digest response? I am reminded of the practice I learned so many years ago in the magic shop.

PRACTICE:
Relaxing the Body

1. GET YOURSELF READY

    A. Find a time and a place to do this practice so that you will not be interrupted.

2. CHOOSE A POSTURE

    A. This practice can be done standing, sitting, or lying down. Before beginning, establish yourself in a posture that is comfortable enough for you to feel relaxed, yet solid and steady enough for you to be alert to your experience.

    B. Straighten your spine and let your shoulders drop. You are looking for a posture of relaxed confidence and gentle strength.

3. BEGIN TO SETTLE

    A. Close your eyes or softly direct your gaze at a point a few feet in front of you. Let your attention turn inward.

    B. Now become aware of the places where your body contacts whatever surface is holding you. Let gravity root you to the earth, and feel the ground pressing upward into your feet. Notice any areas of obvious tension in your body and gently acknowledge them in your awareness.

C. Begin by taking three deep breaths in through your nose and slowly out through your mouth. If you like, you can sigh loudly as you breathe out. Repeat these deep breaths until you get used to this type of breathing so that the breathing itself is not distracting to you.

D. Once you feel comfortable breathing in this manner, specifically notice how you are sitting or lying and imagine you are looking at yourself positioned in that way.

4. START THE BODY SCAN

A. Begin focusing on your toes and invite them to relax. Invite any tension in them to let go. Now focus on your feet, relaxing all the small muscles inside. Imagine the muscles in your feet almost melting away as you continue to breathe in and out. Focus only on your toes and feet.

B. When you begin, your thoughts will naturally wander off and you will become distracted. Don't worry, this is completely natural. When you notice that your mind has wandered, simply begin again, bringing your focus back to the muscles of your toes and feet and relaxing them.

5. CONTINUE THE BODY SCAN

A. Once you have been able to relax your toes and feet and they feel soft, light, and at ease, extend the practice upward, focusing on your calves and thighs. Sense the larger muscles of your legs and invite them each to relax until you feel they have almost melted away as you breathe in and out.

B. Follow the same process with the muscles of your abdomen and chest.

C. Next, focus on your spine and relax the muscles all along your back and up to your shoulders and neck. Remember, the goal is to be both relaxed and alert. If there are any places of obvious or heightened tension, you might experiment with sending your breath directly into those places, inviting them to loosen and let go.

D. Finally, focus on the muscles of your face and scalp and invite them to relax and lighten, releasing any tension they have been holding.

6. BRING AWARENESS TO RELAXATION

A. As you extend the relaxation of your muscles all over your body, notice that there is a calmness coming over your entire body. Notice how this calmness in your body calms your mind. Notice the pleasure and good feelings of being calm in body and mind.

B. At this point, you may feel sleepy or even fall asleep. That's OK. You may continue to feel tense and struggle to connect with any feelings of calm. That's OK, too. It may take multiple attempts to relax the body fully while remaining awake and alert. Be patient. Be kind to yourself, remembering that with every attempt, you are rewiring your nervous system, teaching it to experience a state of peace and regulation.

C. When you have relaxed your whole body to the best of your ability, focus on your heart. Think of your heart as a muscle that you are relaxing as you slowly breathe in and out. You may notice that your heartbeat is slowing down as your body relaxes and your breath slows.

7. DEEPEN THE RELAXATION

A. Imagine your body in a state of complete relaxation. See if you can bring your awareness to a sense of simply *being* as you slowly breathe in and out: nothing to do, nowhere to go, no one to be. Do you feel a sense of warmth or stillness or contentment? You might feel as if you are floating and be overcome with a sense of calmness.

B. Use your intention to take in the feelings of pleasure and peace and install them in your nervous system so you can recall these feelings in the future. Let your nervous system know that this state of relaxation is possible, desirable, and accessible when you need it.

C. On your next exhale, slowly open your eyes. Allow yourself to sit for a few minutes in this state of relaxation with your eyes open, just resting in your experience of being completely at peace.

Begin this practice initially by yourself. Try it for at least a week, even for five minutes at a time. As you find yourself getting rooted in the practice, increase the time to ten, then twenty or thirty minutes. You may discover you actually desire a longer practice; listen to that inner longing. If you found this practice particularly challenging or you struggled to feel a sense of safety and relaxation, you may find it helpful to seek out a group to practice with. You might join a meditation community at a local yoga studio or gather a group of like-minded friends to explore these practices together. As you will see as this process unfolds, enlisting the support you need from others is a crucial skill to cultivate to help you achieve your goals.

VIBRATION

The final component of our physiology is one that comes up often in conversations regarding manifesting: vibrational energy. Although widely misunderstood, there is an entire body of scientific literature that supports the concept that there is a vast circulation of energy that connects everything in the universe, on both the micro- and macrocosmic levels. But what do we mean by vibration?

All things in the universe are constantly in motion, even those that appear inanimate and stationary. One of the more surprising findings that has emerged from physics is quantum coherence, which has given rise to the prediction of nonlocality, or actions at a distance, and instantaneous communication between subatomic particles separated by vast distances. These particles, which compose the fundamental building materials of the physical world, are constantly resonating with each other. Resonance is a type of motion between two states, whether it be called vibration or oscillation, and it occurs at a wide range of frequencies. Thus, every part has a relationship with and is a part of a greater whole, which is again part of something greater. This is true of sentient beings but is also true within and amongst systems—whether in atoms, organisms, social groups, planets, or galaxies. In this context, nothing can be considered separate, alone, or lacking relationships. Each part inescapably affects and is affected by all the other parts.

Like all complex living systems, human beings are composed of numerous dynamic and interconnected networks of biological structures and processes working coherently. Most people know what it feels like to be in this harmonious state, the place where our hearts, minds, and bodies are united in a feeling of wholeness or completeness. We referred to this earlier as "flow" or the "flow state." The term *flow* was first described by Mihaly Csikszentmihalyi in 1975 and has subsequently been widely referred to in a variety of fields beyond psychology. Terms such as "the zone" and "oneness" have also been used to describe this state. The concept, however, has existed for millennia under many other names. In such states, people typically feel connected not only to their deepest selves but to others, even to the earth itself. This state of internal and external connectedness is considered a coherent state of being. Coherence implies correlations, connectedness, consistency, and efficient energy utilization. Coherence is also used to describe the coupling and degree of synchronization between different oscillating systems. It can appear at one level of scale that a given system is operating autonomously, yet it is perfectly coordinated within the whole.

We can witness the emergence of coherence all around us. As the mathematician Steven Strogatz has shown, lasers are produced when photons of the same power and frequency are emitted together, and certain species of fireflies start flashing in sync when they gather in large numbers. In all living systems there are micro-level systems, molecular machines, protons and electrons, organs, and glands each functioning autonomously, doing very different things at different rates, yet all working together in a complex, harmoniously coordinated, and synchronized manner.

On a local level, we can view the workings of the brain itself from the point of view of vibration. Various frequencies are detectable within the brain depending on the activity, with the most common being gamma, beta, alpha, theta, and delta. Gamma waves are the fastest wavelength brain waves and oscillate between 25 and 100 Hz. They are associated with large-scale coordinated brain activities such as focus, attention, learning, problem-solving, and information processing. Beta waves, which oscillate between 12 and 30 Hz, occur during most conscious waking states and are associated with attentiveness, alertness, and concentration that requires maximum brain arousal. Alpha waves are those with a frequency of 8 to 12 Hz and are associated with the brain in an idle state when not concentrating on anything in particular. Theta waves, with a frequency between 4 and 8 Hz, occur during light sleep, deep relaxation, and meditation, while delta waves, which are between 0.5 and 4 Hz, occur during deep states of dreamless sleep.

Researchers such as the neurophysiologist Pascal Fries have explored ways in which patterns of synchronization among these frequencies in the brain produce different types of human consciousness. There are other theories that propose a resonance theory of consciousness that puts the concept of synchronized vibration at the heart of consciousness and even physical reality itself. Although the exact relationship between electrical brain waves and consciousness is still debated, the most important phenomenon of vibration for our purposes is what is known as *neural synchronization*. This occurs when the different frequencies harmonize with each other in terms of shared electrical oscillation rates, allowing for smooth communication between neurons, groups of neurons, and large-scale brain networks. Without this kind of synchronized coherence, inputs arrive at random phases of the neuron excitability cycle and are ineffective, or at least much less effective, in communication. When communication is fragmented or at cross-purposes, the brain cannot produce the synchronized coherence that allows for embedding of salient information into one's subconscious.

Neuroscientists like Antonio Damasio have postulated that it is the underlying state of our physiological processes that determines the quality and stability of the feelings and emotions we experience. The feelings we label as "positive" reflect body states in which "the regulation of life processes become efficient, or even optimal, free-flowing and easy." For the brain and nervous system to function, the neural activity, which encodes information, must be stable and coordinated and the various centers within the brain must be able to dynamically synchronize for information to be smoothly processed and perceived. Ultimately, we are aspiring to make our brain and nervous system vibrate in harmony with the world around us. As Anula puts it, "When you raise your energy by stepping out of the dark cloud, you align yourself with your destiny and things start manifesting."

Amazingly, the most significant vibration of the human body is the one produced by the heart. Many people do not realize that the largest electromagnetic field in the human body is found within the heart. The electrical field as measured in an electrocardiogram (ECG) is about sixty times greater in amplitude than the brain waves recorded in an electroencephalogram (EEG). The magnetic component of the heart's field, which is around five thousand times stronger than that produced by the brain, is not impeded by tissues and can be measured from several feet away from the body. Not only that, but the electrical field also changes along with our emotions, so depending on how we are feeling, we are literally emitting a different quality of vibration from within our chest.

Most people likely assume that the heart rate varies due to exercise or change in one's emotional state, but don't consider that the variability between each beat of the heart is an even more important marker of well-being. As an example, two people could have the same heart rate of sixty beats per minute, but their vibrational energy is completely different, with a vastly different effect on themselves and on others as well. The reason is that one person may have a heart rate of sixty with each beat being one second apart while another may vary between 0.8 and 1.2 seconds. This phenomenon is called *heart rate variability*, or HRV, and has been studied extensively by a number of scientists, including Evgeny Vaschillo, Paul Lehrer, and Rollin McCraty. It may seem paradoxical, but when a person is stressed and anxious, their HRV decreases, meaning the heart beats more steadily and consistently. This is because the stress response stimulates their sympathetic nervous system, which in turn decreases vagal tone. The accompanying rigidity in the heart rate can result in a variety of associated negative mental and physiologic effects. In fact, there is a condition called *broken heart syndrome*, first reported in Japan, in which individuals have sudden cardiac death as a result of severe emotional trauma from a breakup or the death of a loved one.

Conversely, when one is calm, thoughtful, relaxed, and caring, their HRV increases because they are stimulating their PNS by increasing vagal tone. It is when our PNS is stimulated that our physiology works at its best. This phenomenon results in the release of many of our happy hormones, such as oxytocin and serotonin. It also results in the lowering of one's blood pressure, a decrease in one's heart rate, and a decrease in the release of stress hormones and the production of inflammatory proteins. This phenomenon is a result of one's heart rate being coherent, and it is this coherence that creates a measurable energy field that results in improvement not only in our mental and physical well-being but also in that of those around us. When groups of people who are generating this type of coherence come together, the effect becomes larger and more powerful.

It has also been demonstrated that the heart sends more information to the brain than the other way around. When the heart rhythm is coherent, there can be an impact on large-scale brain networks and there also tends to be an increase in heart-brain synchronization. And when heart rate variability increases, one sees an increase in activity and amplitude of brain waves. When Anula began opening her heart to her future patients, she was literally recalibrating the frequency produced by her heart, which in turn had a harmonizing effect on both her physiology and her interactions with others. As we will see later in this book, to harness the full potential of our inner power to manifest our intention, it is necessary to work not just with the brain but with the heart as well.

Now that we have learned the primary components in the body that we will use to deploy our manifestation, we can begin taking the steps to enlist these systems and networks. The first step is understanding how to access our innate power to choose our response to a given situation. In particular, we must reclaim our power to place and hold our attention on whatever object we choose, rather than allow it to be hijacked by our evolutionary baggage: distraction, habit, and the tendency to focus on what frightens us. Learning how this power works and what gets in the way is the key to the entire process of manifesting the life we dream of—and making sure that dream does not become a nightmare. This is the first step I took toward rebuilding my life after it fell apart, and ultimately to creating the family I most deeply longed for.

Chapter 3

STEP ONE

Reclaim Your Power to Focus Your Mind

> *All experience is preceded by mind,*
> *Led by mind,*
> *Made by mind.*
>
> —Buddha, Dhammapada 1–2

THE TWO-WHEELER HOVERBOARD COULD GO OFF-ROAD, GET up to eight miles an hour, and weighed twenty-five pounds. Now Amari held it over his head, ready to swing it smack into Shaun's face.

It was a hot, sunny August day in San Jose, California, at the local pump track in Calabazas Park, a looped sequence of acres and acres of rollers and berms—swoopy, banked turns—designed to maximize momentum, where adventurous cyclists can ride with focus and practice tricks. At thirteen, Amari was the smaller challenger, craning his neck to meet the gaze of the fifteen-year-old, over-six-foot Shaun. As the two young men stood there frozen in conflict, eyes locked on each other, wheels hummed while riders swished by, up and down the small hills, hooting exuberantly as they popped wheelies, bunny hopped, and launched over ramps into 360-degree spins. Amari and

Shaun were there that day to participate in a summer program for neurodivergent students called F+, which stands for Fun Positive. This program combines outdoor activities like dirt biking and dodgeball with improvisational games and meditation training.

Leading this spirited gathering were Dr. Lois Prislovsky, a trained psychologist and expert in ADHD, and Colin Maslan, a former bike mechanic, EMT, teacher, and social worker. Dr. Lois and Colin had met during compassion cultivation training at the Center for Compassion and Altruism Research and Education (CCARE), the center I founded at Stanford, and they shared with me how they bonded over their "redneck proclivities" for BMX biking and snowboarding, as well as a passionate desire to work with youth who were underserved by the conventional educational system. Normally, children diagnosed with multiple behavioral and learning disability issues would be doomed to a summer of dreary analytical worksheets and lifeless PowerPoint presentations, all of it in the indoor imprisonment of sterile classrooms. Many of these students are on the autism spectrum and have experienced the slew of challenges faced by neurodiverse young people. Some had been bullied, others had been the bullies. Some were nonverbal, others suffered from trichotillomania, pulling out the hair on their heads or their eyebrows or eyelashes. For most of them, social interaction was painful, and few of them had any real-life friends. In Lois's view, the system had overpathologized them without listening for what it could do to truly serve their growth and well-being.

"The last thing they need is another freakin' label," says Lois in her lilting Tennessee accent.

So Lois and Colin founded F+ Productions to teach these students self-regulation, compassion for self and others, and a particular brand of short-burst meditation. And dirt biking. People with ADHD—whether they're teenagers, soldiers, athletes, adventurers, or X-games participants—have diffused attention because their brains do not produce dopamine in the same quantities as other people. As a result, their brains crave novelty. Protracted seated meditation in silence was not going to happen with this group.

Instead, Lois recorded personalized meditations for each of the students, usually about two or three minutes long, combining compassion meditation with hypnotherapy. After getting their ya-yas out on the pump track and exploding water balloons over one another's heads, the students practiced these meditations in short bursts in hammocks, up in trees, and on swings. They practiced relaxing their entire bodies, gathering and concentrating their minds, and directing their intention to the kind of person they wanted to be. The exercise on the pump track let them blow off steam and gave them the dopamine hit they needed to be still and practice their inner work.

These practices created an opportunity for transformation to take place. "That's the juice," says Lois.

Lois explained to the students that the human nervous system has two primary modes: the sympathetic and the parasympathetic. She told them how when they get a hit from their amygdala, their bodies go into fight, flight, or freeze mode and they become dysregulated. They needed to calm their minds, open their hearts, and come back to their intention. They used a special biofeedback headset to monitor their brain waves, and when they hit the alpha state associated with relaxation, creativity, and visualization, they heard the trill of birdsong in their ears.

Amari is a warrior type, the kind of boy who grows up to be a Division 1 right guard, going all in to protect the quarterback's exposed rib cage and heart. And Amari was sensitive about his name. Ever since he was young, other kids had been making fun of it, teasing him with singsong nicknames that rhymed. That day at the track, Shaun had failed to read the social cues of the situation and called Amari by one of the nicknames he hated, over and over again. Amari had brushed it off at first, excited to learn how to keep his balance as the hoverboard swooshed around the track. Finally, Shaun repeated the nickname and Amari, wanting to teach his classmate that this was not OK, obligingly raised the hoverboard as if to attack Shaun. So, there they stood, two young men facing off, flooded with testosterone and looking forward to the pleasure of pummeling each other. Other kids had gathered around to watch the rumble.

Lois approached and asked calmly, "How's that gonna work out for the two of you?"

She brought a liberating wildness to the camp that made the students feel at ease. They knew she wasn't afraid to get in the mix with them. One of them had accidentally broken her hand; another had tried to pull her hat off her head but in the process, her glasses had gotten caught on her ponytail and carved a small scar next to her left eye. She'd been upset for about twenty seconds, then got regulated. They saw how she could lose her cool, then find it again.

"Well, I'm going to smash it in his face," said Amari.

Earlier in the day, the students at F+ had been practicing speaking from their hearts. Each one was invited to stand up on a picnic bench and speak authentically. When he first came into the program, Amari could not speak from his heart. He struggled to communicate directly with others, preferring to keep silent. He frequently got in fights and was often in trouble for behavioral infractions.

"When he began working with F+ two years before," says Lois, "he could not practice offering compassion to another human being. So, we started with pets. Once we got living creatures going, we brought in human beings, and then they're offering compassion to the friends they're making for the first time at the camp."

Hoverboard raised above his broad shoulders, temples sweating, Amari considered. He knew his nervous system had flipped its lid and sent him into fight, flight, or freeze mode. He'd been there many times; he knew where it would lead. He saw Lois standing there, waiting cheerfully for his next move.

And then, instead of swinging the hoverboard, he lowered it—and started laughing. Then Lois was laughing, and Shaun was laughing, and all the others who were watching laughed, too. The training had worked.

Finally, Amari spoke from his heart. "Please do not call me by that name," he told Shaun. "I don't like it."

At the beginning of the summer, Lois and Colin had measured Amari's emotional state, and then measured it again at the end. After six weeks, his depression and anxiety had decreased while his compassion for self and others had risen. His parents were thrilled; they knew something magical was happening.

As Amari and the other students had learned to regulate their responses, they slowly regained an extraordinary capacity: they took back their ability to direct attention where they chose—away from stress and conditioning and reaction and toward a new response that embodied the kind of people they longed in their hearts to be. As they reclaimed their attention, choice returned, and choice signaled the presence of an inner power that is the essential element in carrying out any intention. In neuroscience, this inner power is known as *self-agency*.

INNER POWER

Within each of us is an incredible inner power that we limit by our own beliefs. It is the power to endure discomfort, to delay gratification, to decide what we let into our minds from our environment and what we don't, to control our response to any given situation, whether real in the moment or replaying in our minds from the past. This is our power of choice. It is this power that allows us to focus our attention where we choose, no matter how loud or frightening or seductive the external stimuli trying to distract us. This is the power Amari called upon to switch out of fight, flight, or freeze, put down the hoverboard, and speak from his heart. This is the power we can call upon ourselves to direct our attention toward inner intentions that produce powerful positive emotions strong enough to break us out of the emotional addictions that have kept us living small.

As we go about our lives, many of us feel ourselves to be the victims of forces outside of ourselves, or even forces within ourselves that we can't control, tame, or regulate. Our reactions to these forces feel automatic, and we watch helplessly as they seem to steal our inner power away from us. In the moment, these forces feel overpowering and travel deep grooves carved by long-standing habits. The reality is that we can cultivate practices to reclaim our influence over countless processes that appear automatic and inaccessible to conscious control.

Because the power of the practice lies in our mind's belief in possibility and its ability to change our physical reality, it is not limited by anyone else's belief that our desires are not possible, whether that's a skeptical individual or family member or a biased society. Unlike a financial investment, which requires that you already have capital, manifesting demands only an investment of time, energy, attention, and heart; it is an investment *in yourself*. The techniques, although they do require diligence and repetition, do not cost any money to practice and do not require advanced training of any kind.

Now, it may indeed be challenging to surmount deep-seated limiting beliefs about your potential, especially when they are upheld by your family, country, or religion, but thankfully you will discover that your beliefs about yourself are one of the few areas you do have control over. Therefore, if you set your mind to transcending them in yourself, no one else's beliefs will have the power to limit what you can achieve.

In the end, it's not about the universe: it's about you. We may have come to believe that our inner power is limited by our external circumstances or our past conditioning, but it starts in our own minds.

GAMBLING WITH OUR ATTENTION

Much of the time we go through life feeling things are happening *to* us, not motivated *by* us—and certainly not occurring *for* us. This feeling of being a passive participant in an experience is like being the passenger in a car that someone else is driving, either with no intended destination or toward a place that will inevitably cause us pain. It is disheartening, is disempowering, and diminishes our belief in our ability to make choices that serve us. Often we may feel as if some other force has thrown us into the trunk and gone joyriding with the vehicle of our lives, and it can be a long time until we groggily regain consciousness and find ourselves far from where we wanted to be. This is the experience of so many who carry unresolved trauma that continues to dictate their choices unconsciously.

Our attention is not only hijacked from the inside. Many of the most irresistible assaults on our ability to focus our minds come from the world around us. Billions of dollars are spent on advertising designed to persuade us that our lives lack something essential, and to captivate our minds with the one special product that can fill that lack. Social media companies succeed by capturing as much of our attention as they can through psychological processes that mirror addiction, then selling that attention and data to the highest bidders. And news outlets go to great lengths to present stories designed to hijack our amygdala so that we cannot look away.

The typical American spends about 1,460 hours per year on their smartphone, which translates to about ninety-one waking days. We do not give our attention to these devices only because we lack self-control. Our devices are designed to exploit a psychological phenomenon known as a *variable ratio reinforcement* schedule. Imagine a rat in a cage who is taught that if it presses a particular lever three times, it will be rewarded with a food pellet. Now imagine a lever that produces a food pellet at random—sometimes it takes only one press, other times it takes five, other times fifteen. The rat quickly catches on that the faster it pushes the lever, the sooner it will get the next pellet. This is also the principle by which slot machines work.

A human brain, operating at a greater degree of complexity, tries to figure out the pattern that governs the variable rewards. The brain of a compulsive gambler releases dopamine, a reward chemical, to motivate the gambler to pay attention to the seemingly causal connection between pulling the lever and winning the jackpot. Near misses, such as two cherries but not three, deepen the compulsion to keep playing. The apparent causal connection forms between the motivation to seek reward and the deployment of our attention. This is called *incentive salience,* and it creates a pattern of activation in the brain that resembles drug addiction, binge eating, and other compulsive habits.

Similarly, research has shown that as we scroll through our phone, we are essentially manifesting the *Vegas Effect*: notifications produce a sense of anticipation that activates the reward system, which then captures our attention in an endless loop. As we incessantly check our messages or doomscroll through content for the one piece of information that will make us feel OK or will flood us with horror and empathy fatigue at the suffering of the world, we helplessly watch our attention slipping away from us. When we lose the power to direct our attention, we can sink into despair and feel we do not have influence over the course or quality of our lives. Deep down, we know that selective attention is the key investment in building the lives we desire. That is why we say we "pay" attention. Our inner power rests in our ability to make conscious decisions about our investment. If we cannot direct our attention as we choose, it is as if we are giving away the capital we possess to change our circumstances. We are giving away our self-agency.

The reality, though, is that our feelings of disempowerment are often an illusion. If we examine each moment in which we appear to involuntarily give away our power, what is happening is the reactivation of an old habit. Our conditioning to react in a particular negative way to a particular external stimulus is just a pattern of physical, mental, and emotional signals that have become wired together through frequent, unexamined use. Over time, our minds adapt to this ceaseless automatic activity and no longer offer us opportunities for conscious choice. In a sense, it is a subconscious type of negative flow state. When our brain stops believing it is important for us to see chances to change our behavior or environment for the better, we feel stuck, frustrated, and hopeless; we lose sight of our own inner power.

And yet, the feeling of having lost or been deprived of our power does not mean that it is gone. The sense of agency is part of how the brain narrates its experiences, often deriving more from subjective interpretation than actual fact. We may *feel* we have no agency, it may have been suppressed or obscured, but it has never left us. It is a fundamental fact of being human; as long as we have functioning brains capable of growth, we have agency. Therefore, you could say that in our society we are suffering not from a crisis of agency, but from a crisis of the *sense* of agency. Self-agency is the superpower we have forgotten we possess.

THE SENSE OF AGENCY

The sense of self-agency is essentially the feeling of being in the driver's seat when it comes to intending, initiating, and carrying out our actions. This gives us the reassuring sense that we can control the outcome of a given situation through our own actions or our will.

Studies have demonstrated that the sense of agency is much more flexible and adaptable than we might commonly believe and is composed of a variety of elements ranging from high-level cognition (thinking, learning, remembering, reasoning, and paying attention) to low-level sensory and motor systems. The sense of agency is just that: a *sense* that is constructed by our brains from a combination of cues in our experience. The brain examines whether our actions appear to be causing the results we intend them to and influencing our environment as we choose, and then uses that data to assess whether we have agency in the situation. The humbling truth is that our conscious mind does not have access to most of the subconscious processes by which we carry out actions (such as our ability to perform movements), and therefore it can only set an intention, watch its effects, and then interpret them accordingly. In other words, our sense of agency is a *story* our brain tells us about our experience. When the story the brain tells us is that we do not have the power to perform the actions necessary to influence our circumstances for the better, we feel disheartened and lose our motivation; when the story tells us we do have the capacity to act on our desires, we feel empowered, confident, and integrated.

To illustrate the interpretive nature of agency, we can examine the surprising science of how the sense of agency may be present even when physical agency is not. As a neurosurgeon, I have seen many patients, either due to disease or trauma, with a condition known as *anosognosia*. *Anosognosia* comes from the Greek words *nosos* ("disease") and *gnosis* ("knowledge"), so patients with anosognosia do not know or realize they have a particular disease or impairment. One example is hemiplegia, which describes patients who are paralyzed, usually following a stroke. If the stroke also affects those areas of the brain associated with integration of self-awareness, these patients may be unaware on a conscious level that their movements are impaired.

Researchers at the University of Turin examining such patients made a surprising discovery. One woman presented severe and persistent anosognosia for the paralysis on her left side. She never spontaneously reported her motor problems. When questioned about her left arm, she always claimed that it could move without any problem. When asked to actually perform movements with it, she attempted to perform the action, and after a few seconds she appeared to be satisfied with her performance. This woman experienced a sense of agency for movements she was unable to make. Despite all evidence to the contrary, she truly believed she was able to move her paralyzed arm. The researchers concluded that the experience of agency in patients like these is strongly governed by cues in the brain that precede movement, such as intentions and predictions of action, *not* the actual actions themselves. The story the woman's brain was telling her about her power to act was radically different from her physical reality.

The important point here is that the sense of agency is really a perceived *subjective* experience that can be influenced by our own thought processes. Therefore, the depth and efficacy of our sense of inner power comes down to the story we tell ourselves about our ability to express that power. As we will explore in future chapters, the feeling of inner power is ultimately the feeling of being able to direct the full capacity of our brain toward an intention we choose, in particular harnessing the power of our subconscious. And the strange thing about the subconscious is that it runs on beliefs. What we subconsciously believe is often what limits the possibilities of a given situation. There may be a large gap between a person's feeling of inner power and their ability to express that power in practice. In a sense, many of us suffer from the opposite of the patients with anosognosia: we labor under the delusion that we are paralyzed, when we are in fact fully able to act effectively!

In psychology, *self-efficacy* is the belief of an individual in their capacity to act in the ways that are necessary to achieve their goals. Self-efficacy may influence how and why individuals choose to participate in or stick with an activity, and it is believed to be a more accurate predictor of behavior than a person's actual ability.

One may get confused that self-agency implies free will. The nature of free will is a much deeper discussion that brings into play what we know of brain science, psychology, philosophy, and religion. Some hold that we lack free will because so much of our behavior is governed by forces and influences not apparent to the conscious mind, while others argue that all actions are predicated on the interaction of molecules, atoms, and particles, and therefore every event is predetermined—we just ignorantly *think* we are causing our own actions. I am not intending to solve this age-old debate. And happily, for the purposes of our discussion of manifesting, we do not have to solve it. I am simply indicating that we do have choices regarding how we manipulate processes within ourselves to manifest our intentions. It is this cognitive control, rooted in the functioning of the CEN, that enables our ability to adjust and direct cognitive resources to complete the goal-directed task of embedding our intention into the subconscious and therefore optimizing our ability to manifest. One must focus one's attention and make salient that which one wishes to embed in the subconscious by first embedding it into one's working memory. It is sustained selective attention through what is called *effortful control* that results in its power to embed in the subconscious.

It might seem that self-agency or one's inner power is fixed, but one must think of it as a kind of potential energy. Potential energy is a resource that is contained until it is released. The sad reality is that many people do not believe they have such energy and thus end up defining their lives by their limitations and believing change is not possible. Imagine if every day you take a drive in the mountains, and every day it is so foggy that your view down into the valley below is obscured. And, in fact, you've never seen the valley but have only been told it exists. You have been told that in the valley are beautiful waterfalls, lush gardens, beautiful redwood trees, but you have never seen any of that—all you've seen is fog. Eventually, you question if there is any truth to what you've been told. Now imagine that you go on your drive and you reach the top of the mountain and this time, the view is clear and bright and you can see far into the distance. You see that not only does everything you've been told about exists, but it is even more beautiful than you had ever imagined. And you realize that the valley has always been there: you could not see it because of the fog that caused you to doubt, not because its existence was ever in question. Most people live their lives driving in fog. They may have been told of possibilities or seen a bit of the valley, but imagine if they had a crystal-clear view. It is at this point they understand their full potential and realize how much potential energy is within them. They are liberated to use their inner power to change their life.

What does this have to do with manifesting? Our power to manifest the things and experiences we desire comes down to our ability to throw off the narrow mental habits that keep our perception shrouded in fog and tell us we are unable to influence a situation or resist a habitual reaction and instead to embrace our sense of inner power. In order to produce the results we want, we must first believe in our innate ability to affect the outcome of situations through our actions and will. This process starts with our attention. In order to understand why we are so susceptible to fear and negativity hijacking our minds and holding our attention hostage, we need to examine the physiological foundations of our thought processes.

And we will discover that the peace we seek is often only a few deep breaths away.

JUMPING OFF THE TRAIN: METACOGNITION
One of the most significant obstacles to manifesting lies in giving too much power to unpleasant sensory input and not un-

derstanding that our power lies in how we respond to such input. As a result, many of us avoid unpleasant sensory input, but the reality is that to access our inner power we must learn how to sit with unpleasantness and not turn away from it reflexively. By being able to do so, we understand that it is by reclaiming the power to choose our response to discomfort that we access our power to manifest. Consider the example of a Tibetan monk practicing Tummo meditation, a combination of forceful breathing and meditative visualization of flames in certain parts of the body that is often used in cold environments. Using this technique, the practitioner can increase their heart rate, maintain a consistent body temperature even while submerged in ice, and manipulate other physiological processes that most people would argue you cannot consciously access. You, too, can access a whole host of processes that appear to be impossible to access consciously or seem impenetrably automatic. All you need is the right training. We must learn to resist the highly natural urge to escape or deny our discomfort, and instead develop the capacity to stay with it long enough for it to transform and dissolve. This is the key to our liberation and fundamental to manifesting.

The Dutch athlete Wim Hof, also known as "The Iceman," is famous for his endurance when being subjected to extreme cold. He has set world records for swimming under ice and prolonged full-body contact with ice and holds the record for a barefoot half-marathon over snow and ice. He attributes his success to what he calls the Wim Hof Method (WHM), which is a combination of forced breathing, cold exposure, and what some would call a form of meditation. By deliberately hyperventilating, Hof temporarily suppresses his innate physiologic response and raises his heart rate and adrenaline levels. Interestingly, scientists studying Hof concluded that the WHM engages higher-order areas in the cortex (left anterior and right middle insula) that are uniquely associated with self-reflection and that facilitate both internal focus and sustained attention in the presence of adverse (e.g., cold) external stimuli. In other words, Hof's mental *attitude* of confidence and fearlessness about the experience allows him to activate his upper-level capacity for focus, which in turn diminishes his sense of time and space, skillfully drawing his attention away from unpleasant physical sensations and tricking his body into skipping its normal threat response. As a result, he enters and remains in a kind of flow state.

Although we are conditioned to identify with negative emotional responses to the external environment, with practice it is possible for us to recognize our conditioning for what it is, and disidentify from it little by little. Inner power arises when a person learns to discern between their negative conditioning and their inner awareness, and thereby discovers that the emotional reaction is conditioned and not hardwired. The discomfort in the body and in the mind gradually loosen as their sense of identification with their habits dissolves.

The reality of manifesting is that most of us avoid experiences of discomfort. Although loud and compelling to the survival systems of the brain, these uncomfortable feelings, which often derive from painful childhood experiences, are in the end just mental habits often created to protect our childhood self. It is these habits learned as children that determine how we respond to so many experiences we face as adults. These experiences are the subconscious drivers of our behavior that we have never evaluated consciously. If we did, we would quickly discover these habits are not useful solutions to what confronts us as adults. The first key is to transform our relationship with discomfort: we must become aware of our thoughts about it and recognize our ability to work with them. This is the power of *metacognition*, or the practice of consciously viewing your own thinking. Through this process, we can actually set ourselves outside the situation in our minds and look at our thought processes to see exactly how we are thinking. The second key is to learn to recognize our thought processes without becoming overly absorbed in their drama and identified with their stories. Only then are we able to jump off the train of thought. When our attention is no longer hijacked by our thinking being stimulated by our physical and emotional discomfort, we start to have the freedom to turn it toward the goals and objects we wish to manifest.

On the conscious level, manifesting is a process of clear and focused thinking. And the reality is, when you are in survival mode or anxious or stressed, you are literally not thinking clearly and revert to habitual learned ways of behavior. Your body is flooded with cortisol, you are hypervigilant, your upper-level cognitive functions are diminished. Like Anula, we are overcome by physiological reactions that rob us of our natural brilliance, abilities, and intention. We lose our connection with the neocortex and its higher-level abilities of planning, reflection, insight, and even being compassionate. The presence of stress hormones gives cues to our cells to act out of self-preservation, essentially becoming more self-seeking, and thereby endorse our ego to become more self-seeking as well, diverting our attention to our immediate sensory experiences, instead of a broader, more holistic view of reality. The more you are in fear mode, the more your internal thoughts are clouded, and instead of seeing the world through a clear window, that window is opaque.

When a person loses sight of their inner resources, they will find it difficult to consider a choice before they make it, because their high-level cognitive functioning has been hijacked by the survival response of the lizard brain. They become so used to this state of affairs that, on a day-to-day level, they come to identify completely with it. There is no distinction between their habitual negative emotional state and themselves. The feeling can be like being stuck on a train that is about to go over a cliff: although we know we are headed for disaster, we do not believe we have the power to jump off before it goes over the edge.

The first essential step in reclaiming our power is to step back and watch the train. Although it may sound counterintuitive or even foolish, the moment the train is about to go over the cliff is the moment when we most benefit from turning our awareness to our thoughts. With practice, we discover it is possible to view our own thinking objectively and without emotional attachment. When we set ourselves on the train platform rather than on the rushing train itself, we can watch the thoughts as they fly by. Seeing our thoughts for what they are is the first crack in the illusion of our helplessness. When we calm down enough to see them clearly, we make a startling discovery: there are gaps between the stimulus and our response. As we practice for longer, the gaps widen and we gain more and more agency in how we choose to act on our thoughts.

Because the fight, flight, or freeze response often manifests in our conscious mind as rapid-fire, high-volume negativity, the most powerful place to cultivate the sense of inner power, and the most ready-to-hand, is in learning to detach emotionally from our thoughts. When we realize the tricks that evolution and our own physiology have created to make us do certain things or use shortcuts in how we think of things or respond to them, we become empowered to perform a kind of "manual override." When we become aware of the tricks, and see them for what they are, we can start changing them.

There is the standard way in which we respond to a stimulus, but now we also have a new way: we can jump off the train. Jumping off the train is an invitation to the unknown, the untraveled, the unfamiliar but with the possibility of liberation from our self-created prison.

If you are in a state of fight, flight, or freeze activation, and you are thinking to yourself, "But this is all happening *to* me. I am the victim; I do not have the agency and I am making my situation worse with all my negative thinking." And I am saying, "The truth is that your thoughts are influencing your reality. But you have more power over your thoughts than you think, and for that very reason, you have more influence over your reality." I encourage you, when you take stock of your life and consider how to move forward, do not stop at negative external circumstances. Take the inner attitude into account. Do not take external environmental evidence as conclusive or some kind of prophecy of the only things to come. Every day is an opportunity to change how you perceive and react to the world.

Don't get me wrong, experiencing the unpleasant physical sensations of your habitual negative rumination is highly uncomfortable. It can be excruciating and make us want to run for the hills, or regress to our old coping mechanisms. It is a monumental task that requires tremendous discipline and support. For those who are negatively affected by systemic oppression on a societal level, the task of liberating the mind from habitual fear can feel all the more like swimming against the current, because powerful and often violent forces of prejudice are mustered against their sense of individual sovereignty.

However, once you understand that you can relate to your thought processes moment by moment with much greater clarity and power, you can begin experimenting with thoughts that produce a good reality. You will begin to learn how, if you think and act in your old way, it produces one version of reality, and if you learn your lesson and choose otherwise, it produces another, more desirable one. The magic of the process is that it's the same hardware. When you set your mind to a good result, the pathway is exactly the same, but the software is updated through positive neurofeedback. As the Stoic philosopher Epictetus said, it is not events that disturb people, it is their judgments concerning them. It only requires you to take the first step.

PRACTICE:
Building Inner Power

When you feel your body is somewhat more relaxed, reflect on a simple activity that you've wanted to do but for whatever reason you have not done. An example would be to get up early and walk for fifteen minutes or commit to not drinking soft drinks or alcohol.

1. START TO RELAX

- A. Before you go to sleep, sit in a comfortable position in a chair, close your eyes, and focus on relaxing every muscle in your body. Begin at your toes and go all the way to the top of your head while you are slowly breathing in through the nose and out through the mouth.

- B. Once you are relaxed, focus on your breath, slowly breathing in through your nostrils, holding it for five seconds, and then slowly releasing your breath through your mouth.

2. VISUALIZE YOUR INTENTION

A. After you have done this for five minutes, think of yourself doing that simple activity. Don't just think of yourself doing the activity but also see yourself doing it.

3. RECORD YOUR INTENTION

A. Once you have done this, open your eyes and write on a piece of paper your goal or the activity and lay the paper on your nightstand.

4. INSTALL YOUR INTENTION

A. Lie down and close your eyes and slowly breathe in and out for a few minutes as you see yourself carrying out your intention. Let this breathing lead you into sleep.

5. REVIEW YOUR INTENTION

A. When you wake up, sit up and read the paper. Embed the thought of your goal and proceed with your day.

If you've committed to walking in the morning, proceed to do so. If you're not drinking soft drinks, every time there is a choice, pause and choose not to do so. Each time you have done or not done the activity you've chosen, congratulate yourself and then write on a piece of paper, "I congratulate myself for completing this task."

By doing this daily, you demonstrate to yourself that you have the agency to complete a task that you've chosen to focus on. While the task may be simple, the activity of doing so engages those brain processes that are associated with embedding intention into the brain. This is the power of tiny habits.

Continue this task until you no longer think about the process and it comes automatically. This is the power of tiny habits. In fact, my friend BJ Fogg, a behavior scientist at Stanford, wrote a book called exactly that: Tiny Habits. *He even gives us a formula, B=MAP. "Behavior (B) happens when motivation (M), ability (A), and a prompt (P) come together at the same moment."*

Once the mind and body are in a state of balance and peace, and we have access to the power of our imagination, we can start thinking clearly about what we want to manifest in the present and future. Therefore, in our next chapter, we will continue the six-step process of manifestation with Step Two: Clarify What You Truly Want.

Chapter 4

STEP TWO

Clarify What You Truly Want

There is no favorable wind for the sailor who does not know where to go.
—Seneca the Younger

THE INNER COMPASS

In 1980, just before Nainoa Thompson embarked on his historic 2,200-mile wayfinding journey from Hawaii to Tahiti, his teacher, the master Polynesian navigator Mau Piailug, asked him a question.

They were standing at Lanai Lookout on the southeastern shore of Oahu observing the sky as they had done countless times before. Mau instructed Thompson to pay careful attention to every star, every seabird flight, every mare's tail and mackerel cloud whose path predicted the weather.

Thompson was preparing to attempt a feat of seafaring that had not been done since the fourteenth century: a voyage from Hawaii to Tahiti in a double-hulled canoe called the *Hōkūle'a* (Polynesian for the bright star Arcturus) without the use of Western navigational instruments. The trip had a deeply personal meaning for Thompson and his region: to prove that ancient Polynesians had made purposeful trips through the Pacific using sophisticated navigational methods based on the movements of nature, as opposed to passive drifting on currents or sailing from the Americas, as some Western doubters had posited. Mau was among the last living navigation experts in the ancient style from a people on the verge of cultural extinction, and Thompson's training had been the fruition of a lifetime's love for his island and its ocean.

Standing on the shore overlooking the waves Thompson was about to face, Mau asked, "Can you point in the direction of Tahiti?"

Thompson pointed.

"Now," said Mau, "can you see the island?"

Thompson was confused. Of course, he couldn't see Tahiti—it was over two thousand miles away. But he understood Mau meant his question seriously. He considered it for a long time, then answered, "I cannot see the island, but I can see an image of the island in my mind."

Mau said, "Good. Don't ever lose that image or you will be lost."

Then he turned to Thompson and said, "Let's get in the car, let's go home."

This was Mau's last lesson. "He was telling me that I had to trust myself," Thompson said later, "and that if I had a vision of where I wanted to go and held on to it, I would get there."

I first heard this story from a meditation teacher who pointed out that Mau was instructing Thompson to trust his inner compass, the innate and instinctive sense of where he wanted to go that would point him in the right direction and guide him on his journey. The notion of an inner compass has stayed with me and has helped me throughout my life.

As we begin our practice of manifesting, we, too, start by

connecting with our inner compass, our inner image of where we want to go, the island arising in the distance of our own vision. This image fills us with inspiration, energizes us, and guides us through the inevitable ups and downs, opportunities and setbacks we will encounter on our own journey. If we choose a worthy destination, entrust our path to our inner vision, and hold to it even in the face of obstacles that appear insurmountable, through the doldrums where clouds obscure every familiar reference point in the sky, we will be led safely where we need to go by the compass of our hearts. We must then set our minds on a destination that is worthy of our pursuit.

But what is truly worthy of wanting?

WHAT TO WANT?

In today's culture, the conversation about manifesting is focused mainly on the pursuit of fabulous wealth and outward success measured by society's materialistic standards. This is a distortion of the manifesting process and its deeper potential. Sadly, the power of manifesting has been somewhat distorted by the false narrative of our culture, which promises that achieving material success will fill a sense of emotional emptiness. Sitting in my mansion with my head in my hands, I learned firsthand this was untrue. In fact, there is nothing about manifesting that is inherently about acquiring material possessions. In a sense, to envision and seek only material gain is to dream too small. I now find it ironic that when my twelve-year-old self imagined an island, it was to be private, all mine, its luxury a testament to my personal glory alone; when Nainoa Thompson imagined Tahiti, it held a deep symbolic meaning not only for himself but for his entire community and his lineage. Both of us imagined islands, but they were very different destinations.

Knowing clearly what we truly want will allow us to set our inner compass in the right direction; it will be the basis for the intention we will consciously embed in our subconscious. Needs and desires have a way of evolving the more we experience. In the hierarchy of needs as posited by the psychologist Abraham Maslow, we must first meet our basic physical requirements for breath, clean water, food, clothing, and shelter. Only when these basic needs are met can we focus our effort and attention on others, on our need to connect, on those things beyond our basic survival such as the fact that others are suffering. That is our reality. The good news is that manifesting can serve you wherever you find yourself on the hierarchy of needs. Whatever it is you need, manifesting can work to help you find it.

When I was a kid living in poverty, my focus was on manifesting the material needs of my family. I used the same techniques to get into college and later medical school, and later to advance in my professional life, long before I ever thought about self-actualization as a goal. Like all of us, I needed to achieve some degree of stability, prosperity, and worth before I could turn my attention to realizing my higher purpose in the world.

When we first discover the depth and potency of our own inner power to influence our lives for the better through our choices, it can be a dizzying prospect. As we reconnect with our power of agency, we may at first become overwhelmed by the sense that we are responsible for *everything* and blame ourselves for things over which we have little to no control. It can take practice to calibrate our perceptions to a right-sized view of our inner power. In the next chapter, we will address specifically how to overcome these obstacles, release patterns that no longer serve us, and learn others that benefit us.

Alternatively, reclaiming our inner power may fill us with

the sensation of being liberated and drinking in a newfound sense of freedom. We may feel joyful and expansive. The potential seems limitless, and our excitement can carry us away. We rush to pursue all the various dreams and buried hopes and visions that we have carried in our minds; vivid, cinematic images stream across our field of vision.

All of the things we want, or have been taught to want, flood in. It turns out our wants are not as clear as we may have thought. As we attempt to sort through the endless images offered up by our desires, we realize they come from many sources: what our culture values, what our family considers worthwhile, what our friends or social circles prize, and, sadly, what our hurt and pain believe we need in order to be OK, to be secure. More quietly, though, through the static, we can start to receive the deepest longing of our hearts. In trying to make sense of this jostling crowd of wants, we can see the challenge of understanding what we truly want and what is truly worth pursuing. We are gaining clarity about our inner compass.

As a way of starting to make sense of the sometimes-tangled mass of wants and hopes, dreams and aspirations, you might find it useful to reflect on your vision of success. What does success really mean to you? How would it look and feel? This practice gives you the opportunity to examine and explore for yourself the sense of success you are seeking.

PRACTICE:
What Does Success Look Like for You?

1. GET YOURSELF READY

  A. Find a time and a place to do this practice so that you will not be interrupted.

B. Do not start this practice if you are stressed, have other matters that are distracting you, have drunk alcohol or used recreational drugs in the last twenty-four hours, or are tired.

   C. Have a pad of paper and a pen near you.

2. BEGIN TO SETTLE

   A. Sit in a relaxed position with your eyes closed and take three deep breaths.

3. VISUALIZE SUCCESS

   A. Allow your mind to call up an image of what success looks like for you. Don't specifically fixate on one image or thought, but let your mind wander and think of you being successful and what that means or implies to you for a few minutes.

4. BODY SCAN

   A. Sit up straight with your eyes still closed and take three breaths slowly in through your nostrils and slowly out through your mouth. Repeat until this type of breathing feels comfortable for you and is not distracting.

   B. Beginning with your toes, start to relax the muscles of your body all the way to the top of your head, feeling more and more at ease as you focus on relaxing your body. You will find that as you do so, there is a sense of calmness that envelops you, and you feel safe. You are no longer worrying about people judging you or criticizing your dreams and aspirations, as you slowly continue to breathe in and out.

C. You are comfortable and relaxed as you continue to slowly breathe in and out.

5. VISUALIZE SUCCESS MORE FULLY

A. Think again about what success looks like for you. But this time, focus more specifically on your success. Visualize yourself in that position. Watch yourself in your mind's eye being that success. Try to imagine every detail as you slowly breathe in and breathe out. Explore your five senses: What does success look like, feel like, sound like, smell like, taste like? Slowly breathe in and breathe out.

B. Now that you can see every detail, slowly open your eyes and continue to slowly breathe in and out, in and out.

C. You are relaxed and you are calm.

6. RECORD YOUR IMAGE OF SUCCESS

A. Take the pen and paper and write for at least five minutes in your own words what you saw in your mind's eye about your success. Write as many details as possible. Whether it is a few sentences or a paragraph, it only matters that it defines success for you.

B. Now simply sit with your eyes closed, slowly breathing for three to five breaths in through the nose and out through the mouth. Open your eyes.

7. REVIEW YOUR WRITING

   A. First, silently read what you wrote.

   B. Then read what you wrote aloud to yourself.

   C. Sit with those thoughts of your success for a few moments with your eyes closed.

8. APPRECIATE SUCCESS

   A. Feel how relaxed and calm you are with the satisfaction that you are manifesting your success.

I encourage you to keep what you wrote about success somewhere you will see it often. Some people keep theirs taped on the refrigerator or above their desk; others fold it and carry it in their wallet or their purse and take it out and read it over when they are waiting in line. You can make a recording of yourself reading it and play it when you wake up or before you go to sleep. You may even be inspired to create a visual representation of it, either a collage of images from a magazine or a drawing or painting. As we will learn in greater detail later in the book, we train the subconscious to seek our vision by repeatedly coupling images of it in the conscious mind with strong positive emotions in the body.

And remember, our vision of success is constantly evolving. What you wrote today may be a precise representation of everything you truly desire, or it may be more of a jumping-off point for a lifetime of refinement. Success may even feel vague and elusive right now. When I first started manifesting, Ruth taught me to imagine I was looking through a window that was all fogged up, like the inside of a car when it's cold outside. My desire, in this case to become a doctor, was on the other side of the window. The more I practiced visualizing my intention, the clearer the window became.

VALUING FULFILLMENT

My experience of going from poverty to wealth to bankruptcy to wealth again taught me strategies for how to sift through the endless images offered up by our desires. When we begin to practice discernment among our various desires, we may start to hear the deepest longings of our hearts and to appreciate the difference between what we think we want and what we truly need.

The key strategy I propose is reflecting on a time in your life when you felt good, fulfilled, cared about, or truly successful. When we start thinking of what we want to manifest, how to set our intention and where to direct our attention, it can help to cast our mind back to a moment in our lives when we knew in our heart and in our gut that we were on the right track. This will empower us to attune to our inner compass. Ask yourself: What are the things that give me a sense of warmth inside of myself that is long-lasting? When did I feel deeply fulfilled, whole, aligned?

Maybe it was a moment when we were surrounded by loved ones in a warm cocoon of safety and connection; or losing ourselves in an activity, in a state of complete absorption where we blinked and morning had become night in a flash; or being cared for and nurtured by a kind caregiver; or a simple act of kindness we performed ourselves, like making someone a meal or picking up litter in a favorite park or sitting by the bed of someone who is dying and holding their hand; or the sublime sensation of both smallness and interconnection we feel when witnessing a towering mountain or the ceaseless power of a river's current. As you summon these memories in your mind's eye, notice the sensory details—the play of light on water or the tiny movements in a loved one's face. Pay attention to the feeling in your body as well: Can you experience again the warmth, tingling, lightness, spaciousness?

The value of this change in perspective and reflecting on these experiences is that you start to get in touch with some of the powerful, holistic emotions that can arise when the PNS is online: wonder, awe, interconnectedness, gratitude, inspiration. These are feelings that put us in touch with our highest selves, our highest sense of purpose, and the greatness of our hearts. It often turns out that these positive memories contain records of experiences that were not only personally rewarding and fulfilling but also helped other people, whether family, friends, or groups on a larger scale. Reflecting on these positive emotions can be a helpful means of sifting through the mass of desires in our minds and discerning which ones are worthwhile to pursue. We may even have the sense that we are transcending our limited view of existence and become able to appreciate our oneness with everything.

If you find it challenging or painful to look for a positive memory like this, do not be discouraged. It is equally effective to create that vision in your mind's eye. Sometimes you need to use your imagination to experience something for the first time. This prepares us to experience it in reality. The power of the imagination is that, although the images we create are unreal, the emotions we experience when we give ourselves fully to our visions are real. As noted above, the brain does not distinguish between an actual physical experience and one that is intensely imagined. It can be powerful to realize that the important thing is not the particulars or context of the experience that gives rise to the positive emotions, but your body's production of the emotions and the accompanying happy hormones in the first place.

The important point is that *experiences of elevated positive emotion, whether imagined or recalled, teach the subconscious to pay attention.* The release of neurotransmitters such as dopamine and serotonin get the brain's attention, and the subconscious is then primed to seek out similar experiences in reality and pursue them with resilience.

Christine Wamsler is a professor at Lund University in Sweden. She is an expert in sustainable development and associated inner-outer transformation processes. She argues that by tracing the roots of sustainability crises such as climate change through a culturally entrenched story of separateness, we can see the potential of inner transformation through meditation and the development of compassion both for self and others, which then fosters outer connection and transformation in the world. Christine and I became connected when I joined the advisory board for several projects of the Contemplative Sustainable Futures Program.

Through personal explorations involving both visualization and meditation, she experienced firsthand the importance of creating positive emotions. For several years, her inner drive and goal was to relieve suffering and support a more sustainable and just world through a scientific understanding of the mind. Unfortunately, her inner transformation was hampered by current institutional and political structures, which then impacted her ability to create outward transformation.

At first, she had no financing for this type of work. Christine's adolescent daughter gave her twenty euros from her own pocket money to support her, and this gesture touched Christine and inspired her to use her inner power to pursue her goal.

Thus, every night before bed, she decided to visualize a coworker walking into her office and informing her that she had received financial support for her work. She would picture herself sharing her happiness with her colleagues and celebrating with her family, seeing their smiling faces and brightening eyes, and then consciously tune in to the positive emotions in her heart. This would result in her entering a flow state and experiencing a deep sense of well-being and satisfaction.

She remembers that the visualizations caused her to feel so happy and excited, they began to make it difficult for her to fall asleep, to the point that she had to start practicing earlier in the day. The positive emotions sent a powerful signal to her subconscious that successfully getting a grant was deeply meaningful, as it would fund her research that would have a significant impact on society. Within a few weeks, she received multiple grants to support her work, followed by another grant to support her Contemplative Sustainable Futures Program.

The more we are able to direct our attention to our desired intention, through a strong positive emotional association, the more deeply we convey the salience of our intention to our subconscious, which is our most potent ally in realizing our goal. The more closely your inner compass aligns with the longing of your heart, the easier it will be to evoke elevated positive emotions while reflecting on it.

THE POWER OF POSITIVE EMOTION

Positive emotions activate the reward systems of our brains and therefore keep our inner compass set toward our intention. They also help us to free ourselves from the prison of old patterns created in our environment and prior actions. One of the most powerful ways to indicate the value of an intention to our subconscious is through associating it with a strong positive emotion experienced in the present. The more vividly we visualize our intention, the more emotionally heightened our inner experience will be. The more emotionally heightened the inner experience is, the more it has a chance to capture and hold our attention and alert the brain to give attention to it in the future.

Part of how the brain determines how to classify information is through a process known as *value tagging*. Value tagging is part of the salience network and determines the importance of information entering our brain: emotional content concerning our sense of belonging, the strength of our bonds and connections with others, and life meaning, as well as our physiologic functioning and our immediate survival. A strong positive emotion signals to our subconscious that the intention is highly meaningful and deserves to be cultivated through our behavior. For this reason, when we practice visualization, it is essential that in addition to imagining the physical circumstances of achieving our goal or intention in detail, we tune in to our heart and experience the joy, celebration, contentment, and connection in our bodies in the here and now.

This change in the emotional pH of your consciousness, so to speak, is what sends messages to the brain to transform your hardware to prioritize future experiences that give rise to similar positive feelings. Where the emotions come from doesn't really matter as long as you can produce them, recognize their importance, and take the time to savor them. You are teaching your brain to feel and become familiar with feelings of deep, authentic well-being, and having these feelings is what indicates to the brain to form a new neural circuit. Positive emotions increase the salience around an experience and teach the brain that experiences like these are important and worth pursuing. They then become the compass, or north star, for where to direct your intention.

Accessing the power of the imagination is one of the crucial benefits of increasing the tone of the PNS. When the PNS is engaged, the executive control areas of the brain are empowered to make choices that are not automatic but an integration of all of our prior experiences into a holistic picture within our consciousness. And this is how you become creative: by having access to the rich, raw material of your remembered past, present experience, and imagined possibilities, your mind is free to recombine the material to synthesize a new image or sequence or pattern for you to follow.

With its fixation on past and potential dangers, the SNS effectively shuts down our positive imagination and we lose sight of what could be or what is possible, especially in terms of improving our lives and experiencing greater connection, fulfillment, and well-being. Without the power of our imagination, and without a curious, flexible, and open mind to consider its visions, we are deprived of the very engine that can get us out of the vicious cycle of negative experience and negative identity.

In order to free ourselves from being locked in old patterns by our environment or conditioned habits, we must be able to provide ourselves with an inner experience that is vivid, emotionally heightened, and timeless enough to overthrow the emotional addiction that has kept us there. We must no longer be limited by what others tell us we can and cannot do. It is the power and even enchantment of positive emotions, evoked by intensely imagined positive experiences rooted in the compass of our hearts, that will lead us out. Then we can begin to take actions to create those experiences in reality.

As we practice visualizing our desired result over and over again, our intention to experience the fulfillment of our desires is giving our attention (and therefore our subconscious) some velocity to influence the outcome. This is a tried-and-true practice used for years by countless elite athletes, who rehearse successfully executing a skill in their mind's eye before the big game or competition. Research has even shown that just thinking about an action such as building muscles can result in a measurable increase in muscle mass, and thinking about rehearsing the piano can measurably improve a musician's performance, whether they have touched a keyboard or not.

The paradox is that, through mental rehearsal and visualization, we are "reminding" ourselves of how the positive outcome will feel when we experience it in a moment to come. Our minds are literally going back to the future.

PRACTICE:
Eliciting a Positive Emotion

1. GET YOURSELF READY

    A. Find a time and a place to do this practice so that you will not be interrupted.

    B. Do not start this meditation if you are stressed, have other matters that are distracting you, have drunk alcohol or used recreational drugs in the last twenty-four hours, or are tired.

    C. Have a pad of paper and a pen near you.

2. REFLECT ON GOOD FEELINGS

    A. Before we begin, sit in a relaxed position with your eyes closed and think of a time or times when you felt content, happy, and fulfilled.

B. Don't specifically fixate on one image or thought but let your mind wander, thinking of experiences in your life in which you felt safe and protected, and that resulted in you being relaxed, calm, happy, and fulfilled.

C. Sit with these feelings for a few minutes. If you don't believe you have had such an experience, simply imagine what that would feel like.

3. BODY SCAN

A. Sit up straight with your eyes still closed and take three breaths slowly in through your nose and out through your mouth. Repeat until this type of breathing feels comfortable for you and is not distracting.

B. Beginning with your toes, start to relax the muscles of your body all the way to the top of your head, feeling more and more at ease as you focus on relaxing your body. You will find that as you do so, there is a sense of calmness that envelops you, and you feel safe. You feel a sense of warmth and a sense of acceptance and are no longer worrying about people judging you or criticizing your dreams and aspirations, as you slowly continue to breathe in and out.

C. You are comfortable and relaxed as you continue to slowly breathe in and out. Thoughts may arise that seem negative; simply gently acknowledge them without attaching to them and come back to the object of your focus.

4. REFLECT ON FEELING SAFE

A. Call to mind again what it feels like to be safe. For many, this elicits thoughts of their mother or a loved one holding them or embracing them. A feeling of being protected. A feeling of warmth and freedom from concern.

B. If these kinds of feelings do not feel accessible to you through memory, don't worry. Use your imagination to evoke images that provide feelings of warmth, safety, and unconditional care. You might visualize yourself being comforted by spiritual figures or animals, or just the beating heart of life itself.

5. CALL UP GOOD FEELINGS

A. Now focus more specifically, while in this state, on the positive thoughts about yourself, those attributes you like or those events when you yourself have offered love, concern, and nurturing to another.

B. You sense deep contentment and are filled with positive emotions as you slowly breathe in and out. You are enveloped in them, realizing that your own contentment and fulfillment occurs both as you are being held and nurtured but also when you offer the same to another.

C. Watch yourself in your mind's eye as you experience happiness, fulfillment, warmth, and love. Love for yourself. Love for others that is freely given. Try to imagine every detail as you slowly breathe in and breathe out.

6. DEEPEN THE GOOD FEELINGS

A. Slowly breathe in and breathe out. See yourself being loved and giving love. Feel how the sense of happiness, contentment, and fulfillment affect your body. Feel how your heart slows down, how your slow breathing now seems natural. Feel how negative emotions leave you and are replaced with positive thoughts and feelings about yourself, your place in the world, and what you offer to others.

B. Sit with those details. Bathe yourself in those feelings, continuing to slowly breathe in and slowly release your breath.

C. You are relaxed and you are calm.

7. RECORD YOUR EXPERIENCE

A. Take the pen and paper and write for at least five minutes in your own words what you saw in your mind's eye about your positive feelings of who you are, what your abilities are, and how those abilities positively affect others.

B. While you think about these emotions, you feel safe, you feel warm, and you are able to feel deep within you that you are capable of anything.

C. Write as many details as possible. Whether it is a few sentences or a paragraph, all that matters is that you are defining for yourself the power of caring, of nurturing, and how when you do so, it affects your body.

D. Now simply sit with your eyes closed, slowly breathing for three to five breaths in through the nose and out through the mouth.

8. REVIEW YOUR EXPERIENCE

A. Open your eyes. First, silently read what you wrote.

B. Then read what you wrote aloud to yourself. Sit with those thoughts of the power of caring and nurturing for a few moments with your eyes closed.

C. Now think of how that caring and nurturing makes you feel safe.

9. INSTALL YOUR EXPERIENCE

A. Feel how relaxed and calm you are with the satisfaction that you are loved and that you are capable of giving that love to not only yourself but to others, and by doing so, create a deep, positive sense of yourself. Consciously connect these feelings with the sense of your inner compass.

B. It is this inner compass in a state of peace that teaches your subconscious what is important and creates the inner environment for you to manifest your greatest desires and wishes.

TWO KINDS OF HAPPINESS

Philosophers, spiritual teachers, and scientists have identified two forms of well-being: hedonic and eudaimonic. Hedonic well-being, what we often call "happiness," is transitory and characterized by attaining pleasure and avoiding pain, whereas eudaimonic well-being focuses more on meaning, realizing one's potential, and contributing to one's community, and, ultimately, is longer lasting. The debate over which of these two kinds of well-being makes for a truly happy life has raged for centuries. In ancient Greece, the philosopher Aristippus taught that the goal of life is to experience the maximum amount of pleasure, and that happiness is the totality of one's moments of pleasure, while Aristotle argued that well-being is to be found in doing what is truly worth doing. Although these two kinds of happiness are related and often overlap, they can differ sharply and their differences have profound implications for our behavior, relationships, physical health, and our longevity.

In 2013, a group of psychologists surveyed almost four hundred adults, seeking correlations between their levels of happiness and meaning in many aspects of their lives, including behavior, emotions, personal relationships, health, stress levels, work lives, and creative pursuits. They found that although a happy life and a meaningful life are often linked, they don't necessarily go together, and they used statistical analysis to separate out the two kinds of well-being. They discovered that meaning (separate from happiness) is not inherently tied to social benchmarks such as comfort and wealth, while happiness (separate from meaning) is. They also identified major differences between a life full of pleasure and a life full of meaning.

Happiness tends to be focused on the here and now, while meaning comes from reflecting on the evolving relationship between past, present, and future. As noted, happiness is usually experienced as transitory, while the satisfaction of meaning is longer lasting. Happiness from feeling good is often associated with self-centered "taking" behavior, while having a sense of meaning is often associated with selfless "giving" behavior. Where happiness depends on a sense of comfort, ease, or convenience, meaningful lives often include a surprising amount of challenging experiences and even stress, worry, and anxiety. And finally, expressing oneself creatively and caring about personal, cultural, and communal identity were linked to a life of meaning but not of happiness.

Many people seek our materialistic culture's image of "happiness" in the form of hedonic well-being or having all of our wants satisfied. In most cases, this pursuit fails to deliver the sense of a good life in the long term. While it is true that we must have our physical needs met before we are able to focus on seeking meaning and purpose, after a certain point, the satisfactions of physical pleasures drop off. Therefore, health, financial prosperity, and ease in life all ultimately increase hedonic well-being but not meaning. For most of us, only a life of eudaimonic satisfaction involved with meaning, purpose, and service to something we experience as larger than ourselves is the definition of true and sustained happiness.

The differences between these two types of well-being are often written in our cells. In one study, researchers Barbara Fredrickson and Steven Cole examined the self-reported levels of happiness and meaning in eighty-four different participants. To measure the feeling of happiness, they asked questions like, "How often did you feel happy?" "How often did you feel satisfied?" "How often did you feel interested in life?" The more frequently participants reported these feelings of hedonic well-being, the higher they scored on happiness. To measure their sense of meaning, the researchers asked a series of questions examining their orientation toward something larger than themselves. They asked questions like "How often did you feel your life has a sense of direction to it?" "How often have you had experiences that challenge you to grow and become a better person?" and "How often did you feel you had something to contribute to society?"

Once they had noted the levels of happiness and meaning in each participant, the researchers examined how certain genes expressed themselves in the participants' bodies. Cole, a genetics researcher, had previously identified specific gene expressions associated with various kinds of chronic adversity. Experiences of grief over a lost loved one, financial deprivation, loneliness, or military conflict cause the body to go into fight, flight, or freeze mode, the pattern of the nervous system that reflects threat, separation, and disconnection. When the body stays caught in the sense of threat, it triggers a gene pattern with two distinct features: the genes responsible for inflammation increase in activity, while the genes involved in antiviral responses decrease their functioning. In other words, when a body anticipates adversity and isolation, it prepares itself to face bacterial infections, while when it is doing well and feeling connected socially, it prepares to face viruses.

This genetic pattern reveals the imprint of our evolutionary history: early humans who suffered from loneliness and the ill effects of isolation were more likely to get bacterial infections from wounds. But when our ancestors were enmeshed in the social fabric of their tribe or band, they were more likely to contract viruses from prolonged contact with many different people. We continue to carry this genetic legacy and it turns out that it speaks directly to the debate on well-being.

When the researchers examined the genes of their participants, they made a fascinating discovery. It turned out that the people who reported high levels of happiness but little to no sense of meaning had the same genetic pattern expressed by people who are facing chronic adversity such as grief or loneliness. Their bodies, although frequently enjoying experiences of physical pleasure, were genetically disposed to inflammation. From an evolutionary point of view, pleasurable experiences without meaning, whether from alcohol, drugs, casual sex, or pressing "Buy" on an online shopping site, make the body feel like it's been facing chronic adversity. Today, inflammation has been linked to serious health conditions such as heart disease and many cancers. And yet, 75 percent of the study participants reported feeling high in happiness and low on meaning, while only 25 percent reported "eudaimonic predominance," the feeling that they had more meaning in their lives than happiness.

Although many prosperous cultures today value material well-being above all, the health benefits of a life of meaning are undeniable. Participants with a strong sense of purpose, even if they were not especially hedonically happy, showed a genetic expression associated with the deactivation of their stress response and inflammatory process. Rather than preparing for the bacterial infections faced by our ancestors left to tend their wounds alone, their immune systems had shifted to prepare to fight off the viruses that come from being in the middle of the pack and experiencing a wide variety of social connections. Their bodies could tell the difference. We can see in this phenomenon a genetic echo of heart rate variability: the heart that beats dynamically in response to a sense of connection with others produces a coherence that measurably improves physical and mental well-being, while the heart that feels disconnected beats rigidly to its own isolated rhythm, leading to poor cardiovascular and respiratory health and other illnesses.

We might consider these discoveries when we reflect on our own visions of success. When we notice a desire, we might ask, "What is the longing underneath this? Is this desire in alignment with my own deepest well-being? Does this desire serve the life around me and bring me into connection with others? How does this desire live in my cells? What might be the long-term effects on my physical, mental, and emotional well-being?"

As we begin to manifest our intention, it is likely that we will be faced with self-doubt and fear, or feel we are an impostor. This is the mind's natural response to any encounter with the unknown. When we do not believe we have the power to change our situation, we are bound by subconscious habits of a mind rooted in fear. These negative beliefs about ourselves and our world limit the possibilities we see for our future; by limiting our visions of ourselves, they actually determine which desires we have access to and compel us to settle for crumbs or choices that do not feel authentic to us. If we do not believe we are capable of or worthy of having something, it is very painful to go on wanting it. For this reason, we will move on to Step Three: Remove the Obstacles in Your Mind, where we will look closely at the common obstacles and false beliefs that arise in manifesting, and how to work with them with compassion.

Chapter 5

STEP THREE

Remove the Obstacles in Your Mind

The mind must be emancipated from old habits, prejudices, restrictive thought processes and even ordinary thought itself.

—Bruce Lee

WHEN I WAS TWELVE I TRAVELED TO THE UPPER REALMS OF THE atmosphere.

From my bed.

Every week, my brother and I left our apartment and followed the railroad tracks for a mile or two until they met the street the public library was on. The gravel crunched under our sneakers as the Southern California heat haze shimmered above the steel tracks. Grateful for the air conditioning in the library, we lingered among the shelves, then finally we would check out the maximum of ten books each and carry them in our arms all the way back along the tracks to read in the bedroom we shared. Although each of us was on our own mostly private journey (my brother was discovering his talent as a visual artist and exploring his identity as a gay teen), I was still grateful for the way the ritual gave us time to be together, and I remember the pleasure I felt walking slightly behind him on the tracks, our arms weighed down by our latest treasures.

One summer, when I had read every book featuring the Hardy Boys and Sherlock Holmes, I stumbled onto the spirituality shelf at the library and delved into accounts of mystical experiences by the clairvoyant Edgar Cayce, the great yogis Yogananda and Swami Vivekananda, and Paul Twitchell, the founder of the religious movement known as Eckankar, which taught that the soul may be experienced separately from the physical body. Finally, I discovered the Peruvian American mystical teacher Carlos Castaneda and read his first book, *The Teachings of Don Juan: A Yaqui Way of Knowledge*.

Desperate to escape the anguish of my family life, I was intrigued by the promise of transcendence from the limited and painful environment I was living in. Without a wise guide to rein me in, I began experimenting with the practices of "soul travel" and out-of-body experiences. One night, I lay on my bed, did a breathing practice, and attempted to travel with my soul to other planes of reality. At first, nothing happened. Then, with a mixture of delight and uneasiness, I sensed my awareness as it rose up out of my body. My consciousness floated to the windowsill above the battalion of green plastic G.I. Joes and passed through the window and up into the branches of the tree outside, where I could sit and look back down on my own body resting in the bedroom. The sensation of being in two places at once, of experiencing two selves at once, was scary but also exhilarating, and seemed to offer a pathway to the freedom and independence I craved. It would have thrilled me to know that sixteen years later, the CIA would produce an official report on the application of such experiences that predicted teams of agents going out-of-body together and sending their detached consciousnesses across the world to spy on top-secret Soviet military projects in the name of national security. But at the time, I thought I was the only one.

The period of life from early childhood until early adulthood is when the ego develops, and I see now that I was exploring the inner strength and resources that would allow me to maneuver in the wider world. Through these travels with my consciousness and imagination, I was getting the first hint of the power of manifestation.

Motivated by my successes with out-of-body experiences, I was inspired to challenge myself to go further, and I began experimenting with visiting what I believed were different levels of existence through what some people call "astral projection." I kept my journeys secret from everyone including my brother, so I had no teacher or mentor to guide me or advise me to slow down. Now, instead of stopping at the tree outside my window or a physical landmark on earth, I exited my body and rose through the atmosphere until I was so high, I could no longer see my body back in my bedroom. The first stage was total blackness and, no longer aware of the world below, I realized I could move within the blackness and travel to other, further places. I visited levels completely shrouded in fog and began to notice that in some places I felt an incredible sense of love and connection, and in others it was quite the opposite—I had a sense of the presence of various threatening and malevolent spirits floating out there. It was as if I were moving through a room filled with dense smoke, where I couldn't see any forms but could feel their evil presence as they drew closer to me.

Because I had no guide to explain what was going on, these journeys were often terrifying. I would wake up and feel as if I were paralyzed, with a tightness in my chest that made it hard to breathe and full of a great fear that my soul was going to be taken over by one of these spirits. Sometimes I would cry out in terror and wake my brother, but he assumed I was just having a nightmare. Today you could argue that I was having what is known as a *hypnagogic hallucination,* a fleeting perceptual experience that occurs during the transition from wakefulness to sleep, when awareness of the environment drops away but brain stem activity continues. What I didn't know at the time was that these experiences were giving me my first lesson in consciously working with my amygdala, the part of the limbic system in the brain that is responsible for regulating emotions such as fear and anxiety, and that the amygdala is the first gatekeeper in the brain when it comes to manifesting.

My travels became so terrifying that I stopped doing any out-of-body mental practices for several years. I began trying to process the fearful experiences, and to relate to the part of myself that made the whole thing so frightening. Finally I felt confident to try traveling again, and when I returned to my practice, a bit older and stronger, I once again rose into the higher realms and moved through spaces thick with smoky fog. I remember I again sensed the presence of one of the "evil spirits," but my reaction to it was different. This time, I intuitively understood that the manifestation of those entities came from my own vulnerability to the shadow within me: my own fear of the unknown, and the aggression that came from a sense of helplessness, trying to protect my survival. Essentially, I understood I was afraid of my own fear.

With a feeling of compassion, I realized that when the threatening presence approached, I was actually having a moment of recognizing my "shadow" self, as Jung would say. I could choose between resistance and acceptance. In that moment, the evil presence within the smoke-filled room that had terrified me simply came into me, and I absorbed it and no longer feared it. Once I no longer resisted, I no longer felt fear, which then allowed me to integrate it into myself and gave me the insight that, while it was part of me, I did not have to allow it to be in the driver's seat of my life. I also recognized that on some level, it had helped me to survive.

Today I understand this experience as a key to my entire practice of manifesting because I began learning how to work with the amygdala. With practice, we can learn to accept that the amygdala will accompany us on our journeys, doing its job of trying to protect and care for our physical survival, but we do not need to let it make our decisions for us. Specifically, we do not let it choose where we direct our attention. As we will see in the following chapters, the practice of manifestation rests on our ability to direct our attention toward the objects of our intention (selective attention) and away from objects and experiences that distract it. Consciously directing our attention where we choose is the key to our inner power. The more skill we develop in learning to watch our experience without becoming emotionally activated, the more skill we have in placing and keeping our attention on the things we want to manifest.

When we resist events, whether physical or emotional, our resistance stimulates the amygdala. The amygdala is very involved in our salience network (SN), a collection of regions in the brain that decide which stimuli deserve our attention. The SN is constantly filtering the information coming through our senses and making rapid-fire judgments about what is most important to process and respond to. As part of the limbic system, the amygdala has the power to immediately reroute all our cognitive resources to focus exclusively on physical survival. The more fear we bring to an event, the more we are telling the amygdala that the salience of the event is very high and very threatening; and the less fear we bring, the less we are going to activate the threat salience, leaving our attention free to be directed as we choose.

THE NEGATIVITY BIAS

Put simply, if we want to manifest successfully, we must decrease the volume of the voice in our heads that tells us we can't do it. To become free of this inner critic, we must first understand what it actually is, and what its function is in our consciousness.

The power of the inner critic becomes clear when we revisit the role of the SNS. It is based primarily in our brain stem, is the oldest part of our brain, and has been present in our human ancestors for millions of years. Essentially, its job was to keep us alive in our original niche environment. As a result, it is the very thing that has been associated with our survival as a species, and that is why it is so deeply rooted in and attached to us. As the ancient key to our success as organic life, the SNS remains with us today as a prevalent force within our subconscious directing actions it believes are beneficial to our survival. In other words, evolution typically does not discard, it includes. While the attributes of the SNS served a purpose when our species lived on the savanna in Africa, in modern society it results for many in a negative ongoing dialogue in their head. In a sense, negativity is the first language of our species, and we must learn, slowly and painstakingly, to speak a new one.

The problem is, where the SNS once protected our bodies from immediate physical dangers, it has followed us into our modern world and now tries to protect our sense of *self* from the countless small assaults of our interconnected reality. Where the fight response may once have helped us defend ourselves against a marauding tiger, it now causes us to fight against the parts of ourselves that we believe do not measure up, triggering overpowering emotions of shame and the feeling that we are not good enough. The volume of the inner critic and its sense of *relational* threat ("What will people think? Who do you think you are?") is now deployed in a chronic maladaptation; it has undergone the unfortunate metamorphosis into the inner critic we know all too well today. Particularly tricky for us as manifesters is the *negativity bias*, a system of value tagging that makes warnings of danger stand out in our minds as most salient in order to get us to pay attention. From the point of view of the SNS, positivity has no purpose for survival, so it does not merit our attention in the same way as a threat. This is why most news is focused on the negative and not the positive.

One of the side effects of our evolutionary path is that in the process of coming into ourselves as a species, negative self-commentary became classified by the mind in the same way as actual dangers. Therefore, due to what is essentially a glitch in our filing system, our negative commentary sticks to us and stands out disproportionately in the mind. As our intelligence as a species increased, the negativity bias hijacked our thinking mind, and then we started making comparisons and connections that are not really valid. If we tell ourselves "I cannot do this," or "I am afraid of that," or "Gosh, if I do this, there will be this and this and this consequence," these are protective attitudes in some ways. But then you take it to the next level, which is "Well, I cannot do anything. I am not really good enough *as a person*."

What began as a basic survival mechanism has now mutated into a personal identity, as if what we perceive as our personal failings are innate and beyond our control. In fact, it is just that our body and mind have become addicted to the powerful negative emotions of fear, anxiety, and despair, which at one time were associated with self-protection. Therefore, our addiction to fear, and our addiction to a limited sense of self, have become fused as one, to the point where we experience them as seemingly inseparable. As a result, it is as if we have created a prison for ourselves that limits our self-agency.

Each time we believe the inner critic's negative statements, we are adding a brick to the walls of our self-created prison. And the more of these statements we make, the higher the walls get and the darker it becomes. In fact, the walls start coming in on us as we believe every negative thing we are told about ourselves, and by doing so we give up our agency to manifest change. We have given it all away to this voice that we thought meant something when it did not mean anything at all. We have given away our power to that inner critic.

As an example, I was giving a lecture on impostor syndrome to a group of healthcare executives, and a woman in her fifties stood up. She was crying. In a trembling voice, she said, "My father told me I would never be anything and I had to prove him wrong." She is now an RN with a PhD in nursing and in an executive position, yet her father's words had hung over her throughout her entire life. Such a negative childhood experience can indeed be a strong driver of our behavior, but it is often a painful, unhealthy one. This is the power of these negative narratives that get embedded in our heads. Think of how many people are destroyed by such statements and never live up to their potential. Some of us carry these negative stories our entire lives, achieving a "successful" career yet feeling empty and unfulfilled because we cannot escape that negative inner dialogue.

Compare the words of this woman's father to another parent telling his child, "Listen, I love you. You are one of the smartest people I know. You can accomplish anything with your grit and your perseverance and your intelligence. I am so proud of you, and I have no doubt that you are going to be able to do whatever you wish. Know that I will always be there for you, no matter what." When that child faces adversity in pursuit of their goals, the child no longer has that negative voice talking in their head. Instead, they will confront the challenge, thinking, "Well, my parents believed in me. My friends believe in me. They are there for me. I can do this."

TUNING THE DIAL

When we think of the inner critic, we often focus on how badly it makes us *feel*, how discouraging and deflating, but in fact, the truly unhelpful aspect of the inner critic is that it is very distracting. It drains the energy out of your attention and impedes your ability to focus on your intention. The reason we become discouraged is that the inner critic's cruel tirade steals our inner resources and diverts them away from our positive and healthy life goals. Feeding off the power of the fight, flight, or freeze system, the inner critic keeps a stranglehold on our salience network, the part of our brain whose job is to decide what is worthy of our attention. Then, once we are distracted away from our goal and fail to achieve it, the inner critic has a field day torturing us for that, and so on in a vicious cycle.

When we come into the world, we are in an open, flexible, and "unconditioned" state not characterized by habits. Soon thereafter, we begin having experiences with the outside world and with other people, and it is the most negative thoughts and experiences that stick to us. They are like Post-it Notes we stick on the walls of our mind. One note may read "I am not good enough" and another "I am not very smart" and another "My father hates me; therefore, I am not worthy of love." Although each of these notes arises from a particular passing experience, we are so impressionable in our early developmental stages that we imprint the emotional content into our mind as permanent learning. The glue is the fight, flight, or freeze system's exaggerated attention to negative stimuli, and so we emotionally code these messages we believe are essential to our physical survival. These sticky notes, often only accidents of our experience, start to become the basis for deeply rooted habit patterns carved into our neurons, which in turn become the architecture of our sense of self.

We begin to carry these negative thoughts with us everywhere we go, applying them to more and more situations, and accumulating more and more of them until they obscure our vision and we believe they are truth. All we can hear when we listen to our minds are the negative thoughts. We lose sight of the open, curious, responsive state underneath. This sad set of lies starts to define the very way we see ourselves, the way we see the world, and, ultimately, the view of our worthiness to have what we want and need. The negative thoughts become the walls of our prison.

Because we have internalized the beliefs muttered and shouted by the negative thoughts, and acted them out innumerable times, we have come to install them in our subconscious, allowing them to dictate our behavior without even realizing it. And because we are acting under the influence of the negative thoughts when we interact with our environment, other people cannot access us anymore either: they, too, are fooled by the negative thoughts.

Sadly, what the negative thoughts cover over is the radiant, glowing self that is inside each of us, the part that is loving, caring, and already complete. And when we cannot see and connect with our true selves, we lose sight of the inner compass that points us toward what we truly need and how to get it. When you are riddled with negative thoughts, not only can you not see yourself in your shining original state, but the covering blocks your light from shining through to manifest things in your world.

It is almost inevitable that when we begin taking steps to manifest our deepest desires, the negative sticky notes will rear their heads and confront us with their old story about ourselves: our self-doubt, inadequacy, and feeling like an impostor. In our inner experience, negative thoughts show up as the infamous inner critic, a cruel, belittling, frightening tormentor whose loud voice diminishes our ability and willingness to pursue our dreams. For many of us, the biggest obstacle to our inner power to manifest what we desire is this negative inner voice and the fear it evokes in us. The inner critic is the voice telling us we are not good enough to jump off the train of chronic stress into the unknown and unfamiliar that is positive, healing, liberating, and that will ultimately take us to our destination.

THE BODY'S PATH TO LIBERATION

Negative beliefs developed during our childhood are often carried subconsciously into adulthood; we do not spontaneously outgrow them. They are a natural function of our evolution, but we do not need to let them drive us. The challenge of human life is that the vast majority of the habits that shape our lives are established before we are consciously aware of them. By the time we wake up to this fact, usually as the result of our lives not turning out as we would have liked, we discover we have been playing out conditioned patterns subconsciously, and these were the true drivers of our behavior.

If we are unable to identify and understand where our primal negative feelings are coming from, it is easy to keep falling back into their trap because the mind and body naturally return to experiences related to childhood, for better or worse. The early experiences of comfort and safety—or their absence—that occurred when we were children set the stage for how we interact with the world as an adult, and they exercise a powerful gravitational pull on our consciousness, whether we are aware of them or not. The simplest evocative cue or sensory input associated with a traumatic experience can throw us back into the whirlpool of unresolved early emotions. Research has shown that only the upper levels of the brain are able to tell time, while the brain stem, which controls functions like body temperature and heart rate, contains no networks capable of processing the passage of time. What this means in practice is that when trauma is activated in our body and our consciousness shrinks down to its bare survival program, we have no way of knowing that the feelings will not last forever—we experience them as almost eternal, the way an infant would. Because they are tied to our instincts for survival, they can cause us to act from our primal nature, sometimes in ways that are violent and irrational.

Therefore, in order to allow the mind to gather around the intention we want to manifest, we must soothe the primitive nervous system and make it feel safe enough to allow us to take the healthy risks that make us grow.

Because negative beliefs are often imprinted during the critical years of early development, we must work with them on the same deep biological level. Luckily, we find the pathway out of our habitual negativity through a more recent evolutionary innovation: the mammalian caregiving system. As we discovered above in our discussion of the physiology of manifesting, an extraordinary biological transformation was necessary in the evolutionary transition from reptiles to mammals. One of the major adaptations was the evolution of the dorsolateral vagal nerve, a large part of the vagus nerve that links the internal organs with the central control systems in the brain and is the basis for the rest-and-digest response. This adaptation made it possible for mammalian parents to offer the significant postbirth care and investment needed to protect warm-blooded young, to nurture them and be a safe haven for them as they grew. With its ability to signal to the rest of the body that we are OK right now, the vagus nerve will become our greatest physiological ally in the manifestation process.

Once we get the hang of being OK in the present moment, we can cultivate self-compassion, the inner critic's kryptonite. Due to the miracle of neuroplasticity, or the brain's ability to change itself, it is possible through a self-compassion practice to activate the pathways of the caregiving system consciously and intentionally to give ourselves the love, care, and connection we may have been deprived of in our most vulnerable years. We may then work directly with our negative sticky notes, bringing them gently into our awareness, and offer ourselves the safe haven we need to feel unconditionally valued, loved, and cared for. It is then that the notes or negative commentary will begin to recede.

In the following exercise, we engage the same sensitivity to distress that a parent feels for their infant, and, using the same life-giving pathways in our physiology, turn it toward ourselves. Self-compassion has the power to heal the parts of us that make us feel chronically unsafe and unloved and transform them into vital sources of wisdom and compassion to share with others. Learning to connect with other human beings and share in their struggles will also serve us down the line in our manifestation process when we recognize the need to enlist support from others to pursue our goals and meet them with resilience.

THE POWER OF BELIEFS

Often our habitual negativity keeps our lives small through the power of limiting beliefs. These are often beliefs we formed about the world in our early lives. They might have served us in coping with a difficult and painful environment, but they often contain traces of distortions created by our tendency as children to blame ourselves and misunderstand the deeper reality of situations. Our negative beliefs can be about the world around us—"The world is a cruel and unloving place," "Life is unfair, so why try?"—or, most painfully, about ourselves. It takes great effort and care to unmask a long-standing false belief, but freedom from our distorted worldview will create the space to embed the positive beliefs that will give energy to our manifesting.

Shankar Hemmady and I met through the compassion training program I started at Stanford, and he shared his story with me. He grew up in the suburbs of Mumbai, where his father was a mail carrier and his mother worked in the home. Having been abused by her own family, she suffered from PTSD and chronic depression. Shankar describes his early environment as not only financially but also socially impoverished: relatives would often remark that if he only went to the right school or found the right mentor in the right neighborhood, he would do well, but such connections were not easy to find. Early on, he began to develop the core belief "There is not enough," which painfully evolved into "*You* are not enough."

"It was very hard to imagine a glorious or positive future," Shankar says.

Nonetheless, he experienced acts of kindness and generosity in his community. When he was in first grade, Shankar's mother was not always able to make him breakfast due to her debilitating condition, and so she would give him a small amount of money to buy a snack at school, about ten paise, the equivalent of one cent in American currency. During the snack break, he would give his money to one of the security guards at the school, who would go out and buy something for him at the market. Somehow, Shankar's teacher learned about this from the security guard, who told her that Shankar's small amount of money was enough only to buy some candies or cookies, but not enough for something truly nourishing. From her own resources, Shankar's teacher began supplementing his snack with her own money so that he could have raisins and nuts or a piece of fruit to eat on the snack break. Once, when Shankar's mother was visiting the school, she noticed her son's healthy snack and discovered his teacher was paying for his nourishment from her own pocket. This was Shankar's first realization of the kindness and goodwill of others. Its significance, though, only became clear to him in adulthood.

Several members of Shankar's community saw promise in him and introduced him to concentration practices, such as focusing on the breath, and encouraged him to succeed because he had gifts to share with his community. His ability to concentrate on his intention instead of his negative inner dialogue served him well; he was admitted into the Indian Institute of Technology and began a track toward a financially successful career in engineering. This, in turn, led him to move to the Bay Area, where he became an entrepreneur, first in the electronics arena and later in biopharmaceuticals, working to make cancer medicines safer for patients.

As he became more financially secure, Shankar was aware of the inner voice that told him he could not afford to give to others because he would never have enough for himself and for his family. He was still haunted by the old stories of "not enough." He began sitting silent meditation retreats. On one of the retreats, the memory of his schoolteacher's kindness came back to him, and he considered it again with the eyes of an adult. With an aching heart, he saw that his teacher's salary had been about 80 rupees, or ten dollars, a month at that time, and the money she was giving to make sure Shankar had a proper healthy breakfast was a significant percentage of her monthly income.

When he realized his teacher's altruism even when she had little for herself, Shankar found himself crying tears of gratitude for her selfless generosity. This was a profound lesson that allowed him to break the grip of his core belief of inadequacy and scarcity and to begin offering workshops on technological and emotional learning to underserved and remote communities around the world. When he became free from the limiting beliefs conditioned in his mind by his early environment, Shankar was able to focus fully on his earliest intention to offer his gifts in service of young people who feel overlooked and forgotten, allowing them to realize their potential.

PRACTICE:
Beliefs and Their Opposites

Negative beliefs about ourselves are like mushrooms: they grow in the dark. And so it is often very useful to get them out from the darkness of our heads and into the light where we can see them clearly for what they are. The following practice enables you to identify the beliefs and stories that are holding you back, and to consciously work with transforming them so they serve you better.

1. GET YOURSELF READY

   A. Set aside some time to be alone with yourself.

   B. Have a pad of paper and a pen near you.

   C. Divide the paper into two columns: "Beliefs" and "Opposites."

2. BEGIN TO RELAX

   A. Find a comfortable posture, either sitting up straight or lying on your back.

   B. With your eyes closed, take three breaths slowly in through your nose and out through your mouth. Repeat until this type of breathing feels comfortable for you and is not distracting.

   C. Beginning with your toes, start to relax the muscles of your body all the way to the top of your head, feeling more and more at ease as you focus on letting go of tension. You will find that as you do, there is a sense of peace that envelops you, and you feel safe.

3. REFLECT ON A GOOD FEELING

   A. Start to evoke a memory or image of feeling cared for and valued unconditionally. Let the positive feelings suffuse your experience, flowing out from your heart to your organs and all your limbs.

4. REFLECT ON NEGATIVE BELIEFS

   A. Gently invite some of the beliefs about yourself and your life that have caused you difficulty into your mind.

    B. You can imagine you are safely perched at the top of a tree or on a high cliff or balcony and these beliefs are gathering below.

    C. See if you can recognize some of the usual suspects: "I'm not good enough," "I got a raw deal," "I'm too damaged," and others.

    D. Without judging, try to simply see these beliefs clearly; witness them in your mind. You may sense the pain they have caused you. Let it happen.

5. RECORD YOUR OBSERVATIONS

    A. When you are ready, gently open your eyes and begin writing down the beliefs in the "Beliefs" column. Write freely and do not censor yourself. Don't worry about spelling, punctuation, or whether they are the "right" ones or not.

6. REVIEW YOUR WRITING

    A. Read the list of beliefs out loud. Notice your emotions and physical sensations as you read.

    B. Do you feel a contraction in your heart, a knot in your throat, a sense of disappointment, a wave of anger?

7. RETURN TO THE GOOD FEELINGS

    A. If you need to revisit the good feeling you reflected on for support, feel free to do so.

8. RECORD THE OPPOSITES

A. When you are ready, turn to the "Opposites" column. For each belief you wrote, write the opposite: "I am good enough," "I have the inner power to change my circumstances," "I have all the time, love, and support to pursue my goals."

B. Explore what language feels accurate and alive for you and remember you do not need to get it perfectly correct right away.

9. REFLECT ON YOUR PRACTICE

A. Take a few moments to consider the page. Notice how the two columns resonate with each other.

B. Acknowledge that you have begun to transform the beliefs into their opposites simply by becoming aware of them.

THE PATH TO FREEDOM

When we meet someone who is at peace with themselves and relates to us without judgment and with a depth of compassion, we are empowered to relate to ourselves in the same way. When I met Ruth, I experienced what is now called a *sense of psychological safety*. I thought to myself, "Wow, I walked in, and this woman looked up with this radiant smile that embraced me and suddenly I felt calm. I felt I was not being judged. I felt this unconditional love in my interaction with her and that changed everything."

These positive feelings speak to the way out of our habitual negativity through a more recent evolutionary innovation: our PNS.

Many of our deepest wounds that give rise to the loudest negative commentary in our minds arise from distressing experiences in our earliest stages of bonding with our caregivers. We did not feel secure in their love, attention, and care, and they did not offer a secure base or safe haven from which we could confidently explore. These early disappointments and traumas underlie the very beliefs that have become the obstacles to manifesting our goals. Therefore, if we want to treat the obstacle at its root, we must understand that our job is to offer *ourselves* a safe haven in which we feel unconditionally valued, loved, and cared for. We must engage the same sensitivity to distress that a parent feels for its infant, and, using the same life-giving pathways in our physiology, turn it toward ourselves through self-compassion.

There are times when we cannot remove the obstacles in our minds on our own. We need the compassion of others to give us an embodied experience of what it feels like before we can offer it to ourselves.

HELP ON THE PATH

Silvia Vasquez-Lavado never imagined she would be so happy just to see a cigarette butt.

It was pitch-dark in the middle of the night in the remote jungle of Papua, on the western half of the island of New Guinea, and Silvia was lost. She and a local guide had become separated from the rest of their expedition and had spent hours trekking through unfamiliar terrain trying to reunite with them. The landscape seemed to be toying with their minds, tricking them into hope then leaving them stranded. As the sun set, they became more and more uneasy.

"Getting lost in the jungle can mean you die," says Silvia. "You know how Dracula comes out at midnight? That's when all the fun animals come out. And survival chances are very challenging."

The irony was that Silvia had already achieved what she'd come there to do: climb to the top of Puncak Jaya in Papua province, New Guinea, in Indonesia, the highest mountain peak on an island. At over sixteen thousand feet, it is one of the Seven Summits, the highest mountains on each of the seven traditional continents. It was 2015, and Puncak Jaya was the fifth summit Silvia had climbed, having undertaken Kilimanjaro in Tanzania, Mount Elbrus in Russia, Aconcagua in Argentina, and Mount Kosciuszko in Australia.

The climbs were not just recreational; they had a profound symbolic meaning for Silvia. Growing up in Lima, Peru, Silvia was a victim of childhood sexual abuse. The trauma of her abuse and her family's silence around it left deep emotional and psychic wounds. In her twenties, the pain led her into a spiral of serious depression, alcoholism, and broken relationships with women that held her life captive as she concealed her sexuality from her family. Even though she achieved success amidst the male-dominated posturing of the high-tech Silicon Valley world, she knew the untended wounds of her past were threatening to swallow her up. Finally, out of desperation, she accepted her mother's invitation in 2005 to return to Peru to participate in an ayahuasca ceremony during which she had a transformative vision: her younger self appeared to her and called to her to walk together in a valley surrounded by mountains. This experience of illumination and reconnection was the start of a newfound sense of purpose. Silvia would heal herself by climbing the great mountains of the planet. In 2014, she had even started a nonprofit, Courageous Girls, whose purpose was to empower other young survivors of sexual abuse through climbing.

Silvia's calling had brought her to New Guinea with an expedition team of other intrepid mountaineers to ascend the limestone faces of Puncak Jaya. The plan was to travel by helicopter to the base of the mountain, climb it, then trek back through the jungle over seven or eight days, accompanied by members of the Indigenous tribe living at the base of the mountain. The men from the tribe served as porters for the individual and kitchen tents and the women set up the camp and prepared the food. Living in this way in this remote environment, the Indigenous people remained connected to their ancestors through traditions from millennia before, practicing pig husbandry and sweet potato cultivation. The men still walked almost naked and many of the women trekked the entire way barefoot.

The morning after the summit, the locals left first to reach the next destination and set up the spot for that night's camp. Then the rest of Silvia's team did what ambitious mountaineers often do: Boom! They took off, too, driven to reach the next goal, to achieve the next memorable experience, while forgetting about the human connection. Tired out by the climb and nursing sore feet in her muddy hiking boots that were wrong for the terrain, Silvia was slow to get started and the others left her behind with an assistant guide. Silvia was meant to be right behind her team, but when she and the guide set out, they could not find the group's trail. They hiked and doubled back and scoured the virtually trackless landscape for clues but could find nothing. It was as if the others had just vanished. They began to realize they were lost. They'd tried to use a distinctive tree as a landmark, only to circle back and discover five more just like it.

The sun was setting and Silvia knew they were coming dangerously close to violating the most basic rule of trekking by getting lost in the jungle at night. Were the voices in her head that told her she could never achieve her dream right? Had she come all this way, climbed all these mountains, just to be devoured by some terrible night creature and disappear without a trace?

Night fell. With only the glow of their headlamps, Silvia and the guide kept searching. They tried to navigate by sound. Running water? Must be a river. But as they walked toward where they thought the water was, the sound only got farther and farther away. Silvia pushed aside the fear and despair that were starting to well up in her stomach. She had never experienced darkness so thick, like being inside a black hole. What about the remaining summits? And the other young women she had pledged to help?

Silvia and the guide stumbled their way to what looked like it might have been a path. But was it? After so many false starts and short-lived hopes, it was difficult to trust their instincts. And then she saw a tiny flash of something white. She approached and cast the light of the headlamp over it. A cigarette butt! This little scrap of litter, so unnoticeable in daily life and so out of place among the strange trees of the jungle, was finally a sign they were on the right track. They could expect another butt five meters away and follow it like a trail of breadcrumbs. This was the central point they had been lacking. With renewed hope, Silvia and the guide set off again on the trail. In the meantime, the team had realized Silvia was missing and formed a search party to retrace their steps. At last, Silvia saw the light from their flashlights, and she was back in the safety of camp.

The next morning, Silvia was exhausted from the hours of aimless wandering and the adrenaline of believing she might die in the jungle. But the other climbers were packed and ready to go, and instead of taking care to make sure Silvia was all right, the other climbers took off again, leaving her behind. Silvia watched them depart with dismay. Then, to Silvia's surprise, the local women surrounded her. Some stood in front of her, and some stood behind in their multicolored embroidered clothing. Smiling, they made it clear they would be escorting her to the next camp. They would make sure she would not get lost again.

Silvia first came to me as a patient when she was recovering from a traumatic brain injury and wanted advice on how to rehabilitate herself. Since then, we have become good friends and she told me this story. She remembers how, in their bright eyes and open expressions, she could see the women understood: she needed help, and they were responding with compassion.

"I felt a sense of true unconditional care and compassion from these total strangers," she says. "They taught me something about love. You don't need a language for it."

And so, they trekked with her the entire rest of the way out of the jungle, mostly in silence, making sure she reached her destination. Silvia went on to become the first openly gay woman to climb the Seven Summits, carrying with her the sense of being led and held by the Indigenous women. Their unconditional love taught her to offer compassion to herself when she faced adversities.

PRACTICE:
Self-Compassion

Many of us are our own worst critics. While this can motivate people to perform and achieve, the cost is very high in regard to self-esteem. This negative sense of self-worth lives with us always and can gravely impact our health and mental well-being. The negative dialogue often causes further damage because when we tell ourselves we are not capable, we are not worthy, we are not loved and never will be, and that we are an impostor, we limit what is possible for us. The reality is that within each of us there is extraordinary power, but we give that power away by our negative self-talk.

Self-compassion has the power to heal the parts of us that feel chronically unsafe and unloved—the basis for our shadow and our resistance to thriving—and transform them into vital sources of wisdom and compassion to share with others.

This practice is designed to address feelings of unworthiness at the root.

1. GET YOURSELF READY

A. Find a time and a place to do this practice so that you will not be interrupted.

B. Do not start this practice if you are stressed, have other matters that are distracting you, have drunk alcohol or used recreational drugs in the last twenty-four hours, or are tired.

C. Have a pad of paper and a pen near you.

2. BEGIN TO SETTLE

A. Before we begin, sit in a relaxed position with your eyes closed. Let your mind wander, and for a moment listen to all the negative thoughts that go through your head. Don't fixate on a specific image or thought—just relax your mind, feeling how the negative self-talk lives in your body.

B. Is there a particular place in your body where you feel it? What are the sensations?

3. REFLECT ON YOUR EXPERIENCE

A. Sense how this negative self-talk diminishes you and limits you. Think about how you confuse the negative self-talk with reality.

B. Sit with these feelings for a few minutes. How do these thoughts make you feel? Do you feel sadness, anger, numbness, restlessness?

4. BODY SCAN

A. Sit up straight with your eyes still closed and take three breaths slowly in through your nostrils and slowly out through your mouth. Repeat until this type of breathing feels comfortable for you and is not distracting.

B. Beginning with your toes, start to relax the muscles of your body all the way to the top of your head, feeling more and more at ease as you focus on relaxing your body. You will find that as you do so, there is a sense of calmness that envelops you, and you feel safe. You feel a sense of warmth and a sense of acceptance and are no longer worrying about people judging you or criticizing your dreams and aspirations, as you slowly continue to breathe in and out.

C. You are comfortable and relaxed as you continue to slowly breathe in and out. The negative self-talk may

arise, but gently acknowledge it and don't
attach to it; come back to the focus on your breath.

5. REFLECT ON FEELING SAFE

A. Call to mind how it feels to be safe. For many, this elicits thoughts of a mother or a loved one holding them or embracing them. You could also picture yourself in an especially safe place, such as a secluded creek you used to visit or being seated at the table of a warm family dinner. Whatever makes a feeling of being protected come alive for you.

B. Whether safety means being in a relationship or in solitude for you, the effect will be the same. Remember, though, that solitude is different from loneliness. Stay with this feeling of safety and do not be concerned with anything beyond those feelings.

6. DEEPEN THE GOOD FEELINGS

A. While in this state, focus more specifically on positive thoughts about yourself, those attributes about yourself that you like, those events in your life when you have offered love, concern, and nurturing to another. You sense that deep contentment, those positive emotions as you slowly breathe in and out.

B. You are enveloped, realizing that your own contentment and fulfillment occur both as you are being held and nurtured but also when you offer the same to another. Connect with the feeling of your own innate goodness.

7. BATHE IN THE GOOD FEELINGS

A. Watch yourself in your mind's eye as you experience happiness, fulfillment, warmth, and love. Love for yourself. Love for others that is freely given. Try to imagine every detail as you slowly breathe in and breathe out.

B. See yourself being loved and giving love. Feel how the sense of happiness, contentment, and fulfillment affect your body. Feel how your heart rate slows down, how your breathing now seems natural. Feel how negative emotions leave you and are replaced with positive thoughts and feelings about yourself, your place in the world, and what you offer to others.

C. Sit with those details. Bathe yourself in those feelings, continuing to slowly breathe in and slowly release your breath.

D. Realize that the negative self-talk is not you. Understand that from our evolution over thousands of years, negative thoughts and events stick to us to protect us, but in the modern world they only limit us and cause us pain.

8. APPRECIATE YOUR HUMANITY

A. Think specific positive thoughts about yourself. All that you have overcome, all that you have accomplished, and understand that in life there are ups and there are downs, but neither defines us. Understand that this is the nature of our reality as humans. Repeat to yourself that you are worthy of love, that you can accomplish anything, that you are deserving of success, that you are not an impostor.

B. Some of you may struggle to believe what you are telling yourself, and this is natural. For now, it is enough to act as if you do. With time, a deeper trust will come if you are patient. Sit with this reality and feel how calm and satisfied you feel as you continue to slowly breathe in and breathe out.

C. With this feeling of calmness and satisfaction comes a sense of being enveloped by love. You understand the nurturing effect of love and how it allows you to see your power and your potential. Sit with these feelings and continue to slowly breathe in and breathe out. Breathe in and breathe out.

D. You are relaxed and you are calm.

9. RECORD YOUR EXPERIENCE

A. Take the pen and paper and write for at least five minutes in your own words what you saw in your mind's eye about your positive feelings of who you are, your abilities, and how those abilities positively affect others. Consider how, when you think about these feelings, you feel safe, you feel warm, and you are able to feel deep within that you are capable of anything.

B. Write as many details as possible. Whether it is a few sentences or a paragraph, it only matters that it defines for you the power within you and the power of caring, of nurturing, and how when you do so, it affects your body. How by reframing and changing your mindset, it releases you from your self-imposed limitations.

C. Simply sit with your eyes closed, slowly breathing for three to five breaths in through the nose and out through the mouth. Now open your eyes.

10. REVIEW YOUR EXPERIENCE

A. First, silently read what you wrote. Then read what you wrote aloud to yourself.

B. Sit with those thoughts of the power you have within yourself and how offering caring and nurturing for yourself affects your mind and your physiology. Sit with these feelings for a few moments with your eyes closed.

C. Now think of how that caring and nurturing makes you feel safe, how that safety has given you permission to own your own power, and how that power allows you to manifest.

11. APPRECIATE YOUR EXPERIENCE

A. Feel how relaxed and calm you are with the satisfaction that you are loved and that you are capable of giving that love to not only yourself but to others, and by doing so create a deep positive sense of yourself.

B. It is being within this state and mindset that creates the environment for you to manifest your greatest desires and wishes.

Once we start to loosen the distracting grip of the inner critic and consciously care for our wounds of the heart, we become empowered to teach our salience network what is important to us. We learn to hold our inner compass clearly and constantly in our minds. When we are fully free to visualize and rehearse our dreams, the power of our imagination lets us live in them in the present, and this enables us to be in frequent contact with the elevated positive emotions we need to teach our subconscious to pursue the goals and dreams we envision for our lives.

In the next chapter, Step Four: Embed the Intention in Your Subconscious, we will learn how to gain access to the "filing clerk and the bloodhound" of our subconscious mind and give them the scent they need to pursue our intention wholeheartedly and constantly.

Chapter 6

STEP FOUR

Embed the Intention in Your Subconscious

*Concentrate all your thoughts upon the work at hand.
The sun's rays do not burn until brought to a focus.*

—Alexander Graham Bell

JIM CARREY'S $10 MILLION CHECK IS ONE OF THE MOST FAMOUS examples of manifesting in popular culture. But how it came to be is less well known.

As Carrey shared on the *WTF with Marc Maron* podcast, his childhood outside of Toronto was not easy. His mother, Kathleen, suffered from severe depression as well as physical ailments like rheumatoid arthritis and colitis. The child of alcoholics, she became addicted to pain medication and, in Carrey's eyes, emotionally abandoned her children. Carrey's father, Percy, was a gifted professional jazz musician who sold his saxophone to pay his wife's hospital bills. Carrey described his father as an "insanely joyful, incredibly funny animated character that didn't just tell a story—he became the characters. Everything I've done in my comedy career can be traced back to that origin. I love that guy so much."

In his commencement address at Maharishi International

University in 2014, Carrey reflected on how his father could have been a great comedian but his own lack of belief made it impossible. Instead, he chose safety and stability by getting a job as an accountant. Then, when Carrey was twelve, Percy was let go from that job and the family had to scramble to survive. "I learned many great lessons from my father," Carrey said, "not the least of which was that you can fail at what you don't want so you might as well take a chance on doing what you love."

After Percy lost his job at age fifty-one, Carrey's family lived in a Volkswagen camper and in a tent on his sister's lawn in the country. Then they worked, as a family, as janitors at the Titan Wheel tire factory in Scarborough, where his coworkers intentionally defecated in the sinks due to feuds between the families. Carrey's once excellent grades suffered, and he dropped out of high school at age sixteen to work full time. At first these childhood adversities led Carrey to feel a personal vendetta, to "blame the world" for his family's financial and emotional woes. He became convinced that life was unfair and unforgiving.

Beginning in third grade, Carrey started making faces in the mirror for hours, talking to himself in funny voices, and entertaining his family with impressions of neighbors and popular television stars. When his mother was in pain, he jumped up on her bed in his underwear and imitated a praying mantis until she was laughing so hard her belly hurt. He put on outrageous shows for dinner guests, and at age fifteen, Percy took him to appear at a hip underground comedy club in Toronto called Yuk Yuk's. He bombed, but the experience set him on his path toward comedy stardom, ultimately inspiring him to move to Los Angeles to hone his craft full time.

Carrey had a huge vision for himself from the start. "I've always believed in magic," he told *Movieline* magazine in 1994.

He went on to describe how, before he was well known, he began a ritual of driving up Mulholland Drive every night, parking his car overlooking the city, stretching out his arms, and telling himself, "Everybody wants to work with me. I'm a really good actor. I have all kinds of great movie offers." As he repeated these phrases and visualized them coming true in his mind, he started to convince himself he *did* have a couple of movies lined up, and as he drove down the hill, he affirmed to himself, "Movie offers are out there for me, I just don't hear them yet." As he drove back down the hill, he was filled with a sense of well-being, possibility, and even joy, having lived through many celebrations and successes in his imagination. Carrey has acknowledged that these affirmations served as antidotes to the negative beliefs he picked up from his family background.

Years before he became famous or well known, Carrey wrote himself a check for $10 million for "Acting Services Rendered" and dated it "Thanksgiving 1995." He put the check in his wallet where, over time, it became creased and worn. Every time he opened his wallet, the check reminded him of his intention and reinforced the narrative that he had embedded in his subconscious that he had already achieved everything he hoped for, just like Anula's letters to herself that she kept in her purse. In the next three years, Carrey appeared in *Ace Ventura: Pet Detective*, *The Mask*, and *Dumb and Dumber*. The three films broke box office records worldwide and made Carrey one of the biggest movie stars on the planet.

It was from his salary for these three movies that Carrey had manifested his intention. He had $10 million in the bank. Sadly, his father, Percy Carrey, died shortly after the release of *The Mask*. Carrey placed the check he'd written himself for

$10 million ten years before in Percy's pocket, and it was buried with him.

In order to understand how Carrey's process worked, we need to examine in greater detail the systems by which it is possible to install our intention in our subconscious, from the concentrated power of the flow state to hypnosis to the placebo effect. As extraordinary as it may seem from afar, Carrey's experience makes perfect sense when viewed through the lens of the networks in the brain we have been exploring.

THE MISERLY BRAIN

There's a maxim that is often repeated among entrepreneurs: People do business with people they know, like, and trust. This is true for small-business owners and the ambitious entrepreneurs and CEOs of huge companies, but it is also true of the brain.

The brain is constantly blocking stimuli and deliberately filtering out most of our experiences. Like a homebody set in their ways who groans and digs in on the sofa instead of going to the party, the brain resists new experiences that might force it to alter its complex circuitry that has served a purpose, be it healthy or not, over time. The reason for this is that the human brain is designed to be extremely conscientious about its energy use.

For all the thinking power, vision, and abstract reasoning the brain provides us with, it is an energy guzzler. The adult human brain represents about 2 percent of our body weight but, remarkably, accounts for about 20 percent of the oxygen consumed, and therefore the calories—significantly more than any other organ. Within the gray tissue crisscrossed with spongy coils there are over one hundred billion cells, and each of them makes over ten thousand connections within the vast network woven between brain cells. This web produces a thousand trillion synaptic connections, greater in number even than the stars in the universe. About two-thirds of the brain's energy budget goes to helping neurons send signals to each other, and the last third goes to "housekeeping," or cell-health maintenance.

The brain's miserliness is rooted in our evolution as a species. The high energy cost of the brain's labor to form cell connections in service of higher-order processes presented a major problem for our biological predecessors. For the brain to stay "solvent" with such a large energy budget, our ancestors on the savanna had to provide it with vast amounts of fuel. There is even some speculation that the invention of cooked food, especially cooked meat, is directly tied to our ancestors' need for the vast number of calories required to develop brains of such complexity.

But given the tremendous labor required to capture and kill animals, the brain had to significantly streamline its working process. Our brains have no way of storing surplus energy the way our muscles can take on fat. So when our brains need energy, they must draw on a quick-release fuel source: our blood sugar. Any extra work the brain must do pulls on our glucose levels, which is like the premium unleaded gasoline of the body. Such precious fuel is in short supply, and the body relinquishes it only sparingly.

With this evolutionary inheritance, the brain is trying to conserve energy in any way possible, and it does so in a variety of ways. Have you ever noticed you can't remember the name of the plucky kid from your favorite show in childhood? That's because the brain developed not just learning mechanisms but also forgetting mechanisms that erase information it believes has become unnecessary because we have stopped recalling it. The brain also has a variety of shorthand techniques that it uses to encode and process information. Among these are what is known as the *iceberg phenomenon*, where it takes in only the essential information—the "tip of the iceberg"—while allowing the rest of the submerged iceberg to be suppressed. This process is also the source of all kinds of bias, from finding confirmation for our preexisting views to subconsciously choosing one type of person over another because of systemic conditioning. In some ways, our brains are not processing machines so much as predicting machines, using these shortcuts to be more efficient and consume less energy.

What this means for us in the manifestation process is that if the brain is not sufficiently familiar with our goal, it will reject it by default: the new information is just too heavy an energy lift. If your desire is so unfamiliar to the brain that fulfilling it would be a new experience requiring a tremendous amount of energy, your brain would just as soon look the other way. Often, this rejection takes the form of overlooking opportunity. If you are seeking a mate or a better job or a new place to live and feel stuck in a loop of failure and discouragement, it may be because your brain is literally not showing you examples of what you're looking for because it does not yet know you care about them. The brain is only doing its job to make your system run smoothly, suppressing all the information it does not classify as salient. Other times, you may encounter what you believe you desire, but be surprised by a strong sensation of fear that is prompting you to push away what you thought you wanted. This, too, is not unusual, because fear is the brain's way of guarding against the novelty of experiencing your desire.

What we are doing when we engage with visualization practices is teaching the brain to become intimately acquainted with our desire so that it recognizes it instantly. Only after significant repetition can our desire become comfortable to the brain. We want the brain to have to spend as little energy as possible to receive our desire when it comes. We want our desire to be like the well-worn pair of slippers perfectly contoured to the shape of our feet, so the brain slides in easily without any resistance. This is the phenomenon of *cognitive ease*. The more the brain already knows our desire intimately down to the last detail, the less energy it will have to spend to welcome it into our lives. If we invest our energy up front in getting the brain accustomed to our goal ahead of time, it won't have to balk at a large expense in the moment. Then, when our desire shows up to do business with the brain, it will already know, like, and trust it.

Teaching our brain to know our desire consciously is not enough. We want our desire to be encoded in the information that the brain processes automatically. The brain must know our desire deep down, below the surface in the subconscious, so that it is able to seek it out and recognize it even when our conscious mind is focused elsewhere.

THE SUBCONSCIOUS

In terms of the mind, most would argue that we have a conscious, a subconscious (or preconscious), and an unconscious. The automatic parts of our nervous system, composed of the subconscious and unconscious, represent a part of our mind below our conscious awareness. We discussed previously the image of the mind as an iceberg, with the conscious mind (what we are aware of in ordinary waking consciousness) representing that which is above the water and constituting less than 10 percent of the mind, while the subconscious and unconscious make up the remaining 90 percent hidden below the surface of the water. At its simplest, the conscious mind means having awareness of internal and external existence. This awareness is based on the five senses, the qualia (the subjective interpretation of the senses), and the conscious access to memory and prior experience. Today, the definition often includes any kind of feeling, cognition, or perception.

On a conscious level, we can sense events around us, interactions with others, sensory input that is necessary to process for survival, events occurring right now. Yet there are myriad events that typically occur automatically and that are not noted on a conscious level, such as control of body temperature, heart rate, release of hormones, or other factors important to maintaining the homeostatic control of the body itself (autonomic processes). These mechanisms have evolved over millions of years.

Although we may not be conscious of it, that huge 90 percent of the iceberg under the water exerts a powerful influence on our behavior. Thus, the subconscious is working around the clock, taking care of us and making many decisions automatically. On some level, we are consciously aware that there are vast and complex processes churning away below the surface, but our experience of it is that we are often surprised by its workings. The subconscious can seem strange, magical, and even frightening because we are not seeing how it is working or what it is doing. We may even feel it is like a shadow government, pulling the strings of our lives behind the scenes. The sources of most of our reactions to people, places, and things are at a subconscious level, or just beneath the surface, and we do not realize we have any agency over them. Consequently, we often ignore them, with the result being that they drive our behavior without our knowing it.

As we continue in our process of manifesting, part of what

we are doing is making friends with our subconscious mind, respecting its wisdom and its power, and coming to feel through practice that it is serving us, even if its workings are obscure. We humbly acknowledge that we depend on it for our waking mind. In time, we learn to recognize our subconscious as the source of our intuition, our inner guidance, our creativity, and our resilience. In fact, it is our subconscious mind that makes it possible for us to pursue our goals without getting in our own way, because it harnesses the power of our agency without being diluted or distracted by our self-consciousness.

The subconscious system has the power to separate our deeper intentions from the incessant chatter that makes constant demands on our attention. Because it latches on to the intention without being derailed by the chatter, it is capable of extreme focus on the task while remaining free from distraction. In this way, the subconscious *maximizes the meeting between attention and opportunity*.

The trick in working with the subconscious is to teach it what is important to us by changing where our attention is placed and how we feel about the chosen object of our attention. This is how we bring our subconscious in alignment with the directives of our inner compass. If we are constantly distracted, thinking about our job activities, our to-do list, what others think, or the events of the day, then we can't focus on embedding our conscious intention so that it becomes the inner directive of our minds.

We teach our subconscious what is important through repetition and positive emotion. As we repeat our rituals and visualizations, we enter a state of flow, or complete absorption in our inner activity. Deep experiences of positive emotion, whether from real or imagined experiences, teach our subconscious to associate the goals we wish to pursue with the biological reward systems of our bodies. In this state, our sense of self-consciousness is dialed down and we transcend the limiting beliefs of our mental habits and invite guidance from our deeper resources, such as our capacity for compassion or the creations of our imagination. Absorption in our inner vision is the state that connects us to creativity and clarifies our intention in our subconscious. The magic is that, as we go about our daily lives, while we may not be directly thinking about our inner intention with our conscious mind, the subconscious goes on processing it and attuning toward it.

THE FILING CLERK AND THE BLOODHOUND

We might think of the subconscious as comprised of a filing clerk and a bloodhound. The filing clerk oversees a limited filing cabinet governed by the brain's conservation of energy and the needs we've placed on it. Once the filing clerk places a file in the cabinet, the bloodhound gets the scent and relentlessly scans our environment for the slightest whiff of it. The bloodhound will then be on the trail at the subconscious level, attending to manifesting our intention around the clock, employing whatever powers, focus, or opportunities it can find. This is the experience of synchronicity, when seemingly unexpected connections begin to appear in service of a particular desire. This is a fundamental component of manifesting.

As we can see, the real estate of the subconscious is precious and has the power to shape our destiny. *What the subconscious seeks, the conscious mind finds.* So, if we feel threatened and believe on a subconscious level that we live in a threatening world that is out to harm us, our bloodhound will scan for threats and we will find ourselves discovering more and more threatening elements in our outer environment. If we have taught our subconscious mind to seek connection, joy, fulfillment, and thriving, we will naturally find ourselves discovering more and more opportunities to experience those positive emotions in reality. The question is, how do we get access to the file cabinet?

FIFTY BITS

The space in our subconscious filing cabinet is not the only limited real estate. Our conscious attention is highly circumscribed as well. Our system is bombarded by about ten million bits of data per second, the equivalent of ten HD movies. However, it is able to process only about fifty bits consciously. This means that about 99.9995 percent of our brain's bandwidth is not available to our conscious mind.

As a result of this vast gap in processing, the brain is wired for inattention and inertia, rather than attention and choice. Most of our choices are made from unexamined habits or wired responses associated with threat, so we often don't pause in the moment to ask ourselves what we would decide if we were really considering it. Instead, we just let our subconscious make the call. The result is that there is often a disconnect between what we truly desire and what we actually do. Therefore, we must consciously create healthier habits of attention. The more attention we give a particular intention, the more we teach our filing clerk to prioritize it as an inner directive. This is the truth expressed by the phrase "Where attention goes, energy flows." This is the reason the cortex is instrumental in manifesting: it has the power to focus our fifty bits of attention where we choose.

The important thing to understand about the subconscious is that it responds to repetition. The more we focus on a particular outcome, visualize it, imaginatively experience it with our five senses, and repeat the desire to ourselves and to the world, the more the filing clerk will catch on to the salience of our desire and the more our bloodhound will get to work to have our mind manifest our intention.

In order to understand how intentions get embedded in the subconscious, we can use several analogies: flow, hypnotism, and placebo.

RECRUITING THE SNS

The reason negativity and the sense of threat has such power over the subconscious is that, because of the evolutionary structure of the brain, the SNS does not have to go through any neural processing in order to gain access to it. Therefore, the fight, flight, or freeze response to any perceived threat can be triggered with little to no oversight from the conscious mind. As we have considered in previous chapters, the problem is that the SNS is strictly reactive and hijacks everything else to get its agenda going because it is the thing that is protecting us and keeping us alive—at least, in its interpretation of its job, shaped by millennia of threat. Unfortunately, many of the things it does are not helping keep us alive at all, and certainly are not helping us to flourish in today's world. As long as the SNS is curating the subconscious, the filing cabinet will be filled with fears, phobias, insecurities, and habitual beliefs that will be skewing our experience of life to the negative, the frightening, and the limited. Before we bring the light of awareness to our subconscious, we must see that it is really the domain of our survival fears and desires, the legacy of our evolutionary inheritance.

And so the first step in harnessing the power of our subconscious is to sublimate all the whims and wants of the SNS. In practice, this means recognizing that our tendencies to be stressed and anxious derive from the experiences of evolutionary predecessors that have been embedded in the subconscious and become the default software. As we learn how the subconscious works, this gives us the power to get information into the system. We begin to put the information we *choose* into the subconscious and thereby replace the information it is getting by default from the SNS. We are manifesting our own agency.

What we are doing is using the cortex, the higher level control system in the brain, and changing how the vagus nerve responds to our intentions on a conscious level. By doing so we are creating a direct neural route to influencing the subconscious. When we consciously practice repetitive visualization techniques and rituals to conjure powerful positive emotions around our desired outcomes, we are increasing the power of the PNS and diminishing that of the SNS.

The subconscious has both expansive and contractive sides. In other words, the SNS has the power to subconsciously influence the subconscious, while the cortex has the power to *consciously* influence the subconscious. As we access this power, we begin to break up the SNS's unholy monopoly on our subconscious, freeing ourselves from the grip of survival fears that we find hard to ignore and that distract us from our deepest intentions. Using practices of suggestibility and conscious repetition, we limit the SNS's own direct path to the subconscious and gain the power to positively choose its contents.

The power of this choice cannot be overstated. Most of us live our lives with the belief that we have no choice in determining our future because we have no way to positively affect our automatic behaviors. In practice, this means letting our SNS be the primary and default driver of our behavior and thoughts, which manifest into our fears. Compare this to acting on the understanding that our PNS, our executive control areas, change how we react to the world not only on a conscious level but on the subconscious as well. Most people just do not know it, but we all have the power to gain access to the subconscious, and in doing so, change our future.

THE NEUROBIOLOGY OF FLOW

The so-called flow state, a term popularized by the psychologist Mihaly Csikszentmihalyi, is defined as a state of complete engagement with a task accompanied by a lessening in self-referential thinking. It emerges when we have a clear goal that requires action, and we feel that the skills we possess match the challenge we face.

When we are in flow, we often experience a state of self-transcendence: the inner critic's needling voice dies away, our habitual worries and self-consciousness fade, and we feel at one with the moment, with ourselves, and with our environment. We feel in control, no matter how chaotic the factors may be. Time seems to fly, space seems to bend to our will, our actions are guided from a crystalline sense of direction. Artists in the fever of creation, athletes in the zone, a scientist in the process of discovering an innovation—these are our common images of flow. But flow can also arise in more ordinary situations, like completing a task at work or, during leisure time, pulling weeds in the garden. When we are in flow, we can become so lost in a task that we don't notice the day is over, we've eaten nothing, and we're neither tired nor bored. Our work feels effortless when, in reality, the effort we have produced is tremendous. The flow experience often comes with a feeling of healthy achievement, a deepened sense of meaning, and an abiding feeling of joy or rapture that makes life worth living.

Researchers continue to study the neural correlates of flow, but there is a general hypothesis that periods of flow are characterized by lowered activity in the frontal lobes that produce the sense of conscious control. Much of the behavior we perform in a flow state seems to be from the bottom up, initiated automatically from the subconscious. This accounts for the experiences of so many high performers who describe practicing their skills for years only to forget all of their abilities in the moment of performance and just "go with the flow."

Flow is characterized by a strong sense of focus or absorption. To produce this state, the brain's central executive network actively inhibits our experience of stimuli that are not relevant to our task, as well as any thoughts that might distract us. We also experience lowered activity in the default mode network, the part of our brain that wanders and worries when we are not focused on an external cognitive task. This means that in the flow state there is a diminishment of self-referential thinking, and therefore our stress levels go down because we are not self-consciously critiquing our every move. Flow also enlists the brain's dopamine reward system, which tends to coincide with feelings of optimism, hope, possibility, and a feeling of being highly motivated, as well as reducing feelings of fatigue and discomfort. Where the slot machine or phone notification provides a hit of dopamine, flow immerses us in a sustained experience of it. The paradox of flow is that you are going toward the goal but the goal is irrelevant. The promise of rewards inspires the sense of relentless dedication to complete what we need to do, but the satisfaction of one-pointed concentration and the absorption in the process are complete in and of themselves.

In flow, we are free from the baggage we habitually carry around, and there is no interference from outside distractions.

Neurologically, the cortex is reducing input from the sensory centers, which are responsible for your sense of identity, and the circuits in the parietal lobe that process time.

When we practice visualizing our intention with full sensory detail, we strive to enter the flow state *in our imagination*. We want to be as absorbed in our imagined task as we would be in real life. Studies have shown that when the brain is absorbed in states of deep concentration and focus, as when mentally rehearsing a desired outcome, the mind's perception of time and space is reduced. When our physical environment and its concerns take up less space in our consciousness, we give our imagination free rein to carry us wholly into our inner experience of our intention. It is the very act of paying such careful attention that liberates our mind to inhabit the inner vision, just as it liberates the high performer to respond to their task with grace, coordination, and precision.

In a sense, the flow state translates to the complete alignment of our conscious and subconscious minds in service of our intention. In flow, we have a special kind of access to the deeper resources of our subconscious and can draw upon them more directly. We can also seek this kind of VIP access to the subconscious via the techniques of hypnosis, which utilize many of the same regions in the brain.

HYPNOTIZING OUR WAY INTO THE SUBCONSCIOUS

When we are practicing repetitive visualization, the basic technique of manifesting, we are essentially hypnotizing our minds into recognizing that our intention is important. If we go on YouTube, we can find countless examples of performance hypnotists putting audience members into a trance, then guiding them to forget their names, laugh hysterically, collapse into sleep, or feel completely drunk while remaining absolutely sober. Neuroscientists have measured the effects of hypnosis on the brain and made several telling discoveries. Fundamentally, hypnosis is the practice of changing the way we use our minds to control perception and the body itself. Like flow, it works by a state of complete absorption.

Using functional magnetic imaging, which measures brain activity by detecting changes in blood flow, researchers at Stanford University monitored the brains of patients under hypnosis and observed several distinct phenomena. First, a decrease in activity in the dorsal anterior cingulate, part of the brain's salience network, was evident. The reason for this is that in hypnosis, the state of absorption is so thorough that one's attention is focused on the task, with no need to scan the inner and outer environments for further salient stimuli. Further, an increase in connections between two other areas of the brain—the dorsolateral prefrontal cortex and the insula—were noted. These areas working in tandem suggests a connection formed between the brain and body, giving the brain a greater ability to respond to and even exercise some control over the sensations the body is sending it. Finally, reduced connections between the dorsolateral prefrontal cortex and the default mode network were found. This decrease in functional connectivity likely represents a decoupling of the subject's actions from their conscious awareness of those actions. At this point, the subject is no longer thinking about what they are doing: they have entered a state beyond worry or self-conscious commentary and they are simply *doing*.

During hypnosis, this detachment of action from conscious awareness means the subject is highly susceptible to suggestion from the hypnotist or, in the case of self-hypnosis, from themselves. They can more easily engage in activities that might cause a defensive reaction in ordinary life without the self-consciousness that costs so much brain energy. In other words, hypnosis allows us to be completely absorbed in the object of our attention, gain heightened control over our bodies and feelings, and get out of our own way so that we allow the power of our subconscious to work freely. When we deliberately embed an intention in our minds through repeated visualization, we are making use of the same physiological pathways as hypnosis.

Another analogy for the process of manifesting can be found in the phenomenon of the placebo effect. We have all heard incredible stories about patients with chronic illness or pain who were given medicine promising miraculous results. The patients beat their afflictions and healed completely, only to learn they had been taking nothing more than a sugar pill. Simply taking the pill signaled to their bodies a belief in the possibility of healing, which in turn caused their bodies to change on a genetic level, thereby defeating the disease. Similar to the process of hypnosis, the placebo effect arises because the patient's consciousness is communicating with the subconscious and autonomic nervous system and using the mind to reshape their body on a cellular level. The intention of the conscious mind to heal due to the patient's belief in the possibility of healing becomes installed in their subconscious, which can alter the way genes produce cells. Then the patient's body, mind, and heart accept this thought as reality, believe in it emotionally, and eventually come to express it physically by overcoming their symptoms.

What all these processes have in common is the ability of the cortex to lower the volume of the outside world, and by doing so diminish incoming distractions from the senses. This includes tuning down false or distorted beliefs that stand as obstacles to healing and realization. There is also a significant reduction in the activity of the default mode network, which is normally responsible for our self-conscious critique of whatever we are doing. And finally, the positive emotions that flood our bodies as we focus activate the reward centers in the brain, so we become more alert to the possibility of our intention coming true, and more willing to endure discomfort to get it. As a result, consciousness can inhabit a space that is beyond the body, physical environment, and even time itself, and so the inner intention can become more and more of a reality.

THE POWER OF RITUAL

The subconscious responds deeply to strong emotions associated with a particular behavior, which explains why so many manifesting practices revolve around rituals, typically acts that are performed repeatedly in a precise manner. Ritual is one of the most potent ways of aligning our conscious and subconscious minds into focus, allowing us to enter a flow state.

I was introduced to Lynne Twist, founder of the Soul of Money Institute and cofounder of the Pachamama Alliance, through our mutual friend, the author Neal Rogin. Lynne described to me how, before she meets with a potential donor, she writes out her purpose and intended results for the conversation. Then she lights a candle. Whether she is raising money for the Pachamama Alliance to preserve the Sacred Headwaters of the Amazon, the Hunger Project, or the Nobel Women's Initiative, she calls to mind her overarching intention to "facilitate the reallocation of financial resources from fear to love, from destruction to nourishing our communities, our families, and our world." As she contemplates the candle, she clarifies her awareness that she will have the great privilege of speaking to another human being, tuning in to who they really are and the generosity in their hearts, and inviting them to partner with her, rather than manipulating them in any way. From her own private sacred space, she communes with the spirit of the potential donor and envisions the conversation through the lens of her heart, asking them if they would like their money to be a conduit for their love. She visualizes the person's answer, whether they wholeheartedly accept her invitation or decline in favor of putting their money to another purpose. Either way, she pictures them being completely satisfied and fulfilled by their response. This way, if the donor decides not to participate, Lynne is not disappointed; she simply "blesses and releases them."

There are countless rituals, rites, and practices we can make use of to embed our intention into the deeper levels of our minds. Some are ceremonial, like Lynne's, and others are more ordinary. For example, many of us write out our intention and place it somewhere we will see it every day, such as on the bathroom mirror, on the dashboard of our car, or in our wallet. Or we can recall Anula's practice of writing herself letters and carrying them with her. Every time we see the paper with our intention, we can repeat our visualization of achieving our goal, calling into our minds, bodies, and hearts the wonderful feelings we will experience when our goal becomes reality. As we practice remembering our desired result over and over again, our repeated intention to experience the fulfillment of our desires is giving our attention (and therefore our subconscious) some velocity to influence the outcome.

JIM CARREY'S $10 MILLION CHECK

For Carrey, it was necessary to become conscious of the negative and self-limiting beliefs installed in his subconscious during his childhood that were obstacles to him manifesting his desires. Once he was aware of them, he could intentionally offer his subconscious corrective beliefs, which he embedded by means of affirmation, visualization, and repetitive ritualized reminders sitting in his car up on Mulholland Drive. Through associating his intentions with strong positive emotions experienced in the present, he was redirecting his subconscious to pay attention to his desired outcomes and alerting his salience network to scan for opportunities to realize his goals. Evidence confirming the cruelty, randomness, and injustice of the world became less relevant to his mind and made way for hopeful indications of success, synchronicities that advanced his professional dreams, and perseverance in the face of inevitable setbacks.

Carrey combined the sense of empowerment, gratitude, and joy he received from his visualizations (and the neurotransmitters released by these experiences of strong positive emotions) with the fierce work ethic he demonstrated in refining his gifts at the comedy clubs. The positive emotions he lived through in his mental rehearsal signaled to his brain that the experiences he desired were worthy of attention and that mental resources should be devoted to pursuing them. In a sense, he was hypnotizing himself *out* of the grasp his painful childhood experiences exercised over him and *into* the new reality of his future success. His ritual of looking out over Los Angeles and rehearsing his success affected his brain the same way the medical ritual of visiting the hospital and being given a pill affects a patient benefiting from the placebo effect. As a result, when success did indeed come, Carrey's conscious mind had already lived through it as an experiential reality through mental rehearsal and was primed to receive it without fear or resistance.

PRACTICE:
Visualizing Your Intention

For many of us, it is hard to imagine that we have the ability and possess the agency to manifest. It is easy to believe that the drivers of our achievements exist outside of ourselves, but the reality is that within each of us is a superpower that allows us to imagine amazing possibilities for ourselves, and that is the power of visualization. When I first learned these techniques from Ruth in the magic shop, it was before the term visualization *was in common practice or the concept of neuroplasticity was understood. What has been learned since that time is how powerful visualization can be when practiced diligently and with an open heart.*

1. GET YOURSELF READY

A. Find a time and a place to do this meditation so that you will not be interrupted.

B. Do not start this meditation if you are stressed, have other matters that are distracting you, have drunk alcohol or used recreational drugs in the last twenty-four hours, or are tired.

C. Have a pad of paper and a pen near you.

2. START TO VISUALIZE YOUR INTENTION

A. Sit in a relaxed position with your eyes closed, thinking of the goal you wish to manifest while also allowing your thoughts to wander. Often a negative thought or image will occur, but you can direct your attention immediately back to what you wish to manifest.

B. Do this for several minutes, and if your mind wanders (as it likely will), immediately bring it back to the thought of what you wish to manifest.

C. As you are thinking, attempt to provide more clarity to the image of yourself having manifested your goal. See yourself in that image, what you look like, how you feel in your body, what you feel in your heart.

3. NOW RELAX A BIT FURTHER

A. Sit up straight with your eyes still closed and take three breaths slowly in through your nostrils and slowly out through your mouth.

B. Repeat until this type of breathing feels comfortable for you and is not distracting.

C. Beginning with your toes, start to relax the muscles of your body all the way to the top of your head, feeling more and more at ease as you focus on relaxing your body. You will find that as you do so, there is a sense of calmness that envelops you, and you feel safe. You feel a sense of warmth and a sense of acceptance and are no longer worrying about people judging you or criticizing your dreams and aspirations, as you slowly continue to breathe in and out. You now begin to see more clearly what it is you wish to manifest.

D. You are comfortable and relaxed as you continue to slowly breathe in and out. You are now less distracted and more focused.

4. RETURN TO VISUALIZING YOUR INTENTION

A. Again, think of manifesting your intention. Concentrate on that image of you having accomplished the goal that you wish to manifest.

B. Sit with the feeling of satisfaction and accomplishment as you slowly breathe in and slowly exhale. You realize as you do so, the possibilities seem more possible. The vision of you having manifested your intention becomes clearer.

C. You are relaxed, you are calm, and you feel that you can accomplish anything you desire. You feel connected to the endless possibilities that are within you to manifest.

D. Sit with these feelings and continue to slowly breathe in and breathe out. Breathe in and breathe out. Now slowly open your eyes. You feel calm. You have no fear.

5. RECORD YOUR INTENTION

A. Take the pen and paper and write for at least five minutes in your own words exactly how you visualized what you wish to manifest. Be as specific as possible.

B. If it was related to a professional goal, include every possible detail including time and place, the clothes you were wearing, the time of day and how you felt. If it was for an object, include as many details as possible with an in-depth description and how it felt to have that object. See yourself with the object. Imagine every possible detail.

6. REVIEW YOUR INTENTION

A. Silently read to yourself what you have written, close your eyes, and again imagine having manifested it and how it feels for a few minutes.

B. Open your eyes again and now read what you have written aloud to yourself.

C. Close your eyes, again imagine you having manifested and how it feels for a few minutes.

7. REPEAT THIS EXERCISE

A. Some may find doing this meditation once a day for twenty minutes is enough; others may want to do it more than once a day. The reality is that the more often one uses this visualization practice, the more likely it is for one's dreams to manifest.

B. Remember, while it is possible to visualize and manifest things that can benefit only yourself, manifesting is much more powerful and likely to occur when you are able to think of how what you wish to manifest is in service of a goal larger than yourself. That is not to say that such manifestation must be absolutely selfless, but it is more powerful when the goal benefits others as well.

As can be seen in Carrey's example, manifestation is not a one-and-done activity. It is a conscious practice diligently cultivated with care. Rarely do we get what we want right away. Instead, we must stick with it, often through thick and thin, even when our external circumstances (and our own minds) seem to be conspiring to keep us from achieving our goals. And there is almost always a moment when we must enlist the support of others to help us get there. For this reason, we turn in our next chapter to Step Five: Pursue Your Goal Passionately, in which we will learn how the rest-and-digest response lets us connect consciously with others, and how to become the kind of person others want to help through aligning our intention to a higher purpose.

Chapter 7

STEP FIVE

Pursue Your Goal Passionately

Always go with your passions. Never ask yourself if it's realistic or not. Find the place inside yourself where nothing is impossible.
—Deepak Chopra

THE MOST TREACHEROUS PLACE TO SAIL ON EARTH IS THE Intertropical Convergence Zone, known by sailors as "the doldrums." Near the thermal equator, the northeast and southeast trade winds converge, and as the northeast winds die off, they are replaced by long periods of calm followed by severe buffeting squalls and light, baffling winds. It is considered a navigator's nightmare because it is almost impossible to tell which way the current is heading, at what speed, and from what direction the wind blew in the last squall.

On his voyage to Tahiti, Nainoa Thompson dreaded entering the doldrums. Although he put on a brave face for the media and the Polynesians placing their deepest hopes on his success, he doubted his ability to navigate under nearly 100 percent cloud cover with no access to the celestial clues he had learned for guidance. He lacked the confidence to trust his own instincts. He was afraid of sailing blind, and that is exactly what happened.

As he describes it, when they arrived in the doldrums, the sky darkened completely. The rain whipped at their eyes. The wind, about twenty-five knots, was overpowering and kept changing the direction it was coming from.

"That's the worst thing that can happen," says Thompson. "You are going fast, and you don't know where you're going."

He couldn't tell the men steering what direction to steer. Even though he knew he could not afford to give in to fatigue, his body was shot through with tension.

At first, Thompson fought the weather conditions with his mind, straining to grasp some familiar clue in the sky to guide the canoe and the sailors he felt responsible for. Finally he gave up, so exhausted that he backed up against the rail to rest. He abandoned his mental struggle against the weather and let his mind relax. Then, he remembers, something strange happened.

"A warmth came over me. All of a sudden, I knew where the moon was, even though I couldn't see it. The feeling of warmth and the image of the moon gave me a strong sense of confidence and I knew where to go, even when I had already convinced myself prior to the voyage that I would have no confidence in knowing where to go. I turned the canoe on a new course, got things lined up, and felt very, very comfortable in this cold, wet, rough environment. And then—just for a moment—there was a break in the clouds and the light of the moon shone through, just where I expected it to be. I can't explain it, but that was one of the most precious moments in all my sailing experience. I realized there was a deep connection between something in my abilities and my senses that goes beyond the analytical, beyond seeing with my eyes."

It is inevitable that in our process of manifesting, we will encounter obstacles, setbacks, and frustrations. We may even be overcome with self-doubt, losing confidence in our abilities to realize our intentions and losing sight, as Nainoa Thompson did, of the guides and clues we were relying on to lead our journey. When we are facing our own dark night, swarmed by fears and old stories that taunt us with the illusion that we are incapable, unworthy, or wrong, we can turn our attention back to our deepest intention and take refuge in the simple and powerful practices we have been cultivating to express the compass of our hearts. And when we are groping our way through the pitch-darkness of whatever jungle we are lost in like Silvia Vasquez-Lavado, we can look around for the friendly, supportive faces of those who know the way and can guide us out.

We might put extra time into our self-compassion practice or seek new ways to visualize ourselves reaching our goals, or explore new rituals to allow us to enter the state of flow in which we can get out of our own way (and out of our own heads) and let life take its natural course, doing for us what we could never do with only our conscious minds. There are a variety of strategies to help us through the rough patches that will naturally arise when we manifest our intention: starting small, returning to our core practices, activating the social power of altruism, and tuning into synchronicity.

START SMALL

Manifesting is a practice of engagement and, more importantly, understanding the process of placing one's intention into the subconscious, which takes many rounds of repetition. As with any practice, it is wise to start with a small, manageable goal that is not too far out of reach. If we try to jump ahead a million steps and expect spectacular results instantly, we will inevitably feel let down and become discouraged with the entire process. Even worse, we will probably become excessively self-critical and take our disappointment out on ourselves. Achieving a small goal helps us to build confidence in ourselves and in the process itself, and the positive emotions we feel upon achieving the goal buoy us up to pursue the next one. This is the nature of small changes or baby steps. They strengthen us without overwhelming us.

Manifesting is not a one-off practice; it is not a magic wand, and it does not allow us to leap over the laws of physics or the natural stages of human development. There is no ceiling to what we can pursue, but even our wildest dreams can only be realized one step at a time. Although it may sometimes work quickly, manifesting does not just magically happen overnight. It does not go from zero to one hundred in a microsecond. It must also be recognized that manifesting is not a passive endeavor. It is an active process of taking baby steps that lead to the ultimate goal. One must also be committed to the work involved in manifesting, whether that means pursuing an academic achievement or trying to bench-press four hundred pounds. That said, we can manifest extraordinary things, but first they must be embedded in the subconscious. Over time, as opportunities present themselves and we respond, each of these small events ultimately contribute to the manifestation of that intention.

The lessons you acquire over the course of the many small steps will give you the wisdom to persist when you encounter inevitable setbacks of the process. Even more radically, it will help you take the time to enjoy each small gain as it comes, to savor and appreciate it, rather than rush on immediately to the next one. It is not only repetition that forms a habit; it is the positive emotion we attach to doing a good job and completing it.

BE SOMEONE YOU WOULD LIKE TO HELP
You might think the solution to being stuck is to double down on your hustle, to push yourself harder, to be even more relentless. In fact, I would like to offer an alternative strategy that may seem counterintuitive: reflect instead on how you see the world, what you believe about your place in it, and, most importantly, what effect you have on all the people you encounter. Consciously improving our interactions with those around us may turn out to be the key factor in overcoming our obstacles to manifesting. By doing so, you are creating a team of allies to help you.

The nervous system is constantly responding to those around us and our environment, scanning for threats and opportunities. Through the process described by Stephen Porges as *neuroception*, a subconscious system for detecting threats and safety, we classify every encounter with another person as safe or dangerous, subconsciously deciding to approach or move away. When we are in the rest-and-digest mode, our bodies express what is known as the *social engagement system*, accompanied by a series of physiological changes. Our heart rate slows, saliva and digestion are activated, facial muscles are stimulated to express positive mental states, and there is an increase in vocal expressiveness and a willingness to make sustained eye contact with others. These changes affect how we react to stimuli, what kinds of expressions appear on our face, and, most importantly for manifesting, how others respond to us. When we look at the world in a different way, we move through it in a different way, and in turn the world sees us in a different way. One extraordinary example is that the middle-range muscles in our ears come online, and these are the muscles that are designed to hear nuances in the human voice. As researchers into the polyvagal theory have discovered, the human voice sounds special to our ears only when we feel safe. When we are in fight, flight, or freeze, our ears focus only on high and low frequencies because these tend to indicate the approach of predators. In other words, only when we feel safe and taken care of can we truly hear another human being.

In my case, it has been a lifelong practice to learn to listen. I mean really listen, not just sit there watching the other person talk while I prepare my own calculated response. It has often been said about brain surgeons that we are "often wrong, never in doubt." I used to bring this arrogant attitude to all my interactions, and the truth is that I was depriving myself of actual connection with others. The more I practiced just being OK with myself, the more I found I was able to attune to others and really take in what they were saying. In a sense, manifesting is the skill of connecting to those around us, our environment and our context, and kindness and genuine compassion are our direct physiological pathways to that connection. When we express the prosocial physiology of the rest-and-digest response, others instinctively want to help us achieve our goals because they sense our actions are serving the greater good and making a contribution to the whole. In fact, the pleasure and reward systems of our brains light up not only when we are being generous or experiencing the generosity of others but also as a response to food, money, and sex.

When we are in the Green Zone, as discussed in Chapter 2, other people like us and enjoy being around us. Part of the power of the mammalian caregiving system is that when we ourselves are in distress, or we encounter distress in others, we can, if we feel safe enough, choose to self-soothe and practice compassion instead of fighting or withdrawing. Consequently, because we naturally mirror the autonomic state of people around us, our Green Zone state can trigger the Green Zone state in others because they then feel safe, relaxed, and at ease in our presence. Our self-compassion can be contagious, as with the electromagnetic field of the heart in a state of coherence. Feeling safe is necessary to form strong social relationships. Safety allows for physical proximity and the intimacy-building that arises from friendly and caring touch. Positive physical contact promotes the release of oxytocin, which in turn allows for social bonding to take place. We need to feel safe enough to be physically close to others in order to become emotionally close.

As we rehearse the positive emotions of connection, belonging, purpose, and fulfillment in our visualizations and meditations, they become more and more familiar to us, less threatening to our survival. The more we allow these feelings to activate the social safety instinct of the rest-and-digest response, the more others will experience the goodness and benefit of our intention and will then desire to act in service of it because it's serving them as well.

ALIGNING OUR PURPOSE

Remember the moment in Anula's story when she was about to take the MCAT again? Rather than visualizing how a good score might benefit only her personal desires, she shifted the focus to imagine how she could serve her future patients and all the help and healing she could offer them through her care if she became their doctor. Carrying this new heartfelt aspiration into her test-taking, Anula was able to remain more focused on her answers, recall her knowledge more effectively, and ultimately, score higher than before. This is the alchemy that occurs when a desire meets an open-heart yearning for connection. When we reflect on our personal desires, we discover beneath them a deeper longing to contribute to our world. In the manifesting process, this is not just a heartwarming side effect; it is a full-on strategic asset. The world responds favorably and generously to a purpose that heals and invites life to flow. By tuning into how our intention can serve others, we invite benefactors and assistance we could never have imagined if we had pursued our goal only for our own self-interest.

Interestingly, the turning point in Jim Carrey's career also came through a revelation about the greater purpose of his comedy. He describes how, although he was already a popular and successful impressionist—the "man of a thousand faces" imitating Elvis Presley for Johnny Carson on *The Tonight Show*—he decided to strip away his crowd-pleasing persona and go out on stage night after night without any prepared act or jokes and simply improvise to discover his deeper motivation.

"I'd go home [after shows]," Carrey said in the documentary *Jim and Andy: The Great Beyond*, "and I'd lay on my bed and think, 'What do they want? What do they want? What do they want?' It wasn't what *I* wanted. I knew what I wanted: I wanted to be successful, I wanted to be a famous actor. But what do *they* want? What do they want? What do they want? And then one day in the middle of the night I woke up out of a sound sleep, shot up in bed, and went, 'They want to be free from concern,' and the lightbulb went on."

The next night, Carrey went to the Comedy Store and opened with the line "Good evening, ladies and gentlemen, and how are you this evening? *Alrighty then*." The audience roared, and the trademark haughty persona that would soon appear in *Ace Ventura* and launch him into stardom was born. "They knew I didn't care, I didn't give a damn," Carrey said. "What I had decided, in that moment in my bed, was that they need to be free from concern so I'm gonna be the guy that's free from concern." Carrey had discovered that he could align his gifts with the genuine emotional needs of his audience, and in this way, care for them and serve them while being kind to himself. He has even spoken of his work as a comedian as a "ministry."

Years later, at a conference with Eckhart Tolle in 2009, Carrey described reflecting on his life after achieving success. When he considered the past, he discovered a sense of being two different people: one of them was in the living room jumping around for whoever was over, entertaining everyone. The other was trying to relieve the suffering of his mother. He wanted her to feel a sense of freedom, and a sense that "her life was worth something because she gave birth to someone who was worth something." And then he would retreat to his room and sit with a legal pad on his lap and ask the big questions, even as a small child: "Why are we here? What is this?" Later, he read a quotation from the Buddha that said the purpose of all spirituality is to relieve suffering. And he had the sudden realization, *"That's what I'm doing in the other room!* I'm aligned. My purpose is aligned with this."

In other words, once Carrey aligned his comedic gifts with his higher purpose of relieving suffering through freeing people from concern, he started to become the person everyone wanted to work with, just as he had imagined up on top of Mulholland Drive. As he inhabited his new role of ministering to his audience more fully, his dreams began to manifest at an incredible level. "My choosing to free people from concern got me to the top of the mountain," Carrey reflected. "The effect you have on others is the most valuable currency there is... I did something that made people present their best selves to me, wherever I go."

PRACTICE:
How Does My Intention Benefit Life?

One of the most powerful things we can do to increase our inner power is to align our intention with the life around us. In this practice I encourage you to reflect on how your vision is part of something larger than you as an individual.

1. GET YOURSELF READY

    A. Find a quiet place and time where you can reflect.

    B. Take a few deep breaths in and out to settle your mind and return to this moment in your body.

2. REFLECT ON YOUR INTENTION

    A. Call to mind the intention you have been visualizing. Experience it fully in its sensory detail and positive emotion.

    B. Now zoom out a little. In what context is this vision taking place? Who else is connected to the event or goal? What does your intention mean to them?

3. CONNECT YOUR INTENTION TO SOMETHING LARGER

    A. Consider the effect that realizing your intention might have. Maybe achieving your goal will enable you to inspire others like you to pursue their own dreams. Maybe your intention will bring joy or attention or resources to your family or community. Maybe it will address a social or environmental problem that affects many other people.

4. WRITE A STATEMENT

A. Write a statement of intention or a mission statement on how your intention will serve the life around you. This could be in the form of a letter to yourself or to a loved one or to the world, or a personal statement as in a job application, or a series of principles you intend to follow.

B. When you are facing increased doubts or resistance or lethargy, return to this statement for support and inspiration. Remember that what you are manifesting is part of the larger fabric of life. You may read or share your statement with people you encounter to enlist their support for your intention.

SYNCHRONICITY

Another way to approach blocks to manifesting involves making use of our brain's natural ability to scan for clues in our environment. In the previous chapter, we learned about the filing clerk and the bloodhound in our subconscious. Once the filing clerk has classified our intention as salient and given its scent to the bloodhound, the hound will begin to hunt for any trace of opportunity to fulfill our intention. This is the origin of the phenomenon of *synchronicity*, the sudden, often surprising appearance of meaningful coincidences in our lives that we did not notice before. If we are stuck in our manifesting process, we can practice paying careful attention to the subtle hints and unexpected connections we may have dismissed as accidental or irrelevant. Often these strange confluences can be subtle signposts that guide us enigmatically on our path. Only when we look back and reflect on the string of connections do we realize their internal logic.

Consider anything that has happened to you recently that struck you as "weird." Maybe three different people with no relationship to one another have recommended the same book to you, or you have had a recurring dream about a particular landscape that feels full of meaning, or you casually mentioned your intention to someone at a dinner party or work event and they happened to know someone whose help would have a great impact on your project. Maybe a phrase keeps popping into your head and you can't remember the source, or you feel drawn for no rational reason to a particular neighborhood, or you have a sudden inspiration to contact an old friend you haven't seen in years. With its narrow focus on short-term goals, our conscious mind is not always the most reliable judge of what is truly important for us to know and recognize, and so we must make space for the quieter, more intuitive messages of our subconscious that often speak to us through unexpected correlations between people, environment, events, and things.

IN THE FOOTSTEPS OF THE DREAM

Amandine Roche was languishing in law school in France and dreaming of travel when her friend invited her to the Bordeaux Book Fair. It would become the start of a journey that spanned the globe.

Amandine told me her story when we first met in 2014, at an event I was hosting for the spiritual figure Amma, known as the "hugging saint." It turned out that her friend's aunt would be at the book festival, and the aunt was best friends with Ella Maillart. Maillart was a renowned Swiss adventurer and photographer who had undertaken the kinds of extraordinary journeys that Amandine's heart longed to experience. Maillart was best known for traveling 3,500 miles across China with *Times of London* correspondent Peter Fleming in 1935, traversing inhospitable deserts and treacherous passes of the Himalayas by train, truck, yak, and camel and on foot. She had also traveled from Geneva to Kabul by car in 1939 and spent time with nomads in Kyrgyzstan. Amandine said to herself, "This is the life I want to have."

Her friend's aunt gave her Maillart's number to set up an appointment to meet. While Amandine was preparing for the interview and getting to know Maillart's work, Maillart, who was ninety-four, died. Amandine was devastated. That night, Maillart came to her in a dream and said, "Don't worry. You can meet me another way. Take all my books and all my pictures and go back to all the countries where I used to travel and see what has changed in seventy years."

With renewed hope, Amandine put together a proposal and received six grants to follow Ella's footsteps. For eighteen months, she visited all of Central Asia, India, Nepal, Tibet, China, Russia, and Ukraine without taking a plane, living with people she met along the way and using whatever means of locomotion materialized for her, from trucks to sidecars to camels. But she still had to reach Kabul. It was the year 2000 and Afghanistan was under the control of the Taliban. At that time, Amandine was in Tajikistan working with UNICEF. Her boss informed her that a group of Afghan refugees had entered Tajikistan. Because of concerns that the Taliban might have infiltrated the group, the refugees were directed onto two small islands filled with land mines, claimed by neither Tajikistan nor Afghanistan, on the Amu Darya River. As a result, this became an emergency crisis and Amandine was asked to go with three others to give aid and document the situation. She was terrified both by the Tajik-manned Russian tanks on one side, and the Kalashnikovs of the Taliban on the other side. Nonetheless, she accepted the assignment and fell in love with the Afghan people she met, touched by their generous hospitality. She decided she would visit Afghanistan despite the danger. She took leave time and bought a UN plane ticket. But no one would take her there. It was too dangerous.

She spoke to a group of Russian pilots and they told her that the Taliban had just shot down their planes, and they weren't going back. Then she tried to enter the country with an NGO, but she didn't have authorization from the Russians, so she was not allowed to go. After that, she tried to get a ride with Ahmad Shah Massoud, an Afghan military commander, in his helicopter, but her boss told her she was crazy to fly straight into a war zone. Three times she tried, but she could not make it to Afghanistan. Finally, channeling the spirit of Ella Maillart, she took her backpack and went on foot, hitching rides where she could. She arrived in Islamabad, Pakistan, in September 2001, where she met the head of the French alliance in the area. She explained to him her dream to follow in the footsteps of Ella Maillart and enter Afghanistan for her book.

He told her that she was crazy and warned her that the Taliban would kill her. The following day she ran into him again and he asked why she was still there. She repeated her desire. Impressed, he agreed to introduce her to one of his students, Rohullah, whose uncle was Habibullah, the minister of foreign affairs for the Taliban.

Rohullah asked for Amandine's passport and called his

uncle in front of her. He explained how she had tried three times to come to Afghanistan from Tajikistan and now she was trying from Pakistan and asked if he could help her. He agreed and asked her name. Rohullah read her name in Farsi as "Amanuddin Rosh." Habibullah said, "She doesn't need a visa. She's already Afghan."

Amandine was puzzled. "By chance," Rohullah said, "my uncle is coming to Pakistan tomorrow and he would be very honored to give you a visa for free." Now Amandine was baffled. When she met Habibullah, he explained, "Allah sent you to Afghanistan because of your name. *Aman* means 'peace,' *djin* means 'religion,' and *rosh* means 'joy.' Your name actually means the 'happy protector of peace.' That is a sign of Allah, and so you will be our honored guest." Thanks to Habibullah, Amandine crossed into Afghanistan and entered Kabul, completing her journey honoring Ella Maillart's legacy. The date was September 10, 2001.

In the chaos that ensued following the attacks on the World Trade Center, Amandine lost track of Rohullah, but she dreamed of reuniting with the person who had allowed her to complete her quest and repay him. More than ten years later, in 2012, a friend of Amandine called her from France. By this time, Amandine had been living in Afghanistan on and off for the last decade in service to the Afghan people. The friend was writing a book on a famous Pashtun woman and asked if Amandine could invite the woman to her house to assist her with the book contract. Amandine agreed, and her friend sent a translator who turned out to be a translator for the Taliban. "Really?" asked Amandine. "Do you know Habibullah?" The man laughed. "Why are you laughing?" she asked. "Because you are his neighbor. He lives on the corner of your street." Amandine had been in Afghanistan for ten years and had no idea if Habibullah was even still alive, and in fact he was living just down the street. The translator called Habibullah and said, "Habibullah, salaam aleikum. I have a surprise for you."

And Habibullah answered, "Is it Amanuddin?"

Habibullah, it turned out, had been searching for Amandine in the aftermath of the military conflict. She went directly to his house and asked about Rohullah. Habibullah revealed that Rohullah's father had just died, and he was finally back in Afghanistan after years in Norway obtaining a master's degree in peace studies. Habibullah called Rohullah and said, "I have a surprise for you."

And Rohullah answered, "Is it Amanuddin?"

They met again and felt the beauty and incredible fortune of reconnecting. Rohullah was building the Torch of Light School for the children of the Taliban and Amandine was working to create the Amanuddin Foundation to promote peace and nonviolence and to cultivate yoga and meditation practices for local Afghans. They decided to work together.

Three years later, Amandine was in Haiti when she got a call from Rohullah. "Please help me," he said. Because he had been working on women's empowerment with the UN, the Taliban wanted Rohullah killed. He had escaped to Istanbul and was trying to come to France. Amandine used her connections to get him a visa, and today Rohullah is a French citizen. Finally, Amandine was able to offer help in return for his great kindness.

Amandine explains the twists and turns of her story like this: "It's like you are fully connected with your soul, coincidences appear, and everything aligns with your intention. You need to keep your vibration high and put intention on where you want to go, and tune in to your intuition. Meeting Rohullah and Habibullah was a manifestation of my intention and had a big impact on my destiny."

PRACTICE:
Scanning for Synchronicity

Making the most of synchronicity is a habit we can practice. As our subconscious begins tuning in to our environment for opportunities to realize our intention, it is as if we put on night-vision goggles. Whereas before, we were working blind in the middle of the night, unable to see anything around us, but with the goggles on, all kinds of new, unnoticed movements become visible, and suddenly opportunities are everywhere. We are no longer in the dark. This strange intertwining of interests, desires, and events is a phenomenon that often arises when we allow our intention to sink into our subconscious and start interacting with the world at large. Try this practice to increase your own receptivity to the hints your world is offering you.

1. GET YOURSELF READY

A. Find a quiet place and time where you can reflect.

B. Take a few deep breaths in and out to settle your mind and return to this moment in your body.

C. Have a pad of paper and a pen near you.

2. START TO SETTLE

A. Sit in a relaxed position with your eyes closed for a few minutes, allowing your thoughts to settle.

B. Now sit up straight with your eyes still closed and take three breaths slowly in through your nostrils and slowly out through your mouth. Repeat until this type of breathing feels comfortable for you and is not distracting.

3. BODY SCAN

A. Slowly scan through your body, touching each part lightly with your awareness, relaxing each muscle as you go.

B. Allow the relaxation of your body, muscle by muscle, to loosen and open your mind.

4. SCAN FOR SYNCHRONICITY

A. Gently call to mind the events and circumstances of your life. Allow the details of your life to materialize in your mind without judgment. No feeling is too small, no clue is too insignificant. Listen to your life like it is a wise oracle who speaks in a mysterious language.

B. Ask yourself, "Have I noticed any patterns or surprising coincidences?" Reflect on recent conversations you may have had or articles or posts you may have read, memorable dreams, or passing intuitions. Perhaps you have heard the title of the same book from three different people or you can't stop thinking about a certain place, or a long-lost memory of a particularly inspiring experience keeps appearing in your mind.

5. RECORD YOUR OBSERVATIONS

A. Take the pen and paper and write for at least five minutes in your own words what you saw when you visualized your life.

B. Write as many details as possible. Whether it is a few sentences or a paragraph, it only matters that you are writing what your life is trying to tell you.

6. REVIEW YOUR WRITING

A. Sit with your eyes closed, slowly breathing for three to five breaths in through the nose and out through the mouth. Now open your eyes.

B. Silently read what you wrote.

C. Then read what you wrote aloud to yourself. Sit with those images of your life for a few moments with your eyes closed.

7. CONSIDER NEXT STEPS

A. Take a few moments to reflect on how you might follow up on whatever patterns or insights you noticed. Where can you use your own inner power to enhance the web of surprising connections?

B. Spend a few more moments sitting with what you noticed. Recognize that the tiniest connection may be an opportunity to deepen your alignment with your purpose and your vision.

Keep what you wrote somewhere you will see it often to remind you to continue to scan your life for unexpected connections. Synchronicities have a way of multiplying as we give them our attention and respect. Repeat this practice periodically to refine your vision and maximize all the opportunities life has to offer you to realize your goals.

ROLL UP YOUR SLEEVES

Sometimes, to realize our intention, we must commit to putting in some hard work. The process is the same as when building any positive habit. As an example, over the last few years I've gained weight, which, in conjunction with an old skiing accident where I injured my left knee, further limited my desire and motivation to exercise. I live in a hilly neighborhood; when I step out of my house, I am faced immediately with a steep incline. I had not exercised for a while, but I decided to lose weight. By this time I had remarried; I recruited my new wife to help me, and early one morning we went for a walk up the hills. Right away, I was huffing and puffing, and saying, "God, this is not going to work. I can't do this. This is horrible, my knee is killing me."

My body, which wasn't used to pumping blood at that level, rebelled at the discomfort, and that produced mental signals in the form of "I can't do this, I can't take this, it's not going to work." But actually, all that was happening was resistance because I was out of shape. I quickly gave up and went back into the house to lick my wounds. Then one day I woke up at five thirty a.m. and said, "Fuck it, I'm just going to do it." I envisioned myself not only doing it but being in good physical shape. I did the entire walk without stopping, although I was definitely huffing and puffing and my knee was hurting. Now I have been doing it for a few weeks. And the funny thing is, every morning I wake up and say, "I hate this. I do not want to do this; it isn't going to work." And then I just put my clothes on and go do it. I override my pain and my fear of discomfort because I know that in the long run, the exercise is healthy for me, perhaps lifesaving. I teach my body that what it is resistant to doing in the short term will benefit it in the long term. What I realize is that each time I complete my walk, I feel inspired and elevated because I am reminded, first, that anything is possible with the right intention, and second, that my walks up the hill will ultimately benefit me and I can enjoy the sense of well-being that they bring.

TAKE A DEEP BREATH

As a neurosurgeon, I myself have experienced the same sense of insight through internal relaxation as when Nainoa Thompson leaned against the rail of his canoe in exhaustion in the doldrums. There were times when things went wrong in an operation and I was working completely blind on a terrifyingly short clock to save a patient's life. In those moments, while everyone around me was panicking, I returned to my fundamental practices: I calmed my mind, relaxed my body, and opened my heart. I visualized exactly the procedure that I needed to do in order to save my patient's life, and I let myself and my hands be guided by a possibility that is beyond reason, and beyond skill. I let go of my conscious mind's frantic desire to control the situation and make it reasonable and predictable, and I surrendered to the amazing skill of my subconscious, by which life itself could flow through me.

Manifesting is subject to the same rules of life, physics, and reality as everything else. We cannot force a result if it is not in the nature of reality to bring it about. Sometimes we have done everything we can in service of our intention, and it is now out of our hands. At times like this, there is nothing else to do but breathe, calm ourselves, and open our hearts. We now move on to Step Six: Release Expectations and Open to Magic.

Chapter 8

STEP SIX

Release Expectations and Open to Magic

Nothing important comes into being overnight; even grapes and figs need time to ripen. If you say that you want a fig now, I will tell you to be patient. First, you must allow the tree to flower, then put forth fruit; then you have to wait until the fruit is ripe.

—Epictetus

THERE ARE TIMES IN THE PROCESS OF PURSUING OUR VISION we seem to be absolutely stuck or confused, but if we open our hearts and listen, we may discover our very "failure" is leading us to a new opportunity we had not imagined.

Lynne Twist, founder of the Soul of Money Institute, received her vision for forming the Pachamama Alliance while she was still working as an executive for the Hunger Project. She was flying all over the world addressing issues of hunger and poverty in sub-Saharan Africa and the Indian subcontinent, was responsible for operations in over fifty-three countries, and was also raising three kids. This work was the result of her childhood visions of meeting Mother Teresa and joining her ministry, which at the time Lynne believed to be her highest calling in life. She was very busy and her time was stretched, but she agreed to take a short leave to travel to Guatemala to help a close friend co-lead a trip of donors. During the trip, Lynne had an extraordinary experience, led by a shaman in the mountains, which resulted in a series of visions of Indigenous people with orange geometric face paint and feather crowns appearing to her at all hours, almost haunting her. She discovered she was being called to change her life path dramatically and devote her energies to the project of protecting the Sacred Headwaters and its Indigenous people.

The new emerging call to the Amazon rainforest and Indigenous people was confusing for Lynne, as she had no experience in South America, knew nothing about the environment there, and did not speak Spanish. Nonetheless, she began to realize, "This is where my life is going, it's going in this direction." However, she was in great conflict about the Hunger Project, where she had huge responsibilities and a lot of passion and commitment. She did not know how to get out of her obligations to the Hunger Project and change course, but was haunted day and night by the faces calling her to the Amazon. Then she received a gift.

"It sounds terrible," she says, "but the gift I received from the universe was malaria."

In fact, there were two strains of it at once, one from India and the other from Ethiopia.

"And so I had two strains of malaria at the same time," she says, "and I was completely flattened. I could not work for anybody, I could not be on conference calls, I could not think about anything—I could not even sit up."

At first, she believed she only had the flu, and her condition was misdiagnosed several times and not treated properly. Only on the seventh test did her doctors recognize her condition as malaria. Her illness lasted around eight months, and during that time, the Hunger Project had to reorganize to go without her. She had managed hundreds of thousands of volunteers as well as a significant staff, and then suddenly she was gone.

"At that time, it was a blessing," she remembers, "because first of all, I couldn't work, I couldn't think, I couldn't read, I couldn't watch TV. I was super-compromised, so I only had time to be me and think and to reflect. They scrambled to reorganize, and after eight or nine months when I thought, 'Oh, now I've got to go back,' I didn't really need to go back at all."

As Lynne describes it, the mystical power of the rainforest and the power of the Indigenous people's voices drew her toward them, and the seduction of the natural world became almost an obsession. Throughout the months of her illness, she imagined herself in the forest, taking people there, sitting in counsel circles, keeping oil companies and mining companies out, and having the most pristine and biodiverse rainforest on earth protected forever. Up to that point, she had focused on preventing people from starving to death, but now she had visions of being in the forest again and creating something magical that would prevent South America from ending up like Africa and India, which also used to be rainforests.

"I realized that the poverty and hunger I had been working on was actually the effect of two hundred years of massive deforestation. But we still have the Amazon, and I realized I was moving from treatment to prevention, in a way. I'm so grateful that I didn't get diagnosed right away because I would have gotten well too fast. I believe the circumstances of my illness arranged themselves to ensure this huge life pivot or reallocation of who I am and what I was about. The illness took me down and gave me the time I needed to reflect, which I had never given myself because I was so stretched, to actually embrace the new mission."

As counterintuitive as it sounds, part of the manifesting process is the necessity of letting go of our expectations. One of the pitfalls we can easily fall into when we are manifesting is to become overly attached to the outcome of our actions. Attachment to outcome, and the suffering that arises when we are overly attached, takes many forms. We may be attached to a particular timeline, a particular "how," or a particular goal only to discover along the way that life has something different in store for us that we never imagined. In each case, if we remain attached to our preconception of how the outcome should happen, rather than responding to what is changing and evolving and alive for us in the present, we close off possibilities rather than finding our way by living through the experience. If we persist in our grasping at one particular outcome, we are likely to suffer rope burn, and we must practice letting go.

This is indeed a subtle practice, because part of the power of the manifesting techniques is to ground our intention in highly specific and emotionally coded visualizations. However, we have to remember that the high level of detail in our visualizations is for classifying our intention as important within the subconscious, not for actually exerting influence on our external world. In other words, holding a powerfully imagined and emotionally resonant vision of our intention in our minds allows our subconscious to guide our activity, but the results of that activity come from the world around us and what it needs. Frequently, we cannot see far enough ahead to know all the twists and turns of the journey. But if we are willing to attend carefully to the feedback that comes from our environment and the people around us as we pursue our goal, we often discover our inner compass has already plotted the next step on our course, whether we expected it or not. The reality is that we rarely need to know exactly how our intention will be realized or how we will reach our destination. We only need to look for the next right step.

REFINING OUR DESIRE: INNER JUJITSU

I will say it again: manifesting is not a one-off. On the contrary, it's the process of refining one's intention more and more specifically and clearly. As we practice visualizing our intention, putting it out into the world through our speech and actions and seeing what comes back, we create a feedback loop that helps us get in closer touch with our inner compass. When our actions create positive results accompanied by positive emotions, our salience network learns to classify our intention as even more important and to redouble its efforts at realizing it. When, on the other hand, our actions result in frustration, confusion, or even harm to ourselves or others, we can pause to take stock of whether our intention actually serves us, and whether we want to continue to pursue it with passion or resilience, or alter it to better serve the lives we are building and the context in which we want to make a contribution.

There's an interesting paradox to our relationship with others and with ourselves. When we are buying into the negativity of the inner critic inside our minds, we are very self-focused, and the way to get us out of that is to be of service and help others. In the process, we discover, "Oh yes, I'm not the only one suffering, my suffering is part of a much greater whole and I can make a contribution to alleviating it." When we are able to get there in our minds, that allows us to come back inside ourselves with a more positive and wholesome view of ourselves and our possibilities. A kind of inner jujitsu takes place: we have to leave ourselves, through service to others, in order to see the world in a different way, and then by watching how people change through our service, we change and can reflect back on the inner critic and how it limits us. There is a dynamic rhythm to the process, a kind of inhalation-exhalation that allows us to navigate the paradox. It is not linear but a movement of back and forth, in and out.

When I was young, I was given a baseball glove by my father. It is one of the few gifts he gave me and one which I still have. I remember when I first got it. It was stiff and rigid and didn't fit my hand particularly well. This is often how our initial intention feels: ill fitting, imposed by the mind or some external source. As I wore the glove and caught balls and broke it in, it began to soften and stretch, forming around the shape of my hand. In just this way, manifesting is the process I use to mold the leather of my life until the fit is seamless—until it feels like a second skin around my hand. This is how I want the externals of my life to fit the internals.

MOVING PARTS

There is a humility to the process of manifesting when we realize that the larger our goal, the more moving parts it will have, and the more gates there will be to pass through for it to become reality. Lowering one's body temperature, slowing one's heart rate, or even, in some instances, curing oneself of a disease requires passing through the gates only within our own bodies. But some outcomes require help from others that involve a vast range of factors, many of which we have little if any control over.

Often when we look back over past successes, we realize just how many pieces had to fall into places for our intention to be realized. This was true even for Jim Carrey. Even as he honed his outrageous and beloved comedic persona, he still depended on countless other factors outside himself to bring him to success. As Carrey rose to prominence on TV's *In Living Color*, it just so happened that James G. Robinson, the studio chair of Morgan Creek Entertainment in the early 1990s, was looking to make a new kind of comedy full of over-the-top antics and juvenile rudeness: his aspiration, he said, was to "make a film nobody my age gets." It was only after Rick Moranis, star of *Honey, I Shrunk the Kids*, turned down the lead role in *Ace Ventura* that Robinson offered it to Carrey, a decision that, at the time, many saw as the studio taking a disastrous risk on an unproven performer.

None of the players involved could have known then that the culture of Hollywood comedy was reinventing itself and needed a new star to lead the way. For all of Carrey's hard work and brilliance, he was only part of a much larger trend in the entertainment industry into which he fit, and which he served. As Carrey observed later, "Your job is not to figure out how it's going to happen for you, but to open the door in your head. And when the door opens in real life, just walk through it. And don't worry if you miss your cue because there's always doors opening. They keep opening."

DIVERSIFY YOUR OPPORTUNITIES

Several strategies can help us let go of clinging to a particular outcome for our intention. The first is that we have not put all our eggs in one basket, and the second is that our intention is aligned with something larger than ourselves.

At this moment, I am working with friends and colleagues on a number of initiatives that reflect my research and work on the science of compassion at Stanford's Center for Compassion and Altruism Research and Education (CCARE). These include a movie, an animated children's series, and a show highlighting those who are being of service in the world. Additionally, I am working on the creation of a World Compassion Festival, which

I first envisioned in 2012; a Compassionate Countries Index, which I've been working on since 2013; and, since 2018, the idea of an International Compassion Corps similar to the US Peace Corps, but that offers any person from any country the opportunity to be of service anywhere. Many people have contributed to this vision, including a multinational network of thinkers, leaders, educators, activists, entrepreneurs, and organizations dedicated to expanding the practice of compassion globally.

While many of my projects have come to fruition over the years, the truth is that I do not know if or when the others will. Many of the projects I pursue do not happen at all, some happen partially, some happen but only after a long period of time has passed. When everything is riding on a single result, we can't help but put tremendous pressure on ourselves to make it happen, and it's hard not to become tightly attached to the desired outcome. It is important to remember that attachment to results is just another form of fear, and as we have seen in previous chapters, fear is the emotion that most interferes with our agency. When we recognize that we are clinging too tightly to an outcome, we can use relaxation practices to bring ourselves back into balance. When we acknowledge and work with our fear, we can access the natural patience and equanimity that come from being on the right track. This patience is an integral part of the acceptance that separates us from attachment, which is a root cause of suffering for so many.

Throughout the process, I try to cultivate my intention practice in relation to each of the parts of a project, visualize it happening, scan for opportunities, do my best, and try to remember that even when things do not work out the way I had hoped they would, I am still OK. When one door closes, I look for another that is open. The how is not up to me. I can only apply my own inner power and hope for the best. When I am lost, I get back in touch with my inner compass to guide me to the next step. I find this process in and of itself very soothing and observe how it decreases my fear and anxiety.

As you can appreciate, many of our ideas and intentions can take years to become reality, but one must be patient and accept that this is the nature of the process. I believe many of the opportunities in my life have come to me because my intentions are aligned with a larger desire to make a positive contribution to our world. At this point in my life, most of my efforts serve compassion with a capital C, the emotion of care that our world is in dire need of. They do not stop at serving Jim Doty, or my family, or even my circle of relationships. I'm fortunate in that I've met so many who've volunteered to be on this journey with me.

That being said, when others get involved, paradoxically the number of moving parts increases greatly, and the outcome can become more uncertain even as it expands and takes on momentum. Like all people, I am susceptible to my ego, which inflates my identity and invariably leads me astray. Sometimes impatience and anxiety about where it's all going overwhelm me, and I beat myself up for not doing x, y, or z. Other times, things do not go the way I want them to and I get angry. When I am disappointed or defeated, or I feel judged by others for my failures, I practice opening my heart and forgiving myself. Like you, I am only a human being. But when I am balanced in my approach, I have the energy to push forward and the perspective to let go.

Several years ago, I was preparing to speak to incoming medical students at Tulane University's "White Coat Ceremony." I wanted to leave the students with something they could always carry with them, something that would always be there to open their hearts. As a result, I began revisiting the conversations I'd had with Ruth. This led me to create a mnemonic containing ten letters of the alphabet. Where I had once made a list of my material goals, I now made a new list of the ten things that open the heart: Compassion, Dignity, Equanimity, Forgiveness, Gratitude, Humility, Integrity, Justice, Kindness, and Love (CDEFGHIJKL). For me they are an aid to remembering the core values of my life. As I described in *Into the Magic Shop*, I call it the *alphabet of the heart*. I start every day sitting at the side of my bed slowly breathing in and releasing my breath, over and over, and then I think of the joy and awe of being in this incredible world. Once I sit with that for a few minutes, I go through the alphabet of my heart letter by letter, and that sets the tone of my day. When I get frustrated or overwhelmed, I stop, breathe, and then focus on one of the letters and what it means, and it calms me down and resets my intention. Two of these words will serve us particularly well at this point in the journey: gratitude and equanimity.

THE GIFTS OF GRATITUDE

If we find ourselves clinging too tightly to a particular outcome, we may notice that we have lost sight of the good that is already right there in front of us. Significant aspects of our intention may already be materializing in our experience, but we fail to recognize them because they don't fit our exact expectation, or our minds are completely focused on other aspects that have not yet come to fruition. Cultivating gratitude is a simple and effective means to shift our focus from what we still lack to what is already working and energizing in our lives. And gratitude is not just a superficial warm feeling promoted by enthusiasts of positive thinking: it produces a whole range of actual changes in the brain that contribute to physical and mental well-being.

Many studies have found that people who practice gratitude consciously tend to be happier, healthier, and more resilient, even among those suffering emotional challenges. One study set out to measure the effects of a gratitude practice among nearly three hundred college students seeking mental health counseling at their university. These students were recruited before they began their first counseling session, and many of them were struggling with depression and anxiety that had dropped their mental health to clinically low levels. The participants were randomly assigned to three groups. All groups received counseling services, but the first group was given an additional instruction: write one letter of gratitude each week to another person who had helped them in some way for three weeks. The second group was encouraged to write down their deepest thoughts and feelings about daily irritations or memorable negative experiences. The third group did not write at all.

Four weeks after the experiment, the researchers checked in with the students who had written gratitude letters and discovered they reported significantly better mental well-being than those who had either written about negative experiences or received only counseling. When they checked in after twelve weeks, the difference had grown even larger. This increasing benefit is unusual: many other studies suggest that the mental health benefits of positive activities such as pleasurable hobbies decrease over time, while the opposite was true of the gratitude-writing study. Even when the gratitude practice consisted of spending just a few minutes writing down a couple of sentences, the benefits continued. The simple practice of expressing gratitude had amplified the help the students got from the psychotherapy and made it longer lasting.

About three months after the counseling sessions began,

the researchers brought some of the students from the study into the lab to discover if they could detect any changes in the ways their brains were processing information. The students were instructed to do a "pay it forward" task, in which they were regularly given a small amount of money by a kind person known as the "benefactor." The benefactor instructed the students to pass the money on to another person, but only if they felt grateful for receiving it. The students then decided how much money, if any, to pay forward to a worthy cause. They were also asked if their donations were motivated by gratitude or by feelings of guilt and obligation, and how grateful they felt in general. As the students engaged in this experience, the researchers measured their brain activity using an fMRI scanner.

It turned out that the students who wrote gratitude letters showed greater activation in their medial prefrontal cortex when experiencing gratitude in the scanner. This part of the brain is associated with moral and social cognition, reward, empathy, and value judgment. Researchers were then able to conclude that the emotion of gratitude gives the subject a feeling of being supported and a desire to support others, as well as a sense of relief from stress.

This finding is striking for several reasons. First, the scanner was measuring their brains three months after the letter writing started, indicating that the simple practice may have had a lasting effect on their brains. And more importantly, the finding suggests that practicing gratitude had sensitized their brains to look out for gratitude down the line and experience it more readily when an opportunity to feel it happened again. In practice, this also means the brain is being trained to turn attention away from painful emotions such as resentment or envy, increasing the difficulty of ruminating on what didn't work out. The lasting sensitization that gratitude offers has wide-ranging benefits, including psychological protection. Another study found that among adolescents, feelings of gratitude show an inverse correlation with the feeling of victimization from bullying and the accompanying suicide risk. The support we get from feeling gratitude can strengthen us when we face adversity and sweeten our experience of being helped along the way.

Sometimes we need to practice sensitivity to the good in our lives to notice it at all. As we have seen in detail previously, the negativity bias can keep us so blind to the positive that we may start to take it for granted or not catch it when it enters our lives. This is especially true of the relationships that are closest to us. If we are pursuing what feels like a great purpose or passionately chasing a dream, we might lose sight of the ones who quietly support us on the path. When we open to magic, it may involve seeing what is familiar in a new light. Gratitude is a very powerful practice because it requires us to see how we've been supported and affirmed by others. One researcher considers the social dimension of gratitude to be especially important and calls it a "relationship-strengthening emotion." Some studies even link the origin of gratitude among our primate ancestors with the strengthening of bonds between members of the same species who mutually helped and repaid each other's gifts.

With its prosocial reminder that the sources of goodness in our lives are outside of ourselves, gratitude helps us to let our intention be part of the vast web of others like us following their visions. No matter how far along we are, recognizing and appreciating the gifts we've been given naturally inspires us to repay them or find opportunities to pay them forward, which in turn helps others open to the magic in their own lives.

EQUANIMITY

One of the greatest challenges for each of us is to be present with the ups and downs of our circumstances—or at least as present as we can be. No matter how skilled a person is at meditation or other techniques, there will always remain a human instinct to minimize suffering and maximize pleasure. This was an area that I had difficulty understanding and am still struggling to overcome. For many of us, nothing feels better than receiving accolades, being acknowledged, or accomplishing a goal. In fact, there is a term—*completion bias*—that describes the powerful motivation to finish a task that comes from the release of dopamine stimulating our reward centers. The downside of this incentive is that when we do not complete the task, our critical inner voice flares up and leads to rumination, worry, and suffering. These thoughts interrupt our ability to keep our attention focused on our intention and can make it impossible to manifest effectively.

Equanimity is the ability to maintain an evenness of temperament in the face of both the good and the bad that occur in our lives, whether we get what we want, don't get what we want, or get what we do not want. Equanimity is the quality of the mind that lets us be even minded in our reactions toward all experiences or objects, whether they are pleasant, unpleasant, or neutral. In terms of neuroscience, equanimity is associated with a critical change in relation to how we perceive and interpret our own experience. In practice, equanimity is what allows us to pursue our intentions without being the victim of every single tiny vacillation in how things are going. We let experience unfold and do not become overly caught up in our expectations.

At its core, equanimity is the realization of transience or impermanence. While it is wonderful to bask in the glory of accomplishment and have dopamine coursing from our reward centers, that feeling cannot last, and for many this leads to disappointment. Attachment to a positive outcome also leads to not being present as you repeatedly focus on accomplishing a goal to get another reward and feel good again. The flip side is that life naturally contains disappointments, and when we become fixated on our perceived failures, rumination reinforces feelings of discouragement and can lead to depression and further suffering.

What we must learn is to appreciate and enjoy our accomplishments and the associated feelings while understanding that those feelings are transitory. Just as for most of us the feelings that arise when we are disappointed or feel we have failed are transitory as well. Therefore, having an evenness of temperament is critically important. Equanimity is the embodiment of balance and nonreactivity, and it allows us our freedom. It is freedom from attachment that releases the magic within us.

Normally the way emotional experiences take place in the mind is that an event we consider negative triggers a domino effect of secondary reactions: we want to push the negative away or reach tightly to grasp something more positive. The problem is that these secondary reactions cause more reactions like themselves, which in turn provide the basis for further suffering, which in turn—you can see where this is going. But it turns out that if we consciously block the secondary reactions, we can avoid the entire cascading activation.

A group of researchers examined the way long-term meditators reported the pain and intensity of unpleasant experiences compared with novice practitioners. Neuroimaging revealed that the reduction in the unpleasantness of pain while in a meditative state was accompanied by increased brain activation in sensory areas (the posterior insula/secondary somatosensory cortex) and decreased activation in an area associated with executive control (the lateral prefrontal cortex). What this suggests is that the experienced meditators weren't resisting the pain as the novices were, and therefore, the pain was significantly less unpleasant for them.

Similar findings were discovered in studies in which experienced meditators were explicitly told *not* to meditate while experiencing pain from heat stimulation. The experienced practitioners had less sensitivity to the pain while experiencing greater activation in the brain regions that primarily process pain. What this means is that they were feeling their experience more deeply on a sensory level but resisting it with their minds much less. We can see equanimity as the practice of balancing and rebalancing physiological and emotional responses to events that cause us stress: those with an even-minded attitude toward uncomfortable experiences are able to recover more quickly afterward and regain homeostasis.

Equanimity is a key skill when we are pursuing any difficult goal. It lets us focus on our task fully, then helps us let go of our attachment to the result. It is the stance toward life that enables us to feel our experiences fully and with an open heart but take a lighter and more accepting attitude when things do not go our way. And, most importantly, it increases our access to self-forgiveness and gives us the broad perspective to reframe our so-called mistakes as inevitable snags that teach us to do it differently the next time.

GOLDEN CRACKS

There's a story from fifteenth-century Japan about the shogun, or military ruler, Ashikaga Yoshimasa, who had a set of ceramic bowls from China for use in the formal tea ceremony. When one of the bowls was damaged, the shogun sent it back to China to be repaired. The bowl came back with ugly metal staples suturing the crack together, like a poorly closed wound after a shoddy surgery. Disappointed, the shogun recruited a local craftsman to come up with a more aesthetically pleasing method to repair the precious bowls. According to this legend, the craftsman drew on the long-standing practice of using lacquer, a natural resin made from tree sap, to rejoin broken ceramics but transformed the appearance of the seam by sprinkling gold dust into the lacquer. This was the origin of the technique of kintsugi, or "golden joinery." Rather than attempting to hide the previous damage, kintsugi not only accepts the crack but highlights it, allowing us to appreciate the history of the object as part of its beauty. What may have ended up in the garbage has been transmuted into a stronger and more unique work of art.

Whether this legend is true or not, kintsugi contains a profound teaching on how to reframe our so-called mistakes, as well as the inevitable knocks, breaks, and cracks that come with living an engaged life. Kintsugi is part of a Japanese philosophical tradition that includes wabi-sabi, the practice of consciously valuing marks of wear from an object's use in order to embrace what is flawed and imperfect. At the core of wabi-sabi is the humble understanding and realization that we are ourselves incomplete, impermanent, and limited by being bound in time. That is the nature of our existence, and its denial further creates suffering. When we accept this reality, it allows us to move forward without fear.

Kintsugi embodies the recognition that the nature of life results at times in us being broken, but it is the very nature of this brokenness and the repair that defines who we are. These scars define our humanity: every one of us is a frail, fragile human being who is struggling in some way and feels that no one else is struggling as they are. And yet, we can be proud of our scars and not feel insufficient or ashamed and try to hide them. They are living proof of our resilience written on our bodies and hearts. When we relax with our imperfections, we invite others to acknowledge their own scars and come out of hiding to connect with one another. This is the power of us accepting and letting go, and it is a superpower that is contained in each of us. In a sense, we can practice gratitude to our scars for allowing us the opportunity to see our full potential—the scar is what brings out the gold. The awareness I gained from getting everything I thought I wanted and losing it has become a kind of gold thread shining through my life that allows me to appreciate where I am today.

When we believe our vessel is cracked and there's nothing for it but to throw it away, we can instead practice acceptance that leading a life of seamless perfection is neither realistic nor compassionate. Acceptance means taking one foot and putting it in front of the other, and slowly going forward into the unknown. By being willing to forgive myself for all the things I cannot control, as well as for my own mistakes along the way, I take away the power that fear and anger have over my mind, and I allow the inner compass of my heart again to be my guide, trusting I will be led exactly where I need to go.

PRACTICE:
Let Go of Attachment and Open to Magic

1. GET YOURSELF READY

> A. Set aside a time in which you will not be interrupted.
>
> B. Find a comfortable position.

2. QUICK BODY SCAN

A. Close your eyes or direct your gaze softly downward in front of you.

B. Begin by slowly inhaling through your nose and slowly exhaling through your mouth. Do this five to six times. It should not be forced, nor should it be specifically focused on.

C. Take a few minutes to relax your body beginning at your toes and going to the top of your head.

3. REFLECT ON PURSUING A GOAL

A. Think of a goal that you very much wanted to accomplish and how the goal itself became your focus and not the process of accomplishing it. Realize how this reality impacted you being present with your loved ones or coworkers. How this focus separated you from the present moment.

B. Notice how it feels in your body to be attached to an outcome. Where do you feel it? A tightness in your throat, a contraction around your heart, a clenching in your fists? Notice the discomfort this attachment causes for you.

C. Having accomplished that goal, think how wonderful you felt, how elated, how happy you were that you did it. Realize how those feelings were transitory, resulting in you returning to the reality of living your life. Think of how often you wanted those feelings back and that elation you felt.

D. Sit with the realization that it is not possible to have those feelings or to be in flow at all moments. Most importantly, realize that is OK. You are OK regardless.

4. REFLECT ON A CHALLENGE

A. Conversely, think of a time when you pursued a goal and realized, for whatever reason, you were not going to attain it. Again, notice how this feels in your body. For so many, the feeling is devastation, and all their negative self-criticism seems validated. It leads to feelings of being an impostor, feeling not worthy. They sit in this place and ruminate about other failures that have occurred in their lives. It also seems like it will last forever, which only worsens the feeling of worthlessness.

B. Yet two things happen. First is that you realize that the goal wasn't as important as you had made it and that not achieving did not result in the world ending. In fact, the gifts of these situations, on reflection, are often that they gave us the greatest insight and the greatest wisdom and have made us who we are today.

C. Most important, though, is the reality that in almost every case, the experiences were transitory. Again, in the face of not accomplishing your goal, you are OK, and you are, at your core, who you are, meaning you are worthy of love and acceptance. This is the power of having evenness of temperament. The power of equanimity.

5. REFLECT ON THE BIG PICTURE

A. Concentrate on breathing again slowly in and out while understanding that it is OK not to be attached to the goal. Life is not a destination; life is living your life, being present, and being not attached. It is attachment that has caused most of your suffering. It is understanding this reality that will free you from suffering. It is not denying the experience but being able to see it from afar for what it is. Practicing equanimity is what leads to balance and acceptance.

6. SELF-COMPASSION

A. Gently open your heart toward yourself. You might think of someone in your life who has given you unconditional love and made you feel completely accepted. Or you might attune to the physical sensations around the heart of warmth and care. Sit with that feeling of care and acceptance while you slowly breathe in and out.

B. Softly direct those feelings of love and care to the tension you are carrying from holding on to a particular outcome. Remember, it is completely natural to want what you want, and to feel you need to control things or complete them to feel safe.

C. As you reflect on the feelings of being cared for, protected, and loved, notice how these feelings apply and endure regardless of whether plans are going the way you hoped or not. These are feelings that speak to your innate being, who you are in all your imperfections, complexity, and humanness.

D. Sit with yourself in stillness and bathe in the feeling that with your successes and your failures you are worthy of love, you are OK. You are a frail and fragile human being who is doing the best they can. Also know that those who are close to you love you as you are. Who you are is not defined by an event.

7. LET GO OF ATTACHMENT

A. As you surrender to the feeling of being cared for, notice if it is possible for your attachment to a particular outcome to loosen, your burden to lighten. Can you detach your ideas of OKness and worth and safety from external circumstances going only one way? Is there a deeper OKness that can suffuse your life, regardless of outcome?

B. Recognizing the transitory nature of success and failure allows you to no longer be their prisoner.

C. Now take a few more breaths slowly and feel the amazing power of equanimity and of being present.

8. INSTALL POSITIVE FEELINGS

A. Spend a few minutes bathing in these positive feelings. The sense of attachment and the need to control may return, and that is fine. Simply come back to the feeling of being cared for no matter what, protected unconditionally, again and again.

B. As you close this practice and return slowly to your life, notice if the sense of attachment has shifted or transformed in any way. Perhaps you have access now to a new and creative possibility you didn't notice before. Perhaps the stakes don't seem quite so high as they did. Perhaps it feels a little safer to allow events to take their course and meet the magic they have to offer with equanimity.

CONCLUSION

The Journey Home

IT IS THE END OF THE DAY ON A FRIDAY, AND I DRIVE UP THE TREE-lined drive to my home in Los Altos Hills, California. Even as I approach where I live, I begin to be suffused with a feeling of warmth, safety, and peace. Looking over the familiar scene and being greeted by my wife and sons, my heart resonates with the images I pictured for so long in my mind, and I know I belong here.

Where the garden at my former mansion was left to languish and wither, today I am surrounded by living growth: cherry, peach, olive, and pear trees, three varieties of apple trees, lemon trees, and an orange tree, all generously bearing flowers and fruit. Flanking the front of the house are the three parrotia, or Persian ironwood, trees that I had imported for their singular shape and color. I am also struck by the oak tree in the front yard that traveled from San Diego to be part of my home. At the time it was planted, it was ten feet high; it has now grown to over twenty-five feet and, like the parrotias, embraces my home with its branches. As I walk toward the front door, I am greeted by the soothing sound of water flowing over the ancient boulders into the small pond by my house, which tells me I can relax: I am safe. As I do almost every day, I pass by the chicken coop, the beehives, and the treehouse on stilts that I had built for my sons. It is connected to the living trees with a zip line stretched out from the roof across the back of the yard.

I survey the beautiful house we live in, built in a contemporary Asian style according to inspiration from my travels and reading, crafted to provide a soothing atmosphere of tranquility. This house, too, I designed myself and envisioned over and over in great detail before it was constructed. When I first pictured the house, I knew there would be a dramatic centerpiece drawing the eye through the space all the way from the doorway out past the pool. Today, I see the modern cast-bronze statue of a headless Buddha holding a persimmon that I bought at an auction for the Dalai Lama Foundation seated and presiding over the backyard in serenity.

The truth is, staying on course is a daily struggle. I knew I would need a lot of help to continue listening to my own inner compass and not go off track again, and so my home is full of guideposts for myself. The headless bronze Buddha reminds me not to get lost in my head and to always go back to my heart. And the persimmon the Buddha holds has a powerful symbolic meaning, too: persimmons start out as bitter and hard, but if you are patient, they ripen to become soft and intensely sweet. This image inspires me to stick with the hard, resistant, pinched parts of myself and give them care until they soften and reveal their tenderness. Of course, I still go off track, forget to listen to my heart, and act selfishly, but now I know where to come back to, where I am loved and forgiven and where I can forgive myself.

I look at the beautiful stone around the base of my home that is comprised of five different types of granite from different parts of the world and was placed by expert stonemasons in squares and rectangles to form a specific color pattern. I never stopped reading *Architectural Digest* since I first found it among my brother's pile of treasures, and the image of that multicolored granite wall came from there. Long before I oversaw its construction, I held the picture in my mind and taught my subconscious to look for a way to make it a reality.

Whereas the mansion I had lived in was cold and empty of light and joy, my home today is just that: a *home*. My wife's parents, immigrants from Russia, live with us in a guesthouse on our property (although more often than not, they appear in our home unannounced, even when I'm in my underwear). Where I never had the chance to meet any of my grandparents, my sons have lived near theirs for their entire lives. Today, my father-in-law, a former engineer who oversaw the power system in the nation of Georgia, helps my older son with his physics homework, and my mother-in-law helps him with his advanced math. These are two subjects with which I struggled greatly in my own childhood because I had no one to help me. I know that tonight we will all sit in the outdoor cabana with the barbecue grill and pizza oven, enjoying a meal and appreciating the time we spend together. My sons may even take charge and be the pizza cooks for the evening. After dinner, we might play our favorite game, Telestrations, a kind of visual game of Telephone where different pictures go through hilarious and unexpected transformations. Often, my daughter and her husband will visit and share a meal. And in those moments, we will all laugh together and enjoy each other and our surroundings, and I will take in my joy at finding myself in the midst of the warm and loving family I dreamed about.

In my library, I see the framed photograph of myself, my brother and sister, and my parents all sitting together on the couch. It is one of only two photographs from my childhood. Everyone in the photo except me has passed away, and yet, I feel I have finally been able to give us all the home we wanted so badly, like Jim Carrey burying his $10 million check with his father. When I look at the photo, I remember where I came from and the love that we all felt for each other. I remember how we tried to express that love, but our circumstances made it hard to do so. Outside of our bedroom, there is a painting in brown hues done by my brother of a man lying back against a tree while playing a flute and looking out over a lake. No matter how often I straighten it, the painting always gets crooked in the same way. Although I am probably the least superstitious person I know, I have the sense it is my brother making it crooked each time, letting me know he is with me. And while I know on one level it is ridiculous to think that way, on another it warms my heart and reminds me our loved ones are alive for us through our memories of them.

Sitting in the wreckage of my life in the empty mansion, I realized I had accomplished what I viewed as success, but the manifestation of that success was emptiness, and it caused so much pain to those I loved. I still carried the shame of my childhood trauma that drove me to prove myself, and to show others I was worthy; nothing I did was enough, for me or for them. Today, I feel overcome by gratitude for the good things in my life. I am thankful to have been given a second chance at happiness and the tools to apply what I learned from my mistakes to building a new life. I continue to be struck by the paradox my life has taught me: only when we believe we are enough in ourselves do we find the ability to contribute to life, but only in contributing to our world do we discover we are inherently enough. I believe this is what Ruth was trying to teach me all those years ago in the magic shop, and it has taken me a lifetime to understand it.

In my life, I have experienced the power of manifesting in ways that I cannot explain. When I first began the practice, I devoted all my energy and attention and heart to making sure my family's rent was paid so that we would not be evicted from our apartment. Out of the blue, a man who owed my father for a job showed up at our door and handed me an envelope full of money—enough to pay our rent with plenty left over for food. I remember the excitement and joy I felt as I rushed as fast as I could on my bike, with tears in my eyes, to share the news with Ruth. That was my first taste of the true power of the practice. From a neuroscience point of view, I cannot say how I influenced the situation, but the wonder I felt laid the foundation for my belief in manifesting. Since then, I have had countless similar experiences that may defy scientific logic but nonetheless speak to the inner power of setting an intention in the heart and mind.

It is time to break free from the illusion that keeps us from believing in the power of our own possibilities and the extraordinary strength we hold within ourselves, individually and especially together. Waiting for an external force to transform our lives will only distract our attention, drain our energy, and discourage our spirits. For many of us the path is challenging, and it can take years if not decades to gain the insights to know the difference between what we want and what we need. The techniques contained in this book were the path I took to find the answer. As I look out into my backyard at the headless Buddha and the persimmon he holds, I am again reminded to lead with my heart, and to understand that with time those things that caused us pain will give us wisdom and insight.

Lying back and taking in the beauty, abundance, and connection in my life, I remember the good news: it is the realization that the universe isn't separate from you but that you are the universe, and it is only you who can give a fuck. It is only you that can harness the power within yourself. And that is the real magic.

MIND MAGIC: A Six-Week Program to Master Manifestation

AS I NOTED IN THE INTRODUCTION, I HAVE PLACED THIS FINAL section, about the practices I set out previously, into a step-by-step program. It is designed to guide you through the manifesting process. As you proceed, I suggest you keep a specific journal to record your observations, frustrations, progress, doubts, and insights. If it is possible for you in your life circumstances, you may also benefit from setting aside a room or particular area of your home where you can explore these techniques in peace and without disturbance. You might put up quotations that inspire you or images that remind you of your goals, or create a personal altar to focus your mind and give you a sense of support. Or you can set aside a specific time each day, say first thing in the morning, and do your practice at that time. This will prime your brain to be responsive to the practices.

If you already have a meditation practice, the techniques I am suggesting can fit right into it. You might try incorporating one of the visualizations as you sit, or meditating before you do a writing practice. If you don't already meditate, there are countless resources available for cultivating a practice, including many free guided sessions available online. A meditation or contemplative practice is not essential for manifesting, but the two support each other in many ways, from increased relaxation to mental clarity to the boost of self-worth that comes from discipline to the softening of the heart around challenges to deepening the sense that everything is OK no matter what happens.

Some people may find it helpful to read through this program in its entirety to get a sense of what is to come. Others may prefer to focus only on whatever step they are on and not rush ahead. Either way, I recommend following this program in order, as the steps build on each other, each one opening the possibility of and establishing the resources for the next. If you are struggling with a particular step, try returning to the practice in the previous step until it is firmly established, as this will help what is to come arise more naturally and without effort.

It is common to experience some degree of distraction, hesitation, and even fear when starting these practices. The most important thing is to set your intention to manifest your vision and begin your habit of practicing even in very small doses. Remember what we discussed earlier about beginning with small habits.

For the next month, do the practices as outlined in regard to time and duration, as this will ingrain them as a habit. Understand, however, that as you get more proficient, you will naturally adjust the practices in ways that work well for you. And that's OK.

WEEK ONE

Before you embark on manifesting your intention, I recommend you take a moment to examine your life as it is today, in all its imperfection—and, maybe, glory. Appreciate that you have already been manifesting your intention in some form, however imperfectly. Understand that you now have the tools and insights that will allow you to increase the likelihood of manifesting things that will improve your life and the lives of others around you. Also appreciate that you now understand that you have the power to purposefully influence the circumstances of your life, down to the minute details. It may be humbling or discouraging to take a clear-eyed account of the life you have made, but the information you collect will be invaluable when you start to reflect on what you would like to manifest. Trust that you can start exactly where you are.

PRACTICE:

What Am I Already Manifesting?

In this practice, I invite you to assess your current situation with clarity and compassion. The intention here is to be as objective as possible about your circumstances, without any judgment. As you uncover the aspects of your life you are already manifesting, you will discover the places from which you may be withholding your inner power. Don't worry about changing anything right now. All you need to do is offer a kind and clear awareness.

1. GET YOURSELF READY

   A. Find a time and a place to do this practice so that you will not be interrupted.

   B. Do not start this practice if you are stressed, have other matters that are distracting you, have drunk alcohol or used recreational drugs in the last twenty four hours, or are tired.

   C. Have a pad of paper and a pen near you.

2. START TO RELAX

A. Sit in a relaxed position with your eyes closed for a few minutes, allowing your thoughts to settle.

B. Now sit up straight with your eyes still closed and take three breaths slowly in through your nostrils and slowly out through your mouth. Repeat until this type of breathing feels comfortable for you and is not distracting.

C. Beginning with your toes, start to relax the muscles of your body all the way to the top of your head, feeling more and more at ease as you focus on relaxing your body. You will find that as you do so, there is a sense of calmness that envelops you, and you feel safe. You are no longer worrying about people judging you or criticizing your dreams and aspirations as you slowly continue to breathe in and out.

D. You are comfortable and relaxed as you continue to slowly breathe in and out.

3. VISUALIZE YOUR LIFE

A. Gently call to mind your life in its broad strokes. What are your primary relationships? What is your work? What are the locations where your life takes place? Notice the emotions that arise as you consider these questions. Don't specifically fixate on one image or thought but let your thoughts loosely touch on the major elements that make up your life today for a few minutes.

B. Allow any emotions that come up to run their course naturally. You may notice a range of feelings: joy, contentment, sadness, frustration, boredom, anger. Just be with them and the details of your life for a few more moments.

4. VISUALIZE A BIT MORE FULLY

A. Continue to move through the images of your life. You might reflect on these questions: Who are the people who are important to you, who matter? Do you feel truly connected with them? What is your work? Does it provide you with what you need to live? If you have others who depend on you, does your work provide for them? Does how you spend your day feel meaningful and fulfilling to you? What about the locations in which your life takes place? How does it feel for you to be in those places?

B. Visualize yourself within your life and note whatever these images evoke. Watch your life in your mind's eye. Try to imagine every detail as you slowly breathe in and breathe out. Slowly breathe in and breathe out.

C. Now that you can see every detail, slowly open your eyes and continue to slowly breathe in and out, in and out. You are relaxed and you are calm.

5. RECORD YOUR OBSERVATIONS

A. Take the pen and paper and write for at least five minutes in your own words about what you saw and felt when you visualized your life. Write as many details as possible. Whether it is a few sentences or a paragraph, it only matters that you are writing your life as it is for you and how you feel about it.

B. Now simply sit with your eyes closed, slowly breathing for three to five breaths in through the nose and out through the mouth, and then open your eyes.

6. REVIEW YOUR WRITING

A. First, silently read what you wrote.

B. Then read what you wrote aloud to yourself.

C. Sit with those images of your life for a few moments with your eyes closed.

7. REFLECT ON YOUR LIFE

A. Take a few moments to reflect on how your own choices have brought about the life you are living. Where have you made conscious decisions? Where have you allowed others to choose for you, or just taken the path of least resistance?

B. If your life is not how you once expected and imagined it would be, what was your role in how it actually turned out? There is no need to be afraid or condemn yourself for any part of your life today. This is simply a fact-finding practice. It may not feel like it, but you are taking the first step to reclaim your own inner power to shape your life.

8. APPRECIATE YOUR PRACTICE

A. Feel the empowerment and agency that come with examining your life truthfully. Your life is already starting to transform.

What did you notice? Are there areas of your life that elicited a strong emotion when you reflected on them? If an area is painful to contemplate, you may want to make it the focus of your manifesting. If an area was warm and joyful to reflect on, I invite you to consciously bring these images to mind from time to time and feel gratitude, as these feelings can become a powerful support for you.

Keep the notes that you wrote from this practice with you as you proceed through this program. For better or worse, your life today will become the fundamental ground of the new life you aspire to manifest. You may want to read what you wrote to a trusted friend or mentor and share how your discoveries made you feel. This will give you a sense of accountability and enlist external support you may need when you are facing resistance, fear, and doubt. By the end of the program, you will likely be surprised by how much has already changed, and your work with this practice will be a good benchmark for your progress.

You are now ready to take on the first step.

Step One: Reclaim Your Power to Focus Your Mind

The first step is all about accessing the power you have within yourself that is far beyond what you believe. Many people limit their power by believing in an entity outside of themselves that controls their lives. Many people repeatedly beat themselves up, telling themselves that they can't do even a simple task. The first step is to disavow yourself of this belief and realize that even small actions can begin rewiring your brain and creating habits that result in long-term change.

If you are feeling stressed and distracted, it is crucial to make the switch from fight, flight, or freeze to rest-and-digest. The most effective way to do so is by consciously relaxing the body.

PRACTICE:
Relaxing the Body

1. GET YOURSELF READY

A. Find a time and a place to do this practice so that you will not be interrupted.

2. CHOOSE A POSTURE

A. This practice can be done standing, sitting, or lying down. Before beginning, establish yourself in a posture that is comfortable enough for you to feel relaxed, yet solid and steady enough for you to be alert to your experience.

B. Straighten your spine and let your shoulders drop. You are looking for a posture of relaxed confidence and gentle strength.

3. BEGIN TO SETTLE

A. Close your eyes or softly direct your gaze at a point a few feet in front of you. Let your attention turn inward.

B. Now become aware of the places where your body makes contact with whatever surface is holding you. Let gravity root you to the earth, and feel the ground pressing upward into your feet. Notice any areas of obvious tension in your body and gently acknowledge them in your awareness.

C. Begin by taking three deep breaths in through your nose and slowly out through your mouth. If you like, you can sigh loudly as you breathe out. Repeat these deep breaths until you get used to this type of breathing so that the breathing itself is not distracting to you.

D. Once you feel comfortable breathing in this manner, specifically notice how you are sitting or lying and imagine you are looking at yourself positioned in that way.

4. START THE BODY SCAN

A. Begin focusing on your toes and invite them to relax. Invite any tension in them to let go. Now focus on your feet, relaxing all the small muscles inside. Imagine the muscles in your feet almost melting away as you continue to breathe in and out. Focus only on your toes and feet.

B. When you begin, your thoughts will naturally wander off and you will become distracted. Don't worry, this is completely natural. When you notice that your mind has wandered, simply begin again, bringing your focus back to the muscles of your toes and feet and relaxing them.

5. CONTINUE THE BODY SCAN

A. Once you have been able to relax your toes and feet and they feel soft, light, and at ease, extend the practice upward, focusing on your calves and thighs. Sense the larger muscles of your legs and invite them each to relax until you feel they have almost melted away as you breathe in and out.

B. Follow the same process with the muscles of your abdomen and chest.

C. Next, focus on your spine and relax the muscles all along your back and up to your shoulders and neck. Remember, the goal is to be both relaxed and alert. If there are any places of obvious or heightened tension, you might experiment with sending your breath directly into those places, inviting them to loosen and let go.

D. Finally, focus on the muscles of your face and scalp and invite them to relax and lighten, releasing any tension they have been holding.

6. BRING AWARENESS TO RELAXATION

A. As you extend the relaxation of your muscles all over your body, notice that there is a calmness coming over your entire body. Notice how this calmness in your body calms your mind. Notice the pleasure and good feelings of being calm in body and mind.

B. At this point, you may feel sleepy or even fall asleep. That's OK. You may continue to feel tense and struggle to connect with any feelings of calm. That's OK, too. It may take multiple attempts to relax the body fully while remaining awake and alert. Be patient. Be kind to yourself, remembering that with every attempt, you are rewiring your nervous system, teaching it to experience a state of peace and regulation.

C. When you have relaxed your whole body to the best of your ability, focus on your heart. Think of your heart as a muscle that you are relaxing as you slowly breathe in and out. You may notice that your heartbeat is slowing down as your body relaxes and your breath slows.

7. DEEPEN THE RELAXATION

A. Imagine your body in a state of complete relaxation. See if you can bring your awareness to a sense of simply *being* as you slowly breathe in and out: nothing to do, nowhere to go, no one to be. Do you feel a sense of warmth or stillness or contentment? You might feel as if you are floating and be overcome with a sense of calmness.

B. Use your intention to take in the feelings of pleasure and peace and install them in your nervous system so you can recall these feelings in the future. Let your nervous system know that this state of relaxation is possible, desirable, and accessible when you need it.

C. On your next exhale, slowly open your eyes. Allow yourself to sit for a few minutes in this state of relaxation with your eyes open, just resting in your experience of being completely at peace.

Begin this practice initially by yourself. Try it for at least a week, even for five minutes at a time. As you find yourself getting rooted in the practice, increase the time to ten, then twenty or thirty minutes. You may discover you actually desire a longer practice; listen to that inner longing. If you found this practice particularly challenging or you struggled to feel a sense of safety and relaxation, you may find it helpful to seek out a group to practice with. You might join a meditation community at a local yoga studio or gather a group of like-minded friends to explore these practices together. As you will see as this process unfolds, enlisting the support you need from others is a crucial skill to cultivate to help you achieve your goals.

PRACTICE:
Building Inner Power

When you feel your body is somewhat more relaxed, reflect on a simple activity that you've wanted to do but for whatever reason you have not done. An example would be to get up early and walk for fifteen minutes or commit to not drinking soft drinks or alcohol.

1. START TO RELAX

    A. Before you go to sleep, sit in a comfortable position in a chair, close your eyes, and focus on relaxing every muscle in your body. Begin at your toes and go all the way to the top of your head while you are slowly breathing in through the nose and out through the mouth.

    B. Once you are relaxed, focus on your breath, slowly breathing in through your nostrils, holding it for five seconds, and then slowly releasing your breath through your mouth.

2. VISUALIZE YOUR INTENTION

    A. After you have done this for five minutes, think of yourself doing that simple activity. Don't just think of yourself doing the activity but also see yourself doing it.

3. RECORD YOUR INTENTION

A. Once you have done this, open your eyes and write on a piece of paper your goal or the activity and lay the paper on your nightstand.

4. INSTALL YOUR INTENTION

A. Lie down and close your eyes and slowly breathe in and out for a few minutes as you see yourself carrying out your intention. Let this breathing lead you into sleep.

5. REVIEW YOUR INTENTION

A. When you wake up, sit up and read the paper. Embed the thought of your goal and proceed with your day.

If you've committed to walking in the morning, proceed to do so. If you're not drinking soft drinks, every time there is a choice, pause and choose not to do so. Each time you have done or not done the activity you've chosen, congratulate yourself and then write on a piece of paper, "I congratulate myself for completing this task."

By doing this daily, you demonstrate to yourself that you have the agency to complete a task that you've chosen to focus on. While the task may be simple, the activity of doing so engages those brain processes that are associated with embedding intention into the brain.

Continue this task until you no longer think about the process and that it comes automatically. This is the power of tiny habits.

Try this practice every day for one week. At the end of seven days, check in with yourself.

What did you notice? What part of this step was easy for you? What was most difficult? What would it be like to try bringing what you learned from this practice into your daily life?

Ask yourself, is it becoming a little more automatic? If you feel you still need time to reclaim your sense of agency, repeat this practice for another week and reassess. When you are ready and connecting with a sense of inner power that feels natural for you, move on to the next step.

WEEK TWO

Step Two: Clarify What You Truly Want

Now that the body is relaxed and you have an inkling of the power you possess within yourself to change your circumstances according to your intention, you can focus on accessing and calibrating your inner compass. When you start to reflect on what you would most like to manifest, you may discover your head is full of a howling chorus of desires. Loudest of all might be what your family, friends, or the media considers to be of value. But underneath the noise, other quieter voices are murmuring, and that is where you can listen for the sound of your heart's deepest longings. It may take some time to sort through the countless wants, impulses, and cravings to identify what you need most and what will be most fulfilling for you to manifest.

As a way of starting to make sense of the sometimes tangled mass of wants and hopes, dreams and aspirations, it is useful to reflect on your vision of success. What does success really mean to you? How would it look and feel? The following practice gives you the opportunity to examine and explore for yourself the deeper meaning of the success you are seeking.

PRACTICE:
What Does Success Look Like for You?

1. GET YOURSELF READY

A. Find a time and a place to do this practice so that you will not be interrupted.

B. Do not start this practice if you are stressed, have other matters that are distracting you, have drunk alcohol or used recreational drugs in the last twenty-four hours, or are tired.

C. Have a pad of paper and a pen near you.

2. BEGIN TO SETTLE

A. Sit in a relaxed position with your eyes closed and take three deep breaths.

3. VISUALIZE SUCCESS

A. Allow your mind to call up an image of what success looks like for you. Don't specifically fixate on one image or thought but let your mind wander and think of you being successful and what that means or implies to you for a few minutes.

4. BODY SCAN

A. Sit up straight with your eyes still closed and take three breaths slowly in through your nostrils and slowly out through your mouth. Repeat until this type of breathing feels comfortable for you and is not distracting.

B. Beginning with your toes, start to relax the muscles of your body all the way to the top of your head, feeling more and more at ease as you focus on relaxing your body. You will find that as you do, there is a sense of calmness that envelops you, and you feel safe. You are no longer worrying about people judging you or criticizing your dreams and aspirations, as you slowly continue to breathe in and out.

C. You are comfortable and relaxed as you continue to slowly breathe in and out.

5. VISUALIZE SUCCESS MORE FULLY

A. Think again about what success looks like for you. But this time, focus more specifically on your success. Visualize yourself in that position. Watch yourself in your mind's eye being that success. Try to imagine every detail as you slowly breathe in and breathe out. Explore your five senses: What does success look like, feel like, sound like, smell like, taste like? Slowly breathe in and breathe out.

B. Now that you can see every detail, slowly open your eyes and continue to slowly breathe in and out, in and out.

C. You are relaxed and you are calm.

6. RECORD YOUR IMAGE OF SUCCESS

A. Take the pen and paper and write for at least five minutes in your own words what you saw in your mind's eye about your success. Write as many details as possible. Whether it is a few sentences or a paragraph, it only matters that it defines success for you.

B. Now simply sit with your eyes closed, slowly breathing for three to five breaths in through the nose and out through the mouth. Open your eyes.

7. REVIEW YOUR WRITING

A. First, silently read what you wrote.

B. Then read what you wrote aloud to yourself.

C. Sit with those thoughts of your success for a few moments with your eyes closed.

8. APPRECIATE SUCCESS

A. Feel how relaxed and calm you are with the satisfaction that you are manifesting your success.

I encourage you to keep what you wrote about success somewhere you will see it often. Some people keep theirs taped on the refrigerator or above their desk; others fold it and carry it in their wallet or their purse and take it out and read it over when they are waiting in line. You can make a recording of yourself reading it and play it when you wake up or before you go to sleep. You may even be inspired to create a visual representation of it, either a collage of images from a magazine or a drawing or painting. Share it with friends and ask them to remind you of it periodically. You can repeat this practice as many times as you like, noticing what changes and what stays the same. And remember, what you wrote today may just be a jumping-off point for a vision you will refine over the course of your lifetime.

PRACTICE:
Eliciting a Positive Emotion

To clarify your inner compass, reflect on a time in your life when you felt good, fulfilled, cared about, or truly successful. It might be helpful to reflect back to a moment in your life when you knew in your heart and in your gut that you were on the right track. Ask yourself: What are the things or activities or thoughts that give me a sense of warmth inside of myself that is long-lasting? When did I feel deeply fulfilled, whole, aligned? This will empower you to attune to your inner compass. For many people, these feelings naturally come about when they have been of service or done actions for others.

Remember that the experience of strong positive emotion is part of how the brain decides what is important, worth pursuing, and deserving of our attention. The more we pair a strong emotion sensuously experienced in the body with an image in the mind's eye, the more salience the brain will give it and the more resources it will devote to noticing it when it arises in the world.

Do this practice every day for at least one week.

1. GET YOURSELF READY

A. Find a time and a place to do this practice so that you will not be interrupted.

B. Do not start this meditation if you are stressed, have other matters that are distracting you, have drunk alcohol or used recreational drugs in the last twenty-four hours, or are tired.

C. Have a pad of paper and a pen near you.

2. REFLECT ON GOOD FEELINGS

- A. Before we begin, sit in a relaxed position with your eyes closed and think of a time or times when you felt content, happy, and fulfilled.

- B. Don't specifically fixate on one image or thought but let your mind wander, thinking of experiences in your life in which you felt safe and protected, and that resulted in you being relaxed, calm, happy, and fulfilled.

- C. Sit with these feelings for a few minutes. If you don't believe you have had such an experience, simply imagine what that would feel like.

3. BODY SCAN

- A. Sit up straight with your eyes still closed and take three breaths slowly in through your nose and out through your mouth. Repeat until this type of breathing feels comfortable for you and is not distracting.

- B. Beginning with your toes, start to relax the muscles of your body all the way to the top of your head, feeling more and more at ease as you focus on relaxing your body. You will find that as you do so, there is a sense of calmness that envelops you, and you feel safe. You feel a sense of warmth and a sense of acceptance and are no longer worrying about people judging you or criticizing your dreams and aspirations, as you slowly continue to breathe in and out.

- C. You are comfortable and relaxed as you continue to slowly breathe in and out. Thoughts may arise that seem negative; simply gently acknowledge them without attaching to them and come back to the object of your focus.

4. REFLECT ON FEELING SAFE

A. Call to mind again what it feels like to be safe. For many, this elicits thoughts of their mother or a loved one holding them or embracing them. A feeling of being protected. A feeling of warmth and freedom from concern.

B. If these kinds of feelings do not feel accessible to you through memory, don't worry. Use your imagination to evoke images that provide feelings of warmth, safety, and unconditional care. You might visualize yourself being comforted by spiritual figures or animals, or just the beating heart of life itself.

5. CALL UP GOOD FEELINGS

A. Now focus more specifically, while in this state, on the positive thoughts about yourself, those attributes you like or those events when you yourself have offered love, concern, and nurturing to another.

B. You sense deep contentment and are filled with positive emotions as you slowly breathe in and out. You are enveloped in them, realizing that your own contentment and fulfillment occurs both as you are being held and nurtured but also when you offer the same to another.

C. Watch yourself in your mind's eye as you experience happiness, fulfillment, warmth, and love. Love for yourself. Love for others that is freely given. Try to imagine every detail as you slowly breathe in and breathe out.

6. DEEPEN THE GOOD FEELINGS

A. Slowly breathe in and breathe out. See yourself being loved and giving love. Feel how the sense of happiness, contentment, and fulfillment affect your body. Feel how your heart slows down, how your slow breathing now seems natural. Feel how negative emotions leave you and are replaced with positive thoughts and feelings about yourself, your place in the world, and what you offer to others.

B. Sit with those details. Bathe yourself in those feelings, continuing to slowly breathe in and slowly release your breath.

C. You are relaxed and you are calm.

7. RECORD YOUR EXPERIENCE

A. Take the pen and paper and write for at least five minutes in your own words what you saw in your mind's eye about your positive feelings of who you are, what your abilities are, and how those abilities positively affect others.

B. While you think about these emotions, you feel safe, you feel warm, and you are able to feel deep within you that you are capable of anything.

C. Write as many details as possible. Whether it is a few sentences or a paragraph, all that matters is that you are defining for yourself the power of caring, of nurturing, and how when you do so, it affects your body.

D. Now simply sit with your eyes closed, slowly breathing for three to five breaths in through the nose and out through the mouth.

8. REVIEW YOUR EXPERIENCE

A. Open your eyes. First, silently read what you wrote.

B. Then read what you wrote aloud to yourself. Sit with those thoughts of the power of caring and nurturing for a few moments with your eyes closed.

C. Now think of how that caring and nurturing makes you feel safe.

9. INSTALL YOUR EXPERIENCE

A. Feel how relaxed and calm you are with the satisfaction that you are loved and that you are capable of giving that love to not only yourself but to others, and by doing so, create a deep, positive sense of yourself. Consciously connect these feelings with the sense of your inner compass.

B. It is this inner compass in a state of peace that teaches your subconscious what is important and creates the inner environment for you to manifest your greatest desires and wishes.

After a week, reflect on these questions: What did you notice? Were you surprised by what came up in your mind and heart?

Notice the moments, relationships, and situations in daily life that evoke similar positive emotional states, and which ones deplete you and leave you feeling diminished. Make notes in your journal and see if you find patterns after a week. When you are starting to feel distracted, stressed out, or discouraged, you can revisit these experiences of positive emotion and reconnect with your inner compass. If you struggle or have challenges, repeat the practice for another week or until the practice feels comfortable for you. You can also return to the earlier step and continue relaxing your body and reclaiming your sense of inner power. When you feel some confidence as to the direction of your heart's inner compass, it is time to move on to the next step.

WEEK THREE

Step Three: Remove the Obstacles in Your Mind

Now that you have reclaimed your self-agency and clarified your desires, you are likely starting to face some unwelcome visitors to your mind: fear, the feeling that you are an impostor, self-doubt, and resentment.

People like me don't get to have that.
Who do I think I am?
They were right.
It's too late.
This will never work.

And so on. This is the mind's natural response to any encounter with the unknown. Remember that the brain is designed to keep you alive, not keep you happy. Any new direction, no matter how inspiring or enlivening or potent or heartfelt, will inevitably evoke the nervous system's resistance. Your job is not to fight this resistance but to soothe it, coexist with it, and even collaborate with it. The most effective way to respond is to cultivate a sense of self-compassion. Although it may feel buried and inaccessible, the ability to relate to suffering with kindness is a natural capacity installed in us biologically. With practice, you will learn to open your heart to your own experience, no matter the content. In time, resistance will diminish and enthusiasm will increase.

PRACTICE:
Beliefs and Their Opposites

Negative beliefs about ourselves are like mushrooms: they grow in the dark. And so it is often very useful to get them out from the darkness of our heads and into the light where we can see them clearly for what they are. The following practice enables you to identify the beliefs and stories that are holding you back, and to consciously work with transforming them so they serve you better.

1. GET YOURSELF READY

   A. Set aside some time to be alone with yourself.

   B. Have a pad of paper and a pen near you.

   C. Divide the paper into two columns: "Beliefs" and "Opposites."

2. BEGIN TO RELAX

   A. Find a comfortable posture, either sitting up straight or lying on your back.

   B. With your eyes closed, take three breaths slowly in through your nose and out through your mouth.

Repeat until this type of breathing feels comfortable for you and is not distracting.

C. Beginning with your toes, start to relax the muscles of your body all the way to the top of your head, feeling more and more at ease as you focus on letting go of tension. You will find that as you do, there is a sense of peace that envelops you, and you feel safe.

3. REFLECT ON A GOOD FEELING

A. Start to evoke a memory or image of feeling cared for and valued unconditionally. Let the positive feelings suffuse your experience, flowing out from your heart to your organs and all your limbs.

4. REFLECT ON NEGATIVE BELIEFS

A. Gently invite some of the beliefs about yourself and your life that have caused you difficulty into your mind.

B. You can imagine you are safely perched at the top of a tree or on a high cliff or balcony and these beliefs are gathering below.

C. See if you can recognize some of the usual suspects: "I'm not good enough," "I got a raw deal," "I'm too damaged," and others.

D. Without judging, try to simply see these beliefs clearly; witness them in your mind. You may sense the pain they have caused you. Let it happen.

5. RECORD YOUR OBSERVATIONS

A. When you are ready, gently open your eyes and begin writing down the beliefs in the "Beliefs" column. Write freely and do not censor yourself. Don't worry about spelling, punctuation, or whether they are the "right" ones or not.

6. REVIEW YOUR WRITING

A. Read the list of beliefs out loud. Notice your emotions and physical sensations as you read.

B. Do you feel a contraction in your heart, a knot in your throat, a sense of disappointment, a wave of anger?

7. RETURN TO THE GOOD FEELINGS

A. If you need to revisit the good feeling you reflected on for support, feel free to do so.

8. RECORD THE OPPOSITES

A. When you are ready, turn to the "Opposites" column. For each belief you wrote, write the opposite: "I am good enough," "I have the inner power to change my circumstances," "I have all the time, love, and support to pursue my goals."

B. Explore what language feels accurate and alive for you, and remember you do not need to get it perfectly correct right away.

9. REFLECT ON YOUR PRACTICE

A. Take a few moments to consider the page. Notice how the two columns resonate with each other.

B. Acknowledge that you have begun to transform the beliefs into their opposites simply by becoming aware of them.

PRACTICE:
Self-Compassion

Many of us are our own worst critics. While this can motivate people to perform and achieve, the cost is very high in regard to self-esteem. This negative sense of self-worth lives with us always and can gravely impact our health and mental well-being. The negative dialogue often causes further damage because when we tell ourselves we are not capable, we are not worthy, we are not loved and never will be, and that we are an impostor, we limit what is possible for us. The reality is that within each of us there is extraordinary power, but we give that power away by our negative self-talk.

Self-compassion has the power to heal the parts of us that feel chronically unsafe and unloved—the basis for our shadow and our resistance to thriving—and transform them into vital sources of wisdom and compassion to share with others.

This practice is designed to address feelings of unworthiness at the root.

1. GET YOURSELF READY

A. Find a time and a place to do this practice so that you will not be interrupted.

B. Do not start this practice if you are stressed, have other matters that are distracting you, have drunk alcohol or used recreational drugs in the last twenty-four hours, or are tired.

C. Have a pad of paper and a pen near you.

2. BEGIN TO SETTLE

A. Before we begin, sit in a relaxed position with your eyes closed. Let your mind wander, and for a moment listen to all the negative thoughts that go through your head. Don't fixate on a specific image or thought—just relax your mind, feeling how the negative self-talk lives in your body.

B. Is there a particular place in your body where you feel it? What are the sensations?

3. REFLECT ON YOUR EXPERIENCE

A. Sense how this negative self-talk diminishes you and limits you. Think about how you confuse the negative self-talk with reality.

B. Sit with these feelings for a few minutes. How do these thoughts make you feel? Do you feel sadness, anger, numbness, restlessness?

4. BODY SCAN

A. Sit up straight with your eyes still closed and take three breaths slowly in through your nostrils and slowly out through your mouth. Repeat until this type of breathing feels comfortable for you and is not distracting.

B. Beginning with your toes, start to relax the muscles of your body all the way to the top of your head, feeling more and more at ease as you focus on relaxing your body. You will find that as you do so, there is a sense of calmness that envelops you, and you feel safe. You feel a sense of warmth and a sense of acceptance and are no longer worrying about people judging you or criticizing your dreams and aspirations, as you slowly continue to breathe in and out.

C. You are comfortable and relaxed as you continue to slowly breathe in and out. The negative self-talk may arise, but gently acknowledge it and don't attach; come back to the focus on your breath.

5. REFLECT ON FEELING SAFE

A. Call to mind how it feels to be safe. For many, this elicits thoughts of a mother or a loved one holding them or embracing them. You could also picture yourself in an especially safe place, such as a secluded creek you used to visit or being seated at the table of a warm family dinner. Whatever makes a feeling of being protected come alive for you.

B. Whether safety means being in a relationship or in solitude for you, the effect will be the same. Remember, though, that solitude is different from loneliness. Stay with this feeling of safety and do not be concerned with anything beyond those feelings.

6. DEEPEN THE GOOD FEELINGS

A. While in this state, focus more specifically on positive thoughts about yourself, those attributes about yourself that you like, those events in your life when you have offered love, concern, and nurturing to another. You sense that deep contentment, those positive emotions as you slowly breathe in and out.

B. You are enveloped realizing that your own contentment and fulfillment occurs both as you are being held and nurtured but also when you offer the same to another. Connect with the feeling of your own innate goodness.

7. BATHE IN THE GOOD FEELINGS

A. Watch yourself in your mind's eye as you experience happiness, fulfillment, warmth, and love. Love for yourself. Love for others that is freely given. Try to imagine every detail as you slowly breathe in and breathe out.

B. See yourself being loved and giving love. Feel how the sense of happiness, contentment, and fulfillment affect your body. Feel how your heart rate slows down, how your breathing now seems natural. Feel how negative emotions leave you and are replaced with positive thoughts and feelings about yourself, your place in the world, and what you offer to others.

C. Sit with those details. Bathe yourself in those feelings, continuing to slowly breathe in and slowly release your breath.

D. Realize that the negative self-talk is not you. Understand that from our evolution over thousands of years, negative thoughts and events stick to us to protect us, but in the modern world they only limit us and cause us pain.

8. APPRECIATE YOUR HUMANITY

A. Think specific positive thoughts about yourself. All that you have overcome, all that you have accomplished, and understand that in life there are ups and there are downs but neither defines us. Understand that this is the nature of our reality as humans. Repeat to yourself that you are worthy of love, that you can accomplish anything, that you are deserving of success, that you are not an impostor.

B. Some of you may struggle to believe what you are telling yourself, and this is natural. For now, it is enough to act as if you do. With time, a deeper trust will come if you are patient. Sit with this reality and feel how calm and satisfied you feel as you continue to slowly breathe in and breathe out.

C. With this feeling of calmness and satisfaction comes a sense of being enveloped by love. You understand the nurturing effect of love and how it allows you to see your power and your potential. Sit with these feelings and continue to slowly breathe in and breathe out. Breathe in and breathe out.

D. You are relaxed and you are calm.

9. RECORD YOUR EXPERIENCE

A. Take the pen and paper and write for at least five minutes in your own words what you saw in your mind's eye about your positive feelings of who you are, your abilities, and how those abilities positively affect others. Consider how, when you think about these feelings, you feel safe, you feel warm, and you are able to feel deep within that you are capable of anything.

B. Write as many details as possible. Whether it is a few sentences or a paragraph, it only matters that it defines for you the power within you and the power of caring, of nurturing, and how when you do so, it affects your body. How by reframing and changing your mindset, it releases you from your self-imposed limitations.

C. Simply sit with your eyes closed, slowly breathing for three to five breaths in through the nose and out through the mouth. Now open your eyes.

10. REVIEW YOUR EXPERIENCE

A. First, silently read what you wrote. Then read what you wrote aloud to yourself.

B. Sit with those thoughts of the power you have within yourself and how offering caring and nurturing for yourself affects your mind and your physiology. Sit with these feelings for a few moments with your eyes closed.

C. Now think of how that caring and nurturing makes you feel safe, how that safety has given you permission to own your own power, and how that power allows you to manifest.

11. APPRECIATE YOUR EXPERIENCE

A. Feel how relaxed and calm you are with the satisfaction that you are loved and that you are capable of giving that love to not only yourself but to others, and by doing so create a deep positive sense of yourself.

B. It is being within this state and mindset that creates the environment for you to manifest your greatest desires and wishes.

Try this practice daily for at least one week, making notes in your journal after each session. At the end of seven days, consider these questions: What feelings came up as you explored this practice? Was it challenging to feel self-compassion or did it come naturally? What would it be like to take this sense of unconditional care with you back into your ordinary life?

This practice can go deep, and you may choose to linger here longer before moving on to the next step. Self-compassion is itself a lifelong practice of cultivating a supportive and accepting relationship with ourselves. You can revisit this practice anytime you are struggling with negative thoughts, beliefs, and feelings. Over time, you may begin to notice the difference between the discomfort that signals a genuine need for you to take action and the discomfort that is really just the nervous system's natural backlash in response to your growth. This is a powerful skill and will serve you as you pursue greater expansion and larger visions.

For some it may require another week or even more. Be patient and accept that everyone is different. It's OK. When you feel grounded in a compassionate attitude toward yourself and others, it is time to move on to the next step to work directly with your subconscious.

WEEK FOUR

Step Four: Embed the Intention in Your Subconscious

By this point, you have reclaimed your inner power, reflected on what you truly desire, and started to remove the inner obstacles and false beliefs that stand in your way. All of this work has cleared a pathway for the next step: consciously embedding your intention into your subconscious. Because of the barrage of information coming at you at any given moment, the brain needs a way to determine what is important. The way to signal to the brain that your intention is important is by visualizing it and accompanying it with a strongly felt positive emotion. The brain does not differentiate between events you experience in reality and those you experience in your imagination. So, the more vivid you can make your mental picture, the more the brain will respond as if it already lived through your intention becoming reality. As you experience the positive emotions of living your intention, your intention becomes salient and the subconscious starts to allocate resources to seeking it out in reality.

PRACTICE:
Visualizing Your Intention

1. GET YOURSELF READY

    A. Find a time and a place to do this meditation so that you will not be interrupted.

B. Do not start this meditation if you are stressed, have other matters that are distracting you, have drunk alcohol or used recreational drugs in the last twenty-four hours, or are tired.

C. Have a pad of paper and a pen near you.

2. START TO VISUALIZE YOUR INTENTION

A. Sit in a relaxed position with your eyes closed, thinking of the goal you wish to manifest while also allowing your thoughts to wander. Often, a negative thought or image will occur, but you can direct your attention immediately back to what you wish to manifest.

B. Do this for several minutes and if your mind wanders (as it likely will), immediately bring it back to the thought of what you wish to manifest.

C. As you are thinking, attempt to provide more clarity to the image of yourself having manifested your goal. See yourself in that image, what you look like, how you feel in your body, what you feel in your heart.

3. NOW RELAX A BIT FURTHER

A. Sit up straight with your eyes still closed and take three breaths slowly in through your nostrils and slowly out through your mouth.

B. Repeat until this type of breathing feels comfortable for you and is not distracting.

C. Beginning with your toes, start to relax the muscles of your body all the way to the top of your head, feeling more and more at ease as you focus on relaxing your body. You will find that as you do so, there is a sense of calmness that envelops you, and you feel safe. You feel a sense of warmth and a sense of acceptance and are no longer worrying about people judging you or criticizing your dreams and aspirations, as you slowly continue to breathe in and out. You now begin to see more clearly what it is you wish to manifest.

D. You are comfortable and relaxed as you continue to slowly breathe in and out. You are now less distracted and more focused.

4. RETURN TO VISUALIZING YOUR INTENTION

A. Again, think of manifesting your intention. Concentrate on that image of you having accomplished the goal that you wish to manifest.

B. Sit with the feeling of satisfaction and accomplishment as you slowly breathe in and slowly exhale. You realize as you do so, the possibilities seem more possible. The vision of you having manifested your intention becomes clearer.

C. You are relaxed, you are calm, and you feel that you can accomplish anything you desire. You feel connected to the endless possibilities that are within you to manifest.

D. Sit with these feelings and continue to slowly breathe in and breathe out. Breathe in and breathe out. Now slowly open your eyes. You feel calm. You have no fear.

5. RECORD YOUR INTENTION

A. Take the pen and paper and write for at least five minutes in your own words exactly how you visualized what you wish to manifest. Be as specific as possible.

B. If it was related to a professional goal, include every possible detail including time and place, the clothes you were wearing, the time of day, and how you felt. If it was for an object, include as many details as possible with an in-depth description and how it felt to have that object. See yourself with the object. Imagine every possible detail.

6. REVIEW YOUR INTENTION

A. Silently read to yourself what you have written, close your eyes, and again imagine having manifested it and how it feels for a few minutes.

B. Open your eyes again and now read what you have written aloud to yourself.

C. Close your eyes, again imagine you having manifested and how it feels for a few minutes.

7. REPEAT THIS EXERCISE

A. Some may find doing this meditation once a day for twenty minutes is enough; others may want to do it more than once a day. The reality is that the more often one uses this visualization practice, the more likely it is for one's dreams to manifest.

B. Remember, while it is possible to visualize and manifest things that can benefit only yourself, manifesting is much more powerful and likely to occur when you are able to think of how what you wish to manifest is in service of a goal larger than yourself. That is not to say that such manifestation must be absolutely selfless, but it is more powerful when the goal benefits others as well.

BONUS PRACTICE:
Adding Detail

Once you have tried your visualization a few times, I recommend you take some time to thoroughly flesh out your desired intention to make it come alive in your mind's eye as much as possible.

1. GET YOURSELF READY

A. Find a quiet place where you can reflect without being disturbed.

2. START TO SETTLE

A. Sit up straight with your eyes closed and take three breaths slowly in through your nostrils and slowly out through your mouth.

B. Repeat until this type of breathing feels comfortable for you and is not distracting.

C. Imagine you are clearing your mind and the screen of your mind is now blank.

3. RECALL YOUR INTENTION

A. Invite your intention to mind. First just let it materialize however it comes without interfering. Let it disclose itself to you. It may be highly refined already or it may be blurry and vague. Let it come naturally, even if it is only a glimpse or a distant sensation. You may feel a mix of emotions. Let it happen.

B. Once you have let your intention arise in your mind as far as it comes naturally, take a moment to consider it as a whole. What stands out? Are there gaps or fuzzy patches?

4. ADD DETAIL

A. You are now going to fill in and amplify the details of the vision. Start with your five senses. We can get so caught up in how the intention is supposed to look that we forget about other sensuous elements. What does your intention sound like? What does it feel like on your skin and in your body? What does it smell like? What does it taste like?

B. When I visualized becoming a doctor, for example, I not only visualized myself looking down and seeing my white lab coat, but I felt the stiff fabric of the cotton-polyester blend on my arms and shoulders. I smelled the fresh laundry scent as well as the antiseptic cleaner on the hospital floor. And I tasted the residue of that morning's coffee in my mouth. Can you bring your intention to life by fully inhabiting its sensory details?

5. RECORD YOUR DETAILS

A. Write down the details of your intention for each of the five senses in your journal. They can be bullet points or you can experiment with writing out the experience as a stream of consciousness. If your intention is related to a professional goal, include every possible detail including time of day and place, the clothes you are wearing, and how you feel. If it is for an object, include as many details as possible with an in-depth description of how it feels to have that object. See yourself with the object. Imagine every possible detail.

6. REFLECT ON THE FEELINGS

A. Return to your intention and focus on the emotions. When I pictured myself as a doctor, I focused on how I would feel on my first day on the job, zeroing in on feelings of pride, excitement, and compassionate service. I rehearsed the sensation of having an open heart full of gratitude for getting this far, all the people who had helped me, and the enlivening clamor of activity and decisions buzzing all around me. I pictured my first patient and how my heart filled with compassion for them and their unique struggles, how I wanted to move into action to help them get well again.

B. Ask yourself, what are the primary two or three positive emotions I want my intention to elicit in me? Be as specific as possible. Naming the emotions will help you evoke them when you need to. Add these emotions to your description of the sensory details in your journal. As you practice, you will be linking the details with the emotions so they become a single powerful and vivid memory that unites the brain, heart, and body.

7. REVIEW YOUR PRACTICE

A. Return to the sensory and emotional details in your journal periodically to keep your intention fully alive. You may want to make a recording of your intention in your own voice and listen to it often. Or you might try sharing your intention with a trusted friend and encouraging them to ask you questions about it. As new details come to you, add them in.

Try this practice for at least one week. How does it feel to start visualizing and refining your intention? Do the details come easily or do you have to work for them? Do you notice how the intention comes to life in your mind over time?

It is natural for obstacles to return at this point. They may be telling you that you will never realize your intention or that you do not deserve it. As painful as these voices might be, they are a sign you are moving forward with your intention. It is useful during these times to return to the previous steps: consult your opposites list and practice self-compassion. Practicing self-compassion before and after your visualization can provide a powerful support for your intention and give you the feelings of safety and confidence you need to let yourself become immersed in it. You can return to self-compassion for as long as you need to.

When you feel you are ready to move on, be it after one week or more, we will practice sticking with what you've begun and pursuing it with passion.

WEEK FIVE

Step Five: Pursue Your Goal Passionately

Manifestation is not a one-and-done process. Although it sometimes produces overnight success, more often than not it involves many rounds of practice. Now is the time to mobilize your passion and resilience. This step is also about working with others and relating to your environment with harmony. If you know other people who are manifesting their own intentions, start a practice group or find an accountability buddy. Join a chat on social media and share your discoveries. Other people might have tips you had not thought of, and your insights may help others on their way.

PRACTICE:
How Does My Intention Benefit Life?

One of the most powerful things we can do to increase our inner power is to align our intention with the life around us. In this practice I encourage you to reflect on how your vision is part of something larger than you as an individual.

1. GET YOURSELF READY

- A. Find a quiet place and time where you can reflect.
- B. Take a few deep breaths in and out to settle your mind and return to this moment in your body.

2. REFLECT ON YOUR INTENTION

- A. Call to mind the intention you have been visualizing. Experience it fully in its sensory detail and positive emotion.

B. Now zoom out a little. In what context is this vision taking place? Who else is connected to the event or goal? What does your intention mean to them?

3. CONNECT YOUR INTENTION TO SOMETHING LARGER

A. Consider the effect that realizing your intention might have. Maybe achieving your goal will enable you to inspire others like you to pursue their own dreams. Maybe your intention will bring joy or attention or resources to your family or community. Maybe it will address a social or environmental problem that affects many other people.

4. WRITE A STATEMENT

A. Write a statement of intention or a mission statement on how your intention will serve the life around you. This could be in the form of a letter to yourself or to a loved one or to the world, or a personal statement as in a job application, or a series of principles you intend to follow.

B. When you are facing increased doubts or resistance or lethargy, return to this statement for support and inspiration. Remember that what you are manifesting is part of the larger fabric of life. You may read or share your statement with people you encounter to enlist their support for your intention.

PRACTICE:
Scanning for Synchronicity

Making the most of synchronicity is a habit we can practice. As our subconscious begins tuning in to our environment for opportunities to realize our intention, surprising connections appear. This strange intertwining of interests, desires, and events is a phenomenon that often arises when we allow our intention to sink into our subconscious and start interacting with the world at large. Try this practice to increase your own receptivity to the hints your world is offering you.

1. GET YOURSELF READY

A. Find a quiet place and time where you can reflect.

B. Take a few deep breaths in and out to settle your mind and return to this moment in your body.

C. Have a pad of paper and a pen near you.

2. START TO SETTLE

A. Sit in a relaxed position with your eyes closed for a few minutes, allowing your thoughts to settle.

B. Now sit up straight with your eyes still closed and take three breaths slowly in through your nostrils and slowly out through your mouth. Repeat until this type of breathing feels comfortable for you and is not distracting.

3. BODY SCAN

A. Slowly scan through your body, touching each part lightly with your awareness, relaxing each muscle as you go.

B. Allow the relaxation of your body, muscle by muscle, to loosen and open your mind.

4. SCAN FOR SYNCHRONICITY

   A. Gently call to mind the events and circumstances of your life. Allow the details of your life to materialize in your mind without judgment. No feeling is too small, no clue is too insignificant. Listen to your life like it is a wise oracle who speaks in a mysterious language.

   B. Ask yourself, "Have I noticed any patterns or surprising coincidences?" Reflect on recent conversations you may have had or articles or posts you may have read, memorable dreams, or passing intuitions. Perhaps you have heard the title of the same book from three different people or you can't stop thinking about a certain place, or a long-lost memory of a particularly inspiring experience keeps appearing in your mind.

5. RECORD YOUR OBSERVATIONS

   A. Take the pen and paper and write for at least five minutes in your own words what you saw when you visualized your life.

   B. Write as many details as possible. Whether it is a few sentences or a paragraph, it only matters that you are writing what your life is trying to tell you.

6. REVIEW YOUR WRITING

   A. Sit with your eyes closed, slowly breathing for three to five breaths in through the nose and out through the mouth. Now open your eyes.

B. Silently read what you wrote.

C. Then read what you wrote aloud to yourself. Sit with those images of your life for a few moments with your eyes closed.

7. CONSIDER NEXT STEPS

A. Take a few moments to reflect on how you might follow up on whatever patterns or insights you noticed. Where can you use your own inner power to enhance the web of surprising connections?

B. Spend a few more moments sitting with what you noticed. Recognize that the tiniest connection may be an opportunity to deepen your alignment with your purpose and your vision.

Keep what you wrote somewhere you will see it often to remind you to continue to scan your life for unexpected connections. Synchronicities have a way of multiplying as we give them our attention and respect. Repeat this practice periodically to refine your vision and maximize all the opportunities life has to offer you to realize your goals.

This week is all about repetition, so the discipline is to return to the practice in the previous step and spend seven more days visualizing your intention in detail. Let yourself take advantage of the momentum you created by starting. The more you visualize your intention and install it in the filing cabinet of your subconscious, the stronger your inner bloodhound. If your intention starts to materialize, let yourself be excited but do not stop the practice. It is important to follow through fully and demonstrate your commitment to seeing the process to the end.

Once again, if you are struggling with this step, I suggest you re-

turn to the self-compassion practice. You may even want to go back to the beginning and focus on relaxing your body and clarifying your desire. The best chance you can give yourself to achieve your intention is by providing it with a solid foundation in the basics.

Stay on this step for at least one week. When you sense your passion for your intention in your daily activities and that it has started to firmly take root in your subconscious, you are ready to move on to the next and last step.

WEEK SIX

Step Six: Release Expectations and Open to Magic

You are almost done. Take a moment to honor your resolution to get this far. Reflect on how much progress you've made and what you've learned. What feels easier? What still feels difficult?

Go back to the early pages in your journal: What has changed? Does success still look the same? What about the obstacles? Write in your journal for ten minutes about how the work to get here has affected your outlook, your hopes, and the details of your life.

In this final step, you will be called on to face a paradox: after passionately visualizing your intention in all its detail and specifics, it is time to let go of any attachment and become willing to be surprised. This is the magic that comes when we are free of all expectations.

BONUS PRACTICE:
Gratitude Letter

Whether your goal feels near or still far off in the distance, just outside your grasp or impossibly unachievable, you can benefit from taking stock of what you already have and what is working. Gratitude brightens the mind, attunes to the good, and softens frustration and disappointment. It increases our generosity and makes us appreciate the help we have gotten along the way, thereby strengthening the relationships we have in our lives. When we call to mind and savor the warmth, beauty, kindness, and abundance we already have, it is easier to let go of our attachment to a particular outcome occurring at a particular time. We are free to sit back and simply experience without creating suffering for ourselves.

1. Set aside time to reflect in a quiet place with a pen and paper.

2. Relax your body by taking three deep breaths and letting the exhale guide you to settle more deeply in this place and time.

3. Now call to mind someone who has helped you on your journey so far. It could be a parent or family member, a teacher or other mentor, a close friend, a stranger on the street, or a spiritual figure you've never met. It could be an animal or a place in nature.

4. Just as you have practiced visualizing your intention, now see this being in your mind's eye. What qualities of theirs stand out? Their smile, the kindness in their eyes, the warmth of their touch, their laugh, their fierceness?

5. Think of a moment when they helped you and allow yourself to fully reexperience it in your mind. How did it feel to receive their help, care, and support? How does gratitude feel in your body? Stay with the images and feelings for a few minutes.

6. Now take ten minutes to write them a letter expressing gratitude for their help. Be as specific as possible. Feel your own generosity to this being and to yourself for making this act of expression. Let it fill your heart.

7. Reread the letter and let it deepen your gratitude.

It is completely up to you whether you want to give them the letter or not. You may want to share your appreciation with them or keep it to yourself. Either way, the benefit of the practice comes from writing the letter itself. When you are feeling lost or alone or hopeless in your manifesting process, take out the letter and read it again. Consider writing a fresh gratitude letter every couple of weeks going forward to keep the positive feelings alive and close to you.

PRACTICE:
Let Go of Attachment and Open to Magic

One of the greatest challenges for each of us is to be present with the ups and downs of our circumstances—or at least as present as we can be. No matter how skilled a person is at meditation or other techniques, there will always remain a human instinct to minimize suffering and maximize pleasure.

Equanimity is the ability to maintain an evenness of temperament in the face of both the good and the bad that occur in our lives, whether we get what we want, don't get what we want, or get what we do not want. Equanimity is the embodiment of balance and nonreactivity, and it allows us our freedom. It is freedom from attachment that releases the magic within us.

1. GET YOURSELF READY

   A. Set aside a time in which you will not be interrupted.

   B. Find a comfortable position.

2. QUICK BODY SCAN

   A. Close your eyes or direct your gaze softly downward in front of you.

   B. Begin by slowly inhaling through your nose and slowly exhaling through your mouth. Do this five to six times. It should not be forced, nor should it be specifically focused on.

   C. Take a few minutes to relax your body beginning at your toes and going to the top of your head.

3. REFLECT ON PURSUING A GOAL

   A. Think of a goal that you very much wanted to accomplish and how the goal itself became your focus and not the process of accomplishing it. Realize how this reality impacted you being present with your loved ones or coworkers, and how this focus separated you from the present moment.

   B. Notice how it feels in your body to be attached to an outcome. Where do you feel it? A tightness in your throat, a contraction around your heart, a clenching in your fists? Notice the discomfort this attachment causes for you.

   C. Having accomplished that goal, think how wonderful you felt, how elated, how happy you were that you did it. Realize how those feelings were transitory, resulting in you returning to the reality of living your life. Think of how often you wanted those feelings back and that elation you felt.

D. Sit with the realization that it is not possible to have those feelings or to be in flow at all moments. Most importantly, realize that is OK. You are OK regardless.

4. REFLECT ON A CHALLENGE

A. Conversely, think of a time when you pursued a goal and realized, for whatever reason, you were not going to attain it. Again, notice how this feels in your body. For so many, the feeling is devastation, and all their negative self-criticism seems validated. It leads to feelings of being an impostor, feeling not worthy. They sit in this place and ruminate about other failures that have occurred in their lives. It also seems like it will last forever, which only worsens the feeling of worthlessness.

B. Yet two things happen. First is that you realize that the goal wasn't as important as you had made it and that not achieving did not result in the world ending. In fact, the gifts of these situations, on reflection, are often that they gave us the greatest insight and the greatest wisdom and have made us who we are today.

C. Most important, though, is the reality that in almost every case, the experiences were transitory. Again, in the face of not accomplishing your goal, you are OK, and you are, at your core, who you are, meaning you are worthy of love and acceptance. This is the power of having evenness of temperament. The power of equanimity.

5. REFLECT ON THE BIG PICTURE

A. Concentrate on breathing again slowly in and out while understanding that it is OK not to be attached to the goal. Life is not a destination; life is living your life, being present, and being not attached. It is attachment that has caused most of your suffering. It is understanding this reality that will free you from suffering. It is not denying the experience but being able to see it from afar for what it is. Practicing equanimity is what leads to balance and acceptance.

6. SELF-COMPASSION

A. Gently open your heart toward yourself. You might think of someone in your life who has given you unconditional love and made you feel completely accepted. Or you might attune to the physical sensations around the heart of warmth and care. Sit with that feeling of care and acceptance while you slowly breathe in and out.

B. Softly direct those feelings of love and care to the tension you are carrying from holding on to a particular outcome. Remember, it is completely natural to want what you want, and to feel you need to control things or complete them to feel safe.

C. As you reflect on the feelings of being cared for, protected, and loved, notice how these feelings apply and endure regardless of whether plans are going the way you hoped or not. These are feelings that speak to your innate being, who you are in all your imperfections, complexity, and humanness.

D. Sit with yourself in stillness and bathe in the feeling that with your successes and your failures you are worthy of love, you are OK. You are a frail and fragile human being who is doing the best they can. Also know that those who are close to you love you as you are. Who you are is not defined by an event.

7. LET GO OF ATTACHMENT

A. As you surrender to the feeling of being cared for, notice if it is possible for your attachment to a particular outcome to loosen, your burden to lighten. Can you detach your ideas of OKness and worth and safety from external circumstances going only one way? Is there a deeper OKness that can suffuse your life, regardless of outcome?

B. Recognizing the transitory nature of success and failure allows you to no longer be their prisoner.

C. Now take a few more breaths slowly and feel the amazing power of equanimity and of being present.

8. INSTALL POSITIVE FEELINGS

A. Spend a few minutes bathing in these positive feelings. The sense of attachment and the need to control may return, and that is fine. Simply come back to the feeling of being cared for no matter what, protected unconditionally, again and again.

B. As you close this practice and return slowly to your life, notice if the sense of attachment has shifted or transformed in any way. Perhaps you have access now to a new and creative possibility you didn't notice before. Perhaps the stakes don't seem quite so high as they did. Perhaps it feels a little safer to allow events to take their course and meet the magic they have to offer with equanimity.

MORE MAGIC

You have now reached the end of this program. Do you see changes in yourself and your life? Do you feel more confident about using your inner power to focus your mind? Are you clearer on what you want? Do the obstacles feel less intimidating? Has your ability to seize opportunity become more automatic? Do you have more access to your passion? Are you more able to let go of expectations that things happen in a particular way? Use your journal for at least ten minutes to explore the changes you observe.

As I have said before, manifesting is an ongoing process. The six steps inform each other and flow into each other. They are more like a wheel than a straight line. Opening your mind to the magic of your ability to manifest naturally leads us back to the inner power we started by reclaiming.

At its heart, manifesting is a practice of well-being for orienting harmoniously with life. There is no end. As long as we are breathing, hoping, struggling, and persisting, we are manifesting our lives. You may want to go back to the beginning of this program and start again or focus on a particular step that felt rewarding or challenging. You may want to take a break and just let life happen for a period.

Whatever you choose, I hope that these techniques that have helped me so much are of benefit to you, and that they bring you the safety, peace, connection, and resources you need to take care of yourself, to open your heart, and to allow your own mind to manifest its magic.

Acknowledgments

While writing my first book, *Into the Magic Shop: A Neurosurgeon's Quest to Discover the Mysteries of the Brain and the Secrets of the Heart*, it became evident that an important theme was the reality that one could manifest one's intentions. I realized this concept was critically important, as so many readers commented on it and wanted to learn more. Yet there seemed to be confusion as to exactly what manifestation was, and many connected it with the idea that somehow the universe or some external force would grant them their wishes—which often related to obtaining wealth, power, or position—and by doing so, they would be happy. This idea has been promulgated by many who have promoted the concept of the Law of Attraction and the notion that if I just got more for myself, then I would be happy. Nothing could be further from the truth, and sadly, this idea reinforces a narrative that leads to emptiness and unhappiness, which is the opposite of creating a life of meaning, purpose, and, ultimately, happiness.

As a scientist, the other aspect that I wanted to explore was the neural basis of how one is able to embed one's intentions into the brain to actually allow for manifestation to occur. This took me on a long trek involving history, philosophy, psychology, and neuroscience. But even beyond this, it resulted in me exploring in depth the concept of self-agency and the power each of us has within us to change our brains, which led me back to many of the things I discussed in my first book. So it seems that I have come full circle.

When I first came up with the idea for this book, I discussed it with my literary agent, Doug Abrams at Idea Architects, who was enthusiastically supportive. We created a proposal that we presented to the amazing Caroline Sutton, editor-in-chief of Avery (an imprint of Penguin Random House), the publisher of my first book. She was immediately on board. Her support, encouragement, and guidance has been greatly appreciated.

Of course, translating a concept into a narrative is not simple or straightforward. One of the first things I did was a deep dive into the science behind the topic, reading many books and hundreds of articles. My dear friend Monica Bucci, MD, kindly offered to read through the books and articles as well, and helped me by organizing and summarizing the literature and giving me much appreciated input and advice as the project progressed. Next, Idea Architects was kind enough to recommend Alexander Nemser to collaborate with me, not only in regard to organizing my thoughts but also to assist in turning what could have been a somewhat dry topic into a compelling narrative, intertwining the science with stories that I had shared with him. In the process, Alexander has become a close friend.

I would also like to thank my extraordinary wife and life partner, Masha, whose support I try not to take for granted. My wife has always remained supportive of my endeavors in promoting the power of compassion to change lives. For this I am forever grateful.

Notes

Introduction: The Real Secret

ix. ***manifesting* is defining an intention:** Many have used the terms *subconscious* and *unconscious* interchangeably. The subconscious typically refers to the part of our mind that holds our beliefs about the world and self, remembered traumas, long-term memory, fears, and desires, as well as semiautomatic physiologic processes. On some level, our conscious mind can access aspects of the subconscious. The unconscious mind refers to the part of the psyche that is inaccessible to consciousness and that contains our forgotten traumas, instinctual responses, cellular memory, early memories and impressions, and automatic physiologic responses. For simplicity's sake, I will only use the term *subconscious*. See Step Four for a more thorough discussion of the subconscious.

xi. **researchers in the field of epigenetics have discovered:** Stanley Krippner and Deirdre Barrett, "Transgenerational Trauma: The Role of Epigenetics," *Journal of Mind and Behavior* 40, no. 1 (Winter 2019): 53–62, https://www.jstor.org/stable/26740747.

xii. **we cultivate *dispositional optimism*:** Michael F. Scheier and Charles S. Carver, "Dispositional Optimism and Physical Health: A Long Look Back, a Quick Look Forward," *American Psychologist* 73, no. 9 (December 2018): 1082–94, https://doi.org/10.1037/amp0000384.

xiii. **The Mundaka Upanishad:** Mundaka 3, chapter 2, verse 10; Mundaka 3, chapter 1, verse 10.

xiii. **The Buddha similarly commented:** *Dvedhavitakka Sutta*, MN 19; cited in Bodhipaksa, "We Are What We Think," *Tricycle*, Fall 2014, https://tricycle.org/magazine/we-are-what-we-think.

xiv. **the function of large-scale brain networks:** Steven L. Bressler and Vinod Menon, "Large-Scale Brain Networks in Cognition: Emerging Methods and Principles," *Trends in Cognitive Sciences* 14, no. 6 (June 2010): 277–90, https://doi.org/10.1016/j.tics.2010.04.004.

xv. **through a process called *value tagging*:** Tara Swart, *The Source: The Secrets of the Universe, the Science of the Brain* (New York: HarperOne, 2019).

xix. **my alphabet of the heart concept:** James R. Doty, MD, *Into the Magic Shop: A Neurosurgeon's Quest to Discover the Mysteries of the Brain and the Secrets of the Heart* (New York: Avery, 2017), 242.

Chapter 1. Out of the Wreckage: What Am I Already Manifesting?

1. **"It is in the knowledge of the genuine":** Simone de Beauvoir, *The Ethics of Ambiguity* (New York: Philosophical Library, 1948).

Chapter 2. Networks and Vibrations: The Physiology of Manifesting

21. **"Any man could, if he were so inclined":** Santiago Ramón y Cajal, *Advice for a Young Investigator* (1897; Cambridge, MA: MIT Press, 2004), xv.

36. **This label has since been discarded as misleading:** R. Nathan Spreng, "The Fallacy of a 'Task-Negative' Network," *Frontiers in Psychology* 3, no. 145 (May 2012), https://doi.org/10.3389/fpsyg.2012.00145.

37. **99.9995 percent of the stimuli:** Bob Nease, *The Power of Fifty Bits: The New Science of Turning Good Intentions into Positive Results* (New York: Harper Business, 2016).

43. **It was necessary for mammals to evolve physiological traits:** James N. Kirby, James R. Doty, Nicola Petrocchi, and Paul Gilbert, "The Current and Future Role of Heart Rate Variability for Assessing and Training Compassion," *Frontiers in Public Health* 5, no. 3 (February 2017), https://doi.org/10.3389/fpubh.2017.00040.

49. **As the mathematician Steven Strogatz has shown:** Steven H. Strogatz and Ian Stewart, "Coupled Oscillators and Biological Synchronization," *Scientific American* 296, no. 6 (December 1993):

102–9, https://www.scientificamerican.com/article/coupled-oscillators-and-biological/.

49. **In all living systems there are micro-level:** Steven Strogatz, *Sync: How Order Emerges from Chaos in the Universe, Nature, and Daily Life* (New York: Hachette Books, 2003).

50. **Researchers such as the neurophysiologist Pascal Fries:** Pascal Fries, "A Mechanism for Cognitive Dynamics: Neuronal Communication Through Neuronal Coherence," *Trends in Cognitive Sciences* 9, no. 10 (2005): 474–80, https://doi.org/10.1016/j.tics.2005.08.011.

51. **"regulation of life processes become efficient":** Antonio Damasio, *Descartes' Error: Emotion, Reason and the Human Brain* (New York: Harper Perennial, 1995).

52. **This phenomenon is called *heart rate variability*:** Paul Lehrer et al., "Heart Rate Variability Biofeedback Improves Emotional and Physical Health and Performance: A Systematic Review and Meta Analysis," *Applied Psychophysiology and Biofeedback* 45, no. 3 (2020): 109–29, https://doi.org/10.1007/s10484-020-09466-z.

53. **a result of one's heart rate being coherent:** Rollin McCraty and Maria A. Zayas, "Cardiac Coherence, Self-Regulation, Autonomic Stability, and Psychosocial Well-Being," *Frontiers in Psychology* 29, no. 5 (September 2014): 1090, https://doi.org/10.3389/fpsyg.2014.01090.

Chapter 3. Step One: Reclaim Your Power to Focus Your Mind

63. **we are essentially manifesting the *Vegas Effect*:** Luke Clark et al., "Pathological Choice: The Neuroscience of Gambling and Gambling Addiction," *Journal of Neuroscience* 33, no. 45 (November 2013): 17617–623, https://doi.org/10.1523/JNEUROSCI.3231-13.2013.

64. **The sense of agency is part of how the brain narrates its experiences:** Elisabeth Pacherie, "Self-Agency," in *The Oxford Handbook of the Self*, ed. Shaun Gallagher (Oxford, UK: Oxford University Press, 2011), 442–65.

64. **Studies have demonstrated that the sense of agency:** James W. Moore, "What Is the Sense of Agency and Why Does It Matter?,"

65. **Researchers at the University of Turin:** Anna Berti, Lucia Spinazzola, Lorenzo Pia, and Marco Rabuffetti, "Motor Awareness and Motor Intention in Anosognosia for Hemiplegia," in *Sensorimotor Foundations of Higher Cognition*, ed. Patrick Haggard, Yves Rossetti, and Mituso Kawato (Oxford, UK: Oxford University Press, 2008), 163–81.

69. **scientists studying Hof:** Otto Muzik, Kaice T. Reilly, and Vaibhav A. Diwadkar, "'Brain over Body': A Study on the Willful Regulation of Autonomic Function during Cold Exposure," *NeuroImage* 15, no. 172 (May 2018): 632–41, https://doi.org/10.1016/j.neuroimage.2018.01.067.

74. **As the Stoic philosopher Epictetus said:** "The chief task in life is simply this: to identify and separate matters so that I can say clearly to myself which are externals not under my control, and which have to do with the choices I actually control. Where then do I look for good and evil? Not to uncontrollable externals, but within myself to the choices that are my own." Epictetus, *Discourses* 2.5.4–5; Epictetus, *Discourses II* 5.8; Epictetus, *Enchiridion* 5.

Chapter 4. Step Two: Clarify What You Truly Want

77. **"There is no favorable wind":** Seneca the Younger, Letter LXXI: "On the supreme good," line 3.

78. **"He was telling me that I had to trust":** "Hawaiian Voyaging Traditions," accessed February 10, 2023, https://archive.hokulea.com/index/founder_and_teachers/nainoa_thompson.html.

91. **just thinking about an action such as building muscles:** Vinoth K. Ranganathan et al., "From Mental Power to Muscle Power—Gaining Strength by Using the Mind," *Neuropsychologia* 42, no. 7 (2004): 944–56, https://doi.org/10.1016/j.neuropsychologia.2003.11.018.

91. **thinking about rehearsing the piano:** Alvaro Pascual-Leone et al., "Modulation of Muscle Responses Evoked by Transcranial Magnetic Stimulation During the Acquisition of New Fine Motor

Skills," *Journal of Neurophysiology* 74, no. 3 (September 1995): 1037–45, https://doi.org/10.1152/jn.1995.74.3.1037.

96. **correlations between their levels of happiness:** Roy F. Baumeister, Kathleen D. Vohs, Jennifer Aaker, and Emily N. Garbinsky, "Some Key Differences Between a Happy Life and a Meaningful Life," *Journal of Positive Psychology* 8, no. 6 (October 2012): 505–16, https://doi.org/10.1080/17439760.2013.830764.

97. **The differences between these two types of well-being:** Barbara L. Fredrickson et al., "A Functional Genomic Perspective on Human Well-Being," *Proceedings of the National Academy of Sciences* 110, no. 33 (July 2013): 13684–689, https://doi.org/10.1073/pnas.1305419110.

Chapter 5. Step Three: Remove the Obstacles in Your Mind

101. **"The mind must be emancipated":** Bruce Lee, *Tao of Jeet Kune Do* (Burbank, CA: Ohara, 1975).

102. **the CIA would produce an official report:** Wayne M. McDonnell, "Analysis and Assessment of Gateway Process," https://www.cia.gov/readingroom/docs/CIA-RDP96-00788R001700210016-5.pdf.

112. **only the upper levels of the brain:** Rhailana Fontes et al., "Time Perception Mechanisms at Central Nervous System," *Neurology International* 8, no. 1 (2016): 5939, https://doi.org/10.4081/ni.2016.5939.

112. **innovation: the mammalian caregiving system:** James N. Kirby, James R. Doty, Nicola Petrocchi, and Paul Gilbert, "The Current and Future Role of Heart Rate Variability for Assessing and Training Compassion," *Frontiers in Public Health* 5, no. 3 (2017): 40, https://doi.org/10.3389/fpubh.2017.00040.

113. **offer ourselves the safe haven:** Stephen W. Porges, "Love: An Emergent Property of the Mammalian Autonomic Nervous System," *Psychoneuroendocrinology* 23, no. 8 (November 1998): 837–61, https://doi.org/10.1016/s0306-4530(98)00057-2.

Chapter 6. Step Four: Embed the Intention in Your Subconscious

132. **"Concentrate all your thoughts":** Alexander Bell, interview in Orison Swett Marden, *How They Succeeded: Life Stories of Successful Men Told by Themselves* (Boston: Lothrop, 1901), chapter 2.

132. **as Carrey shared on the *WTF with Marc Maron* podcast:** Marc Maron, "Jim Carrey," July 16, 2020, in *WTF with Marc Maron*, podcast, 1:28:05, http://www.wtfpod.com/podcast/episode-1140-jim-carrey.

133. **"I've always believed in magic":** Stephen Rebello, "Carrey'd Away," *Movieline*, July 1994.

134. **[Carrey] put the check he'd written:** *Jim & Andy: The Great Beyond*, directed by Chris Smith (Netflix, 2017).

135. **The brain is constantly blocking out stimuli:** Marcus E. Raichle and Debra A. Gusnard, "Appraising the Brain's Energy Budget," *Proceedings of the National Academy of Sciences* 99, no. 16 (July 2002): 10237–239, https://doi.org/10.1073/pnas.172399499.

136. **About two-thirds of the brain's energy budget:** Fei Du et al., "Tightly Coupled Brain Activity and Cerebral ATP Metabolic Rate," *Proceedings of the National Academy of Sciences* 105, no. 17 (April 2008): 6409–414, https://doi.org/10.1073/pnas.0710766105.

136. **invention of cooked food:** Suzana Herculano-Houzel, "The Remarkable, Yet Not Extraordinary, Human Brain as a Scaled-Up Primate Brain and Its Associated Cost," *Proceedings of the National Academy of Sciences* 109, supplement 1 (June 2012): 10661–668, https://doi.org/10.1073/pnas.1201895109.

138. **This is the phenomenon of *cognitive ease*:** Richard Thaler, *Nudge: Improving Decisions About Health, Wealth, and Happiness* (New York: Penguin Books, 2009).

138. **The automatic parts of our nervous system:** The origin of the modern concept of being conscious is often attributed to John Locke, who defined consciousness as "the perception of what passes in a man's own mind" in his *Essay Concerning Human Understanding* in 1689. That being said, writings of a similar vein date as far back as Aristotle in the fourth century BCE and even

earlier. The eighteenth-century German philosopher Friedrich Schelling first coined the term *the unconscious mind*, defining it as those processes that exist under the surface of conscious awareness. Paracelsus is credited as the first to describe an unconscious aspect of cognition in his work *Von den Krankheiten* in 1567, but unconscious aspects of cognition have been referred to in the Indian Vedas and other texts dating back to at least 2,500 BCE. In psychology, the discovery of the concept of the unconscious is popularly attributed to Sigmund Freud, but William James had already extensively examined how a long tradition of European philosophers had used the term *unconsciousness* in his 1890 treatise *The Principles of Psychology*. In fact, historian of psychiatry Mark Altschule observes that "it is difficult—or perhaps impossible—to find a nineteenth-century psychologist or psychiatrist who did not recognize unconscious cerebration as not only real but of the highest importance." Altschule, *Origins of Concepts in Human Behavior* (New York: Wiley, 1977), 199.

Today, the definition of the "conscious" mind often includes any kind of feeling, experience, cognition, or perception. This does not negate the influence that the subconscious or unconscious mind has on conscious behavior. This statement will often result in a discussion of free will both on the level of influences not apparent to the conscious mind that affect decisions, but also on a deeper level of believing that all actions are predicated on the interaction of molecules, atoms, and particles, and thus every event is predetermined. A large amount has been published in this area and is beyond the scope of our discussion.

142. **This means that about 99.9995 percent:** Bob Nease, *The Power of Fifty Bits: The New Science of Turning Good Intentions into Positive Results* (New York: Harper Business, 2016).

145. **The so-called flow state:** Mihaly Csikszentmihalyi, *Flow: The Psychology of Optimal Experience* (New York: Harper Collins, 1990).

146. **Researchers continue to study the neural correlates of flow:** Dimitri van der Linden, Mattie Tops, and Arnold B. Bakker, "The Neuroscience of the Flow State: Involvement of the Locus Coeruleus Norepinephrine System," *Frontiers in Psychology* 12 (2021): 645498, https://doi.org/10.3389/fpsyg.2021.645498. See also Martin Ulrich et al., "The Neural Correlates of Flow

Experience Explored with Transcranial Direct Current Stimulation," *Experimental Brain Research* 236, no. 12 (September 2018): 3223–37, https://doi.org/10.1007/s00221-018-5378-0.

148. **monitored the brains of patients under hypnosis:** Heidi Jiang et al., "Brain Activity and Functional Connectivity Associated with Hypnosis," *Cerebral Cortex* 27, no. 8 (July 2016): 4083–93, https://doi.org/10.1093/cercor/bhw220.

149. **the phenomenon of the placebo effect:** Joe Dispenza, *You Are the Placebo* (New York: Hay House, 2014).

Chapter 7. Step Five: Pursue Your Goal Passionately

158. **"Always go with your passions":** Deepak Chopra, quoted in Roger Gabriel, "How Passion Activates Purpose," chopra.com, July 9, 2021, https://chopra.com/articles/how-passion-activates-purpose.

158. **Nainoa Thompson dreaded entering the doldrums:** "Hawaiian Voyaging Traditions," accessed February 10, 2023, https://archive.hokulea.com/index/founder_and_teachers/nainoa_thompson.html.

162. **Through the process described by Stephen Porges as neuroception:** Stephen W. Porges, "Polyvagal Theory: A Science of Safety," *Frontiers in Integrative Neuroscience* 16 (May 2022): 871227, https://doi.org/10.3389/fnint.2022.871227.

163. **the human voice only sounds special:** Porges, "Polyvagal Theory."

166. **at a conference with Eckhart Tolle:** Eckhart Tolle, "Jim Carrey's Full Introduction for Eckhart Tolle," January 20, 2010, Vimeo video, 2:43, https://vimeo.com/8860684.

Chapter 8. Step Six: Release Expectations and Open to Magic

179. **"Nothing important comes into being overnight":** *The Golden Sayings of Epictetus*, trans. Hastings Crossley (New York: Macmillan, 1925), verse XXXIX.

184. **As Carrey rose to prominence:** Alan Siegel, "Comedy in the '90s, Part 2: The Year Jim Carrey Arrived," *Ringer*, August 28, 2019, https://www.theringer.com/movies/2019/8/28/20835101/jim-carrey-comedies-1994-ace-ventura-mask-dumb-and-dumber.

185. **"Your job is not to figure out":** Maharishi International University, "Jim Carrey at MIU: Commencement Address at the 2014 Graduation," May 30, 2014, YouTube video, 23:32, https://www.youtube.com/watch?v=V80-gPkpH6M.

189. **the effects of a gratitude practice:** Y. Joel Wong et al., "Does Gratitude Writing Improve the Mental Health of Psychotherapy Clients? Evidence from a Randomized Controlled Trial," *Psychotherapy Research* 28, no. 2 (March 2016): 192–202, https://doi.org/10.1080/10503307.2016.1169332.

191. **feelings of gratitude show an inverse correlation:** Lourdes Rey et al., "Being Bullied at School: Gratitude as Potential Protective Factor for Suicide Risk in Adolescents," *Frontiers in Psychology* 10 (March 2019): 662, https://doi.org/10.3389/fpsyg.2019.00662.

191. **One researcher considers the social dimension of gratitude:** Sara B. Algoe, Jonathan Haidt, and Shelly L. Gable, "Beyond Reciprocity: Gratitude and Relationships in Everyday Life," *Emotion* 8, no. 3 (June 2008): 425–29, https://doi.org/10.1037/1528-3542.8.3.425.

193. **long-term meditators reported the pain:** Gaëlle Desbordes et al., "Moving beyond Mindfulness: Defining Equanimity as an Outcome Measure in Meditation and Contemplative Research," *Mindfulness* 6, no. 2 (January 2014): 356–72, https://doi.org/10.1007/s12671-013-0269-8.

Index

absorption, 147, 148–149
Ace Ventura (film), 166, 185
Adding Detail (practice), 244–247
ADHD, 56–59
agency, sense of, 64–68. *See also* self-agency
alchemy, xiii
alphabet of the heart, 188
amygdala, 24–25, 27, 38–39, 104, 105–106
AN (attention network), 22–23, 36, 40, 42
anosognosia, 65–66
anxiety (chronic), 23–26, 28, 32–35, 51, 53
Aristippus, 96
Ashikaga Yoshimasa, 194–195
astral projection, 103–105
attachments. *See* materialism; releasing expectations
attention, xv, 39–40, 61–64, 105, 109–111, 142–143
attention network (AN), 22–23, 36, 40, 42
autism spectrum, 56–57
autonomic nervous system (ANS), 26–32. *See also* parasympathetic nervous system; sympathetic nervous system

bacterial infections, 98, 99
Beliefs and Their Opposites (practice), 116–119, 230–233
Bell, Alexander Graham, 132
bloodhound analogy, xv–xvi, 141–143, 168–169, 252
brain. *See also* program for mastering manifestation
   ADHD and, 57
   agency and, 64–68
   attention and, 62–64, 109–111
   autonomic nervous system and, 26–32 (*see also* parasympathetic and sympathetic nervous systems)
   brain waves, 50–52, 57
   energy consumption and conservation by, 135–138, 141–143
   equanimity and, 193–194
   flow state and, 31–32, 145–147
   gratitude and, 188–191
   heart and, 51–52, 53, 57
   hypnosis and, 148–150

brain (*cont.*)
  negativity bias and inner critic, 106–109, 113
  neural networks, 22–23, 35–42, 67, 89, 105–106
  out-of-body experiences and, 104
  positive emotion and, 88–91
  synchronicity and, 168–169
  trauma and, 112–114
  visualization and, 6, 9–10, 86–87, 137–139, 152
brain stem, 26, 104, 106, 112
breath meditation, 33–34, 69–70, 188
broken heart syndrome, 52
Buddha, xiii, 55, 166, 203
Building Inner Power (practice), 74–76, 218–220
Byrne, Rhonda, xiii

Calloway, George, 21–22
Carrey, Jim, 132–135, 151–152, 165–167, 184–185
Carrey, Kathleen, 132, 133, 166
Carrey, Percy, 132–133, 134–135
Castaneda, Carlos, 102
Cayce, Edgar, 102
CDEFGHIJKL (alphabet of the heart), 188
Center for Compassion and Altruism Research and Education (CCARE), 185–186
central executive network (CEN), 22–23, 39, 41, 42, 67
childhood self, 70–71, 108–112, 132–133, 151–152, 204–206
Chopra, Deepak, 158
Christian gospels, xiii

chronic anxiety, 23–26, 28, 32–35, 51, 53. *See also* stress
clarification process, 77–100
  happiness types, 95–100
  inner compass for, 77–81, 85, 87–88, 91–95, 220
  positive emotions and memories for, 86–95
  practices and program for, 81–85, 91–95, 220–229
  valuing fulfillment, 85–88
cognitive ease, 38, 138
coherence, 49–50, 51, 53
cold temperatures, 69–70
Cole, Steven, 97–99
compassion
  ADHD and, 59
  in alphabet of the heart, 188
  author's research on, 185–186
  metta and, 33–34
  self-compassion, 113–114, 124–131, 160, 164, 199–200, 247
  for shadow self, 104
Compassion, Dignity, Equanimity, Forgiveness, Gratitude, Humility, Integrity, Justice, Kindness, and Love (CDEFGHIJKL), 188
Compassionate Countries Index, 186
completion bias, 192
conscious mind
  agency and, 64–68
  defined, 270
  flow and, 147
  hypnosis and, 148–150
  iceberg phenomenon, 137, 138–139

intentions and, 138–139, 141–143
placebo effect and, 149–150
synchronicity and, 169
visualization and, 43, 152
consumerism, xiv, xviii, 79, 97
Contemplative Sustainable Futures Program, 87–88
Covey, Stephen R., 27
Csikszentmihalyi, Mihaly, 49, 145
current manifestation state, 1–20
author's personal story, 1–6
author's starting point, 13–16
author's wounds of the heart, 6–13
practices and program for, 16–20, 208–213

Damasio, Antonio, 51
DAN (dorsal attention network), 40
default mode network (DMN), 22–23, 35–37, 39, 42
discomfort, 60, 69–73, 177, 239
disempowerment, 61–64
dispositional optimism, xii–xiii
dopamine, 31–32, 57, 62, 87, 146, 192, 193
dorsal attention network (DAN), 40
dorsolateral vagal nerve, 43, 113
Dyer, Wayne, 27

Eckankar, 102
effortful control, 67
Eliciting a Positive Emotion (practice), 91–95, 224–229
embedding intention. See intention, embedding of

emotional discomfort, 70–73
emotions
equanimity and, 192–194, 255
positive emotions, 86–95, 140–141
subconscious and, 140–141
endorphins, 31–32
Epictetus, 74, 179
equanimity, 188, 192–194, 255
eudaimonic well-being, 95–100
expectations. See releasing expectations

fear, 104, 105–106, 107–108
fight, flight, or freeze response
background, 27, 28–30
biofeedback for, 57
gene patterns for, 98
hearing during, 163
switching to rest-and-digest response, 44–48, 57–59, 60, 72–74
filing clerk analogy, 141–143, 168–169, 252
flow state (the "zone"), 31–32, 49–50, 70, 145–147
focusing the mind, 55–76
for ADHD teens, 55–59
disempowerment vs., 61–64
inner power, 59, 60–61, 63–64, 70
inner power, sense of, 64–68
metacognition, 68–74
practices and program for, 74–76, 213–220
Fogg, BJ, 76
Frankl, Viktor, 27
Fredrickson, Barbara, 97–99
free will, 66–67

frequencies, 50–51
Fries, Pascal, 50
fulfillment, 85–88

genetic patterns of meaning and happiness, 98–99
"giving" pleasure, 97–99
goal orientation, 158–178
   author's personal story, 176–177
   breathwork, 178
   in footsteps of dreams, 169–173
   intention and, 164–167, 248–249
   manifestation definition and, x
   Polynesian sea journey, 158–160
   practices and program for, 174–176, 248–253
   social engagement and, 162–164
   start small, 160–162
   synchronicity and, 168–169, 174–176, 250–253
golden joinery, 194–196
Gratitude Letter (practice), 253–255
gratitude practice, 188–191, 196, 253–255
Green Zone, 42–44, 163–164

hallucination, hypnagogic, 104
happiness, x, xi, 95–100
heart
   alphabet of, 188
   brain and, 51–52, 53, 57
   physiology of, 51–53
   "wounds of the heart," 11–13
heart rate variability (HRV), 52–53, 99
hedonic well-being, 95–100

hemiplegia, 65–66
Hemmady, Shankar, 114–116
hierarchy of needs, 80, 97
Hill, Napoleon, xiii
Hinduism, xiii
Hof, Wim "The Iceman," 69–70
homeostasis, 27
How Does My Intention Benefit Life? (practice), 167–168, 248–249
HRV (heart rate variability), 52–53, 99
Hunger Project, 179–181
hypnagogic hallucination, 104
hypnosis, 147–150

iceberg phenomenon, 137, 138–139
imposter syndrome, 108
inattentional blindness, 39–40
incentive salience, 62–63
inflammation, 98, 99
inner compass
   clarification process and, 77–81, 85, 87–88, 91–95, 220
   expectations and, 182–183, 187, 196
   intention and, 140
inner critic
   author's personal story, 10–11
   equanimity and, 192
   flow and, 145
   inner jujitsu and, 183–184
   negativity and, 100, 106–109, 111, 113
   physiology of, 36, 106–107
   practices and program for, 125–131, 233–240
inner intention. *See* intention, embedding of

inner jujitsu, 183–184
inner power (self-agency)
　attention and, 63–64
　background, xvii, 59, 60–61
　building, 74–76, 218–220
　free will comparison, 66–67
　manifestation and, x
　metacognition and, 70
　reclaiming, 80–81
　sense of, 64–68, 80
intention, embedding of, 132–157
　Jim Carrey's experience with, 132–135, 151–152
　conscious attention, 142–143
　flow and, 145–147
　manifestation definition and, ix–x
　miserly brain and, 135–139
　optimism and, xii–xiii
　overview, 156–157
　practices and program for, 153–156, 167–168, 240–247
　ritual and, 150–151, 152
　subconscious and, 9–10, 138–143
　sympathetic nervous system and, 143–145
　value tagging and, xv–xvi, 89, 107
International Compassion Corps, 186
Intertropical Convergence Zone, 158–160
Into the Magic Shop (Doty), xvi–xix, 25, 188
intrinsic (large-scale) brain networks, 22
Invisible Gorilla experiment, 39–40

Jim and Andy (documentary), 165

kintsugi, 194–196

large-scale (intrinsic) brain networks, 22
Law of Attraction, xiii–xiv
Lee, Bruce, 101
Let Go of Attachment and Open to Magic (practice), 196–201, 255–260
long-term nonspecific optimism, xii
loving-kindness (metta)/compassion, 33–34

Maharishi International University, 132–133
Maillart, Ella, 170–172
manifestation
　accessibility of, xx
　defined, ix–xi, 264
　external source and, ix, x
　historical context, xiii
　Law of Attraction and, xiii–xiv
　mastering, 207–261 (*see also* program for mastering manifestation)
　networks and vibrations of, xiv–xv, xx, 21–54 (*see also* physiology of manifestation)
　starting point, 1–20 (*see also* current manifestation state)
　steps for (*see* clarification process; focusing the mind; goal orientation; intention, embedding of; obstacle removal; releasing expectations)

Maslan, Colin, 56–57
Maslow, Abraham, 80
materialism, xiv, xviii, 79, 97
Mau Piailug, 77, 78
meaning, happiness vs., x, xi, 96–99
medial frontoparietal network (M-FPN), 35. *See also* default mode network
meditation, 26, 33–34, 57, 69–70, 188, 193–194
metacognition, 68–74
metta (loving-kindness)/compassion, 33–34
mind-wandering, 36–37
Mother Teresa, 179
Mundaka Upanishad, xiii

near misses, 62
negative beliefs, power of, 109–111, 114–116
negative self-talk. *See* inner critic
negativity bias, 106–109, 111, 113
networks. *See* physiology of manifestation
neural synchronization, 50–51
neuroception, 162–164
neurons. *See* physiology of manifestation
neuroplasticity, xiv–xv, xvii, 113
neurotransmitters, 30–32
New Thought movement, xiii

obstacle removal, 101–131
   author's personal story, 101–106
   beliefs, power of, 109–111, 114–119
   help for, 120–124
   liberation, 111–114, 119–120
   negativity bias and inner critic, 100, 106–109, 111, 113
   practices and program for, 116–119, 124–131, 229–240
   self-compassion and, 113–114, 124–131
openness to magic. *See* releasing expectations
optimism, xii–xiii
oscillation (vibration), 48–54
out-of-body experiences, 102–105
oxytocin, 28, 31–32, 43, 53, 164

Pachamama Alliance, 150–151, 179–181
parasympathetic nervous system (PNS)
   about, 26–32, 43, 52–53
   fulfillment and, 86
   positive emotions and, 90
   sense of psychological safety, 119–120
"pay it forward," 190
Peale, Norman Vincent, xiii
physical discomfort, 69–71, 177
physiology of manifestation, 21–54
   autonomic nervous system, 26–32, 35–42
   background, 21–23
   chronic anxiety and, 23–26, 28, 32–35, 51, 53
   Green Zone, 42–44, 163–164
   overview, 53–54
   practices and program for, 44–48, 213–218
   vibration, 48–54
placebo effect, 149–150, 152
pleasure, 96–99
PNS. *See* parasympathetic nervous system

Polynesian sea journey, 77–78, 79, 158–160
Porges, Stephen, 162
positive emotions and memories
  fulfillment and, 86–88
  power of, 88–91
  practice for, 91–95
  subconscious and, 140–141
potential energy, 67–68
The Power of Positive Thinking (Peale), xiii
practices
  Adding Detail, 244–247
  Beliefs and Their Opposites, 116–119, 230–233
  Building Inner Power, 74–76, 218–220
  Eliciting a Positive Emotion, 91–95, 224–229
  Gratitude Letter, 253–255
  How Does My Intention Benefit Life? 167–168, 248–249
  Let Go of Attachment and Open to Magic, 196–201, 255–260
  Relaxing the Body, 44–48, 214–218
  Scanning for Synchronicity, 174–176, 250–253
  Self-Compassion, 124–131, 233–240
  Visualizing Your Intention, 153–156, 240–244
  What Am I Already Manifesting?, 16–20, 209–213
  What Does Success Look Like for You?, 81–85, 221–223
Prislovsky, Lois, 56–59
prisoner of war (POW), xii
program for mastering manifestation, 207–261
  about, xxi, 207–208
  as ongoing practice, 260–261
  week one, 208–220
  week two, 220–229
  week three, 229–240
  week four, 240–247
  week five, 248–253
  week six, 253–260
prosperity gospel (materialism), xiv, xviii, 79, 97
psychological safety, sense of, 119–120
Puncak Jaya, 121–124

Ramón y Cajal, Santiago, 21
relational threat, 107
relaxation techniques, 33–34
Relaxing the Body (practice), 44–48, 214–218
releasing expectations, 179–206
  attachments and, 196–201, 255–260
  author's personal story, 185–188
  diversification and, 185–188
  equanimity and, 188, 192–194, 255
  golden joinery for, 194–196
  gratitude and, 188–191, 196, 253–255
  inner jujitsu and, 183–184
  moving parts and, 184–185
  overview, 182–183
  practices and program for, 196–201, 253–260
  Twist's personal story, 179–181
rest-and-digest response, 27, 29–30
ritual, 150–151, 152

Robinson, James G., 185
Roche, Amandine, 169–173
Rogin, Neal, 150

salience bias (cognitive ease), 38, 138
salience network (SN), 22–23, 37–40, 42, 89, 105–106
Scanning for Synchronicity (practice), 174–176, 250–253
scars, golden joinery for, 195–196
The Secret (Byrne), xiii, xx
selective attention, xv, 39–40, 105
self, sense of, 37
self-agency. *See* inner power
self-compassion, 113–114, 124–131, 160, 164, 199–200, 247
Self-Compassion (practice), 124–131, 233–240
self-consciousness, 36, 42, 140–141
self-doubt, 100
self-efficacy, 66
self-referential processing, 35
Seneca the Younger, 77
sense of psychological safety, 119–120
sense of self, 37
serotonin, 28, 31–32, 53, 87
shadow self, 104
shame, 107
SN (salience network), 22–23, 37–40, 42, 89, 105–106
SNS. *See* sympathetic nervous system
social engagement system, 162–164
Soul of Money Institute, 179–181
soul travel, 102–106

starting point. *See* current manifestation state
Stoicism, 74
"story of oneself," 35
stress, 28–29, 71. *See also* chronic anxiety
Strogatz, Steven, 49
stroke, 65–66
subconscious mind
  agency and, 64–67
  clarification process and, 80, 84, 87–91
  flow and, 147
  goal orientation and, 160–163, 168–169, 174–176
  hypnosis and, 147–150
  iceberg phenomenon, 137, 138–139
  intentions and, 9–10, 138–143
  manifestation definition and, x
  metacognition and, 70–71
  neural networks and, 27, 37–42, 106–109
  placebo effect and, 149–150
  sympathetic nervous system and, 143–145
  synchronicity and, 168–169
  value tagging and, xv–xvi, 89
success, determining what it looks like, 81–85
sustainability crises, 87–88
sympathetic nervous system (SNS)
  about, 26–32, 36, 42
  evolutionary perspective on, 106–107
  inner critic and, 106–107
  intentions and, 143–145
  neural networks and, 36
  positive emotions and, 90

synaptic cleft, 31
synchronicity, 168–169, 174–176, 250–253

Tahiti, 77–78, 79, 158–160
"taking" pleasure, 96–99
"task-negative network," 36
The Teachings of Don Juan (Castaneda), 102
Think and Grow Rich (Hill), xiii
Thompson, Nainoa, 77–78, 79, 158–160, 178
Tiny Habits (Fogg), 76
Tolle, Eckhart, 166
transcendentalism, xiii
Tummo meditation, 69
Twist, Lynne, 150–151, 179–181
Twitchell, Paul, 102

unfairness, x, xi–xii

vagus nerve, 26–27, 43, 113
value tagging, xv–xvi, 89, 107
valuing fulfillment, 85–88
variable ratio reinforcement schedule, 62
Vasquez-Lavado, Silvia, 120–124
Vedic scriptures, xiii
ventral attention network (VAN), 40
vibration (oscillation), 48–54
Vietnam War POW, xii
viral infections, 98

visualization. *See also* intention, embedding of
author's personal story, 5–6, 9–10
for clarification, 87–91
conscious mind and, 43, 152
flow and, 147
meditative, 69
for obstacle removal, 131
physiology of, 6, 9–10, 32–35, 38, 86–87, 137–139, 152
practices and program for, 153–156, 240–247
for releasing expectation, 182–184
Visualizing Your Intention (practice), 153–156, 240–244
Vivekananda, Swami, 102

Wamsler, Christine, 87
well-being, types of, 95–100
What Am I Already Manifesting? (practice), 16–20, 209–213
What Does Success Look Like for You? (practice), 81–85, 221–223
Wim Hof Method (WHM), 69–70
World Compassion Festival, 185
WTF with Marc Maron podcast, 132

Yogananda, 102

the "zone" (flow state), 31–32, 49–50, 70, 145–147